Bridges Instead of Walls

Christian-Muslim Interaction in Denmark, Indonesia and Nigeria

Lissi Rasmussen, Editor

Lutheran University Press
Minneapolis, Minnesota

Bridges Instead of Walls
Christian-Muslim Interaction in Denmark, Indonesia and Nigeria
Lissi Rasmussen, editor, on behalf of The Lutheran World Federation

Editorial assistance and layout: LWF-DTS
Design: LWF-OCS
Artwork on cover: "It is Time to Smile" by twelve-year-old Fadhila Annisa, Banda Aceh, Indonesia, 2005. The painting was selected from 3,000 children's drawings exhibited at "Tsunami Children Artworks" organized by Guntomara "The Kingdom of Art" (Banda Aceh) and sponsored by a number of international NGOs.

Published by Lutheran University Press under the auspices of:
The Lutheran World Federation
150, rte de Ferney, PO Box 2100
CH-1211 Geneva 2, Switzerland

This book is also available in Europe using ISBN 978-3-905676-56-3.

Library of Congress Cataloging-in-Publication Data

Bridges instead of walls : Christian-Muslim interaction in Denmark, Indonesia and Nigeria / Lissi Rasmussen, editor.
p. cm.
Includes bibliographical references and index.
ISBN-13: 978-1-932688-29-0 (alk. paper)
ISBN-10: 1-932688-29-3 (alk. paper)
1. Islam—Relations—Christianity. 2. Christianity and other religions—Islam. I. Rasmussen, Lissi.
BP172.B74 2007
261.2—dc22
2007035024

Lutheran University Press, PO Box 390759, Minneapolis, MN 55439
Manufactured in the United States of America

Contents

Bridge Models
Stories of Relationships

Foreword

Karen L. Bloomquist

The Lutheran World Federation (LWF) has been carrying out interreligious work for many years. Most pervasively and practically this occurs through its many field programs (of the Department for World Service). Here Christians regularly work alongside those of other faiths such as Muslims, Buddhists, Hindus, as well as with others in civil society for the sake of alleviating poverty, empowering communities and pursuing justice, peace and reconciliation, particularly in multifaith settings.

In 1985, the LWF Department for Theology and Studies began an extensive series of studies and consultations that initially focused on "Theological Perspectives on Other Faiths," specifically on Islam, Hinduism, Buddhism, Confucianism and African Religion. Numerous publications included *Theological Perspectives: Toward a Christian Theology of Religions, LWF Documentation 41/1997* and *Dialogue and Beyond: Christians and Muslims Together on the Way, LWF Studies 01/2003*. In order to overcome traditional apologetics and polemics and to establish new relationships with people of other faiths, these study programs encouraged the churches to promote dialogue in a spirit of mutual respect and hospitality. Some face-to-face dialogues with people of other faiths have also taken place under LWF auspices. Increasingly recognized was the importance of developing a practical theology of living together, *diapraxis*, especially with Muslims.

The LWF study program "Christian-Muslim Relations: Conflict and Peace" (2002–2006)

In 2001, based on this prior work and in the wake of the charged atmosphere after 9/11, Ingo Wulfhorst, LWF study secretary for the Church and People of Other Faiths, proposed, organized and began carrying out a new study program that became the basis for this book. It asked, What roles do Christians and Muslims play today in conflicts and attempts to overcome such? How do they contribute toward peaceful coexistence for the sake of the common good? A study team comprising five Muslims and five Lutherans from Denmark, Indonesia, Nigeria and USA was appointed.

These questions were explored through case studies in three quite different areas—Europe (Denmark), Asia (Indonesia) and Africa (Nigeria)—where tensions have escalated since the mid-1990s. The sites selected have a considerable number of Lutheran Christians, but the proportion of Christians and Muslims varies dramatically. Whereas Indonesia is overwhelmingly Muslim, Denmark is overwhelmingly Christian. Nigeria has approximately an equal number of Christians and Muslims, although the study took place in the North, where Muslims are in the majority.

The case studies were developed in close cooperation with local churches, Muslim communities and interfaith organizations. We are grateful to all who were willing to talk, arrange meetings and be interviewed by study team members. Team members were challenged by first-hand input from the grass roots as well as by religious and political leaders in Denmark (22–27 October 2003), Indonesia (5–15 June 2004) and Nigeria (1–13 March 2005).

We are grateful to all who participated in this process, especially to Lissi Rasmussen of the study team, who offered to carry out the challenging and time-consuming task of writing and bringing together the analyses and reflections from the case studies in this book, as well as to staff who completed the editorial work. We hope that the findings here will challenge some assumptions and prejudices and open up new insights into how walls of violence, suspicion and tension between Muslims and Christians might be transformed or demolished and bridges be constructed instead.

Setting the Stage

Lissi Rasmussen

Religion is the great catchall term for conflicts in our time and the prism through which wars, conflicts and clashes between people are understood. Many people believe that without religion the world would be a better and more peaceful place.

The LWF study team's studies and experiences have shown that it is not quite as simple. Distinct demographics and histories have given rise to various patterns in Christian-Muslim relations, different types of conflict and resolution of such, and therefore we need more than one model for cooperation and dialogue. Nonetheless, the similarities between the conflicts in the three countries visited—especially between Nigeria and Indonesia—with regard to their origin and course and what was required for their resolution, were striking. Certain parallels in the human mechanisms involved were noticeable; namely that it was not religion as such but economic inequalities, political ambition, feelings of neglect and exclusion, as well as ethnic, cultural or social envy that fuelled the conflicts. These may have been framed in religious terms and religion used as a tool in the struggle. Nonetheless, to think of religion as the root cause would be to oversimplify the many ways in which religion works and has worked in practice.

Methodology

The three countries were selected for a number of reasons. First, they are on different continents and home to a considerable number of Lutherans. Moreover, they reflect certain numerical symmetries: Indonesia has an overwhelming Muslim majority whereas Christians constitute ten percent of the population, including a minority of Lutherans. In Denmark, the opposite is true: eighty-three percent of the population are Christian and only 3.8 percent are Muslim. Nigeria has an almost equal number of Christian and Muslim citizens, but in Northern Nigeria, where the studies took place, Muslims constitute the majority.

Instead of studying Christian-Muslim relations at the national level, the team decided to focus on six case studies. These tell the stories of events and processes which enabled us to compare the role religion plays in Denmark, Indonesia and Nigeria, and how it has influenced the construction of walls and the building of bridges.

Collectively and individually the team interviewed politicians, scholars, religious leaders and dialogue practitioners. Visits were made to villages, boarding schools, universities, political parties, grassroots movements and religious organizations. The team took part in each other's religious ceremonies such as church services and Friday prayers.

In Nigeria, the team joined a four-day conference in Gusau, Zamfara State,[1] with the theme "Sharî'a and Christian-Muslim Relations in Nigeria." Arranged by the Association of Christian-Muslim Mutual Relations in Nigeria, the conference brought together eighty Christians and Muslims from around the country, many of whom work in the field of Christian-Muslim relations.

In Indonesia, the team was invited to participate in a one-day Peace and Reconciliation Conference at the State University (Stain) at Surakarta (locally referred to as Solo), Central Java, 12 June 2004.[2] In Denmark, the team attended two seminars at the Islamic-Christian Study Centre (IKS), Copenhagen, with a broad Christian and Muslim participation, and two regular meetings for Lutherans involved in Christian-Muslim relations at the national and regional levels (Diocese of Copenhagen). The national meeting took place in Odense within the framework of the Evangelical Lutheran Church in Denmark's Committee for Church & Encounter with other Religions (Stiftssamarbejdet "Folkekirke & Religionsmøde").[3] Here

---

[1] Zamfara State was the first Northern Nigerian state to implement Sharî'a criminal laws in 1999. The dialogue conference was financed by the state governor of Zamfara.

[2] A research team, set up by a Protestant (Universitas Kristen Duta Wacana, Yogyakarta) and an Islamic university (State Institute of Islamic Studies, Solo), wanted to share with the LWF study team the results of a research project on the roots of interreligious conflict and violence in Solo and Yogyakarta. This program is part of a cooperation in interreligious MA and Ph.D. programs.

[3] **www.religionsmoede.dk**. The committee is supported by eight of ten dioceses and was established in 2001 with the following aims: 1) to motivate and inspire congregations to engage in encounter with citizens of different faiths; 2) to equip congregations to present and represent Christian faith in the encounter with people of other faiths; and 3) to be church in a multireligious society in a responsible and insightful way, marked by respect and openness.

the team was introduced to the various initiatives that have been taken in the Lutheran church to establish contact with Muslims.

These meetings gave the team the opportunity to listen to numerous interesting papers and speeches, to follow internal discussions and to meet and interview many people including scholars, pastors, imams and other representatives from different religious organizations and backgrounds, politicians, media workers and others interested in this topic.

The purpose of our visits was to glean an impression of Christian-Muslim relations in the three countries, to get a sense of the complexity of the causes of the conflicts and to see how religion was both barrier to and resource for overcoming them.

The book's coherence

This book, to which different people from the LWF study team have contributed, is not an anthology of more or less unrelated contributions, but aims at offering a consistent analysis. It is based on direct experience, observations, interviews and formal and informal discussions with a range of relevant people whom we met during our stay in the three countries between 2003 and 2005. Furthermore, it is grounded in shared discussions on the book's content and informed by primary and secondary sources.

In addition to the team, three people have to be thanked for their assistance and advice regarding the manuscript: Musa Gaya (University of Jos, Nigeria), Kristian Morville (University of Copenhagen, Denmark) and Simone Sinn (LWF). This book would not have been possible without the gracious hospitality of local Christians, Muslims and others who supported the team by arranging interviews and meetings and freely sharing information. To them we owe our deepest gratitude.

The two main sections of the book include three case studies from each of the countries and their contextualization followed by comparative reflection. The first section deals with conflicts, the second with different models for conflict resolution and bridge building. A chapter on Sharî'a is included in the first section since the various ways of dealing with this issue highlight some of the important aspects at stake in Christian-Muslim relations. The introduction of Sharî'a law has been one of the remote causes of the crises in Nigeria and Indonesia and has contributed to intensifying certain fears in Denmark.

Many things have changed since the team visited the three countries. Issues relevant at the time may play a lesser role today and vice versa. We have continued to follow events and developments through visits, local contacts and media and have wherever possible updated our material accordingly.[4]

Walls and bridges

On our journeys, we encountered many obstacles or walls: tensions and conflicts that in combination with global events have resulted in an increasing fear of "the other" among Christians as well as Muslims. But we also saw how bridges were being built through efforts to bring people together in order to enable mutual understanding, and grassroots activities with the aim of securing peace and harmony and preventing future conflicts.

Christians and Muslims alike have been involved in constructing walls and building bridges. Religion has been both a help and complication during the course of the conflicts. During our travels, we sensed that many religious leaders and lay people do not only want to be reactive but more proactive in the peace building process.

We are convinced that we have a lot to learn from one another, and that by looking at mechanisms and developments in other countries it might become easier to see and understand those operating in one's own country. Often we do not recognize that bridges are very much a part of our realities. By focusing on that which divides us, the walls, we ignore the fact that existing bridges sometimes prevent both parties from falling into a deep crater. It is our hope that this book will contribute to strengthening those bridges as well as to keeping them in good repair. We hope that our shared journey will generate new insights and inspire many more Christians and Muslims to journey together so that fear can be dismantled and a shared future be built.

[4] The team was not present in Denmark during or after the cartoon crisis but in 2004 witnessed the atmosphere leading up to it.

Three countries—three contexts

In the following brief introduction to the three countries visited, we shall focus on the history of Christianity and Islam and on the political and economic developments over the last two decades. A survey included at the end of this book provides further useful information.

With 140 million inhabitants, Nigeria is Africa's most populous nation. Every fifth African is Nigerian. It comprises more Muslims than any Arab country and is the world's eighth largest exporter of oil. One of Nigeria's most pressing problems is the unequal distribution of its resources, not least the oil in the Niger Delta, which has led to several clashes between the oil producing states and the federal government.

The presidential elections on 24 April 2007 were the first civil-to-civil transfer of federal power in Nigeria. Olusegun Obasanjo of the People's Democratic Party (PDP), Nigeria's first democratically elected president, had to step down after Nigeria's longest ever uninterrupted civilian rule (since 1999), and to hand over power to one of his party colleagues, the former state governor from the predominantly Muslim North, Umaru Musa Yar'Ardua.

Indonesia is the largest archipelago in the world. It consists of five major islands and about thirty smaller groups (17,508 islands in total). It comprises more Muslims than any country on earth, and with a total population of over 200 million sports a rich ethnic and cultural diversity. Until today, one of Indonesia's main problems remains the regional struggle for political autonomy. Indonesia's president, Susilo Bambang Yudhoyono of the Partai Demokrat, was elected in 2004. He is the first directly elected president of the country.

Indonesia is a secular state based on *Pancasila* which teaches freedom of religion for followers of Islam, Protestantism, Catholicism, Hinduism, Buddhism and Confucianism.[5] *Pancasila* continues to have a strong impact on most Indonesians.

A decentralization process known as *pemekaran* (literally: blossoming) was initiated in 1998 with the passing of a bill on regional autonomy

[5] The word *Pancasila* consists of two Sanskrit words, *panca* meaning five, and *sila* meaning principle. It comprises five principles thought to be interrelated. The five principles are: 1) belief in the one Supreme God; 2) a just and civilized humanity; 3) the unity of Indonesia; 4) democracy led by the wisdom of unanimity arising from deliberations among representatives of the people; and 5) social justice for the whole people of Indonesia.

that permits the division of provinces, districts and sub-districts into smaller units. The number of districts has increased from 292 in 1998 to 483 in early 2007.[6] This process continues to affect social cohesion and in some areas is eroding interreligious harmony.

Until the 1970s, Denmark, with its population of 5.4 million, has been an exceptionally monocultural and homogeneous nation-state. Today, eight percent of the population are immigrants, less than half of whom (3.8 percent) have a Muslim background. The size of the population is undoubtedly one of the reasons why the country has had difficulties adjusting to a more pluralistic situation.

The present government, a two-party coalition, took office a few months after 9/11. The two parties in power, the Liberals and the Conservative Party, depend on support from the extreme right-wing Danish People's Party in which two Lutheran pastors have played a powerful central role. The party exerts a strong influence and has been instrumental in pushing for tougher anti-immigration policies. Prime Minister Anders Fogh Rasmussen is a member of the Liberal Party.

The history of Islam and Christianity

Islam came to Nigeria in the eleventh century when Arab and Berber merchants and scholars from northern Africa made their way across the Sahara desert to the Kanem-Borno Empire. In the fourteenth and fifteenth centuries, Fulani pastoralists gradually migrated from the Senegal valleys settling in towns in Hausaland. Islam first appealed to the rulers and for a considerable period remained the religion of the kings' courts.

A series of Fulani-led *jihâds*—the most important being Usman Dan Fodio's *jihâds* in 1804—conducted with the aim of establishing a more just society based on the Islamic ideology of the *umma*, heralded the second phase of Islam. These *jihâds* resulted in the establishment of the Sokoto caliphate. During this period, the Muslim Brotherhoods, *turuq*, especially the Qadiriya, played a central role and Islam became a faith of the people.

[6] "Indonesia: Decentralization and Local Power Struggles in Maluku," in International Crisis Group, *Asia Briefing*, no. 64 (Jakarta/Brussels: 22 May 2007), p. 1.

Islam spread to Southern Nigeria only much later. Hausa cola nut traders and scholars brought Islam to Southern Nigeria in the middle of the seventeenth century.[7] It spread gradually in most of the major Yoruba cities, with the highest concentration in Ilorin and Ibadan, but remained a minority religion.

Toward the end of the nineteenth century, the British established a system of indirect rule in Northern Nigeria, allowing traditional Muslim rulers to continue to govern and reinforcing their positions and establishing a very strong Muslim élite. Since independence in 1960, the traditional rulers have ceded much of their power to the Northern Muslim politicians

Although Portuguese missionaries came to Benin and Warri already in the sixteenth century, it was not until the mid-nineteenth century that mission societies started their work there and Christianity began to gain ground in the South. Formal missionary activities in Northern Nigeria only occurred in the early twentieth century.

The Danish United Sudan Mission (DFSM) began its work in Adamawa in 1913. In 1954, it became an independent Nigerian church with the name Lutheran Church of Christ in Sudan (and later Nigeria), LCCN.

In many ways, Nigeria is a divided nation. A divide between the predominantly Muslim North and the predominantly Christian South has existed since colonial times, when missionary presence was banned from the Muslim areas in the North, creating an educational imbalance between North and South. Over the years, the divide has deepened, tensions increased and religion has come to be used more and more to fuel conflict. This occurred for instance during the Biafra civil war (1967–1970).

Long before the introduction of Islam in the eighth century by Muslim traders, Indonesia was home to Hinduism and Buddhism. It was not until the thirteenth century that Islam began to spread significantly among the local population, and Islamic kingdoms were gradually established between the fifteenth and seventeenth centuries. Rather like in Nigeria, Islam was first embraced by the local rulers (sultans) and only later by the population. This early form of Islam was pluralistic and tolerant of other traditions and became the basis for the development of a wide

---

[7] Muhib O. Opeloye, *Building Bridges of Understanding between Islam and Christianity in Nigeria*, (Lagos: Lagos State University, 2001), p. 3. See also T. G. O. Gbadamosi, *The Growth of Islam among the Yoruba 1841-1978* (London: Longman, 1978).

range of local Muslim traditions influenced to a varying degree by Sufism (Islamic mysticism) and local tradition, *adat*.

By the seventeenth century, the sultanate of Aceh, in the northern part of Sumatra, had become the most influential center of Islamic learning and for a time was known as the "Gate of Mecca."

Under Dutch colonial rule, Islam became regulated, bureaucratized and directly suppressed. The Dutch preferred local customs to Sharî'a making these the basis of law in the Dutch East Indies (unlike the British in West Africa). Islam, however, remained a strong force of resistance against the Dutch.

During the nineteenth century, the rural boarding schools, *pesantren*, developed into central institutions for transmitting Islamic knowledge in Indonesia. Here students studied religious subjects combined with mystical practices. The system was founded on a close relationship between teacher, *kyai*, and student, *santri*.

In the sixteenth century, Roman Catholic missionaries who had accompanied Portuguese explorers in search of valuable spices brought Christianity to Indonesia. Christian settlements were established on many of the islands, but Christianity did not spread until colonization in the early eighteenth century when many European and American missionaries established thousands of congregations.

Today, Christians account for no more than ten percent of the overall population. In some regions, Christians constitute a considerable number (and in certain areas even the majority). This is not only the case in several regions in Maluku and Sulawesi but also in Yogyakarta[8] where Christians add up to twenty percent of the population. Like Islam, Christianity is influenced by local tradition, and recent years have seen a growth of Pentecostal churches and an increasingly radical discourse. In places where forty percent of the population live with less than 2 USD a day, there is a tendency to go along with religious systems that promise greater social security.

Contrary to Nigeria, Indonesia is not divided into two distinct blocks. Nonetheless, there has been a Christian-Muslim divide to some extent due to a Christian overrepresentation in public positions during the Suharto administration (1966–98), and Suharto's exploitation of

[8] Yogyakarta has around 500,000 inhabitants.

religious tensions in the 1990s when he pitted one religious community against the other.[9]

Since King Harald Bluetooth's baptism in 960, Christianity has been accepted as the official religion in Denmark. Until then, the ancient Nordic religion prevailed. Until 1849, when Denmark received a Constitution that granted freedom of religion, all Danes had to be members of the Danish state church. Today, over eighty religious communities are registered including Muslims, Hindus, Buddhists, Sikhs, Baha'i, etc. The communities have the right to conduct marriage ceremonies and their congregations may donate money to them. These donations are tax deductible and religious communities are exempt from property tax.

The Danish church was part of the Roman Catholic Church until the Reformation in 1536 when it became the Evangelical Lutheran Church in Denmark. The church founded the first schools and hospitals, thus leaving a strong mark on society. In most Danes' minds, Christianity is part of their historical cultural heritage and therefore their identity. However, Denmark is not a Christian country in the sense that the gospel has penetrated people's consciousness, and only a small percentage of all church members are regular church goers. Most are so-called "cultural Christians," using the church when they need it, such as for baptisms, weddings and funerals.

Historically there has been a strong connection between the ruler and religion. This tradition has continued, and the ties between church and state remain close. The Constitution obliges the state to support the established church (of the people) by providing economic support via the tax system. This gives the established church a special status. The Ministry for Ecclesiastical Affairs is responsible for much of the administration and pastors are trained at the universities. The Constitution also demands that the church is Lutheran, and until this day the church is responsible for recording births and deaths.

---

[9] Suharto's close association with ultra-conservative leaders during this period was motivated by his determination to win Muslim support for his reelection as president and to undermine growing democratic opposition. A number of extreme Islamic organizations were formed during this time. Bob S. Hadiwinata, "Muslim-Christian Relations in Indonesia. Political or Religious Conflict?," in Institute of Political Science, Indonesia Research Unit, *IRU-Series on Indonesia*, (2005-04), at **www.indonesia-research-unit.com**. Robert W. Hefner, "Introduction: Multiculturalism and Citizenship in Malaysia, Singapore, and Indonesia," in Robert W. Hefner (ed.), *The Politics of Multiculturalism. Pluralism and Citizenship in Malaysia, Singapore, and Indonesia* (Honolulu: University of Hawaii Press, 2001), p. 35.

The first wave of Muslim immigration began in the late 1960s when labor was being imported in the form of guest workers from Turkey, Pakistan, Morocco and Yugoslavia. The import of foreign labor stopped in 1973 and since then Denmark has officially not been a country of immigration. Today the only way to enter Denmark is through permitted family reunions and the granting of political asylum.

When Muslim immigrants began to bring their families after 1974, their Islamic identity became more important to them; they needed institutions such as schools and mosques and Muslim organizations. Some of the immigrants became Danish citizens.

A second wave of immigration in the early 1980s comprised asylum seekers mainly from urban areas in Iran, Lebanon, Iraq, Bosnia, Somalia and Iraq. Many of them became more interested in Islam when they came to Denmark, since Islam had become a symbol of their identity. It is becoming harder to obtain political asylum in Denmark and to get permission to bring spouses and other family members into the country.

The Muslim community in Denmark is divided. There is no overall Muslim organization and no one to speak on behalf of most Muslims. Young Muslims born in Denmark are more aware of this problem and are trying to organize themselves across ethnic differences. They are bound together by their Danish Muslim identity and a growing number of ethnic Danish converts to Islam contribute to this development.

Political transition

In Nigeria and Indonesia, Christian-Muslim relationships had been more or less positive, especially at the grass roots, until the transition from a controlled state to more democratic rule in the wake of the new millennium. In both countries, the breakdown of state authority led to a sense of insecurity. After nearly thirty years of authoritarian control—in Indonesia under Suharto and in Nigeria under military rule—the two countries entered an open political order which led to a crisis in national cohesion, mutual suspicion and communal discord.

In both countries, tensions had been ignored and political forces suppressed. In 1999, with the advent of democracy in Nigeria, tensions erupted. The discontent that had built up over the years surfaced. After

Suharto's fall in 1998, Indonesia experienced similar upheavals, including bitter struggles for political leadership compounded by a serious economic crisis.

Both countries suffered similar consequences. In 1999, the governors of twelve out of thirty-six Northern Nigerian provinces adapted their legal systems to conform to parts of Sharî'a. This occurred first in Zamfara State (see pp. 107ff. and note 1). In Indonesia, bylaws based on Sharî'a were introduced in a number of provinces after 2000.[10] Aceh was given the right to apply Sharî'a in full. This new political environment enabled Muslim extremists to exert greater influence and to pursue their intent to undermine the country's pluralist political institutions and establish an Islamic state.

However, in Indonesia, mainstream Islam has remained anchored in pluralist principles. The state philosophy of *Pancasila*, the embodiment of basic principles of an independent Indonesian state, has had a strong impact and represents the national consensus of religious communities. In spite of strong critique against *Pancasila* over the years, especially from radical Muslim groups who advocate for an Islamic state and therefore find the principles too secular and inclusive, the philosophy and its principle of unity in diversity remain a part of many Indonesians' self-understanding. In the 1999 and 2004 national elections, radical Islamic parties only captured a small percentage of the votes.

During the 1990s, nationalism began to be used as a tool in Denmark in order to obtain political power. The Danish People's Party increasingly promoted itself as the defender of "Danishness" as a national cultural homogeneity opposed to the values of "foreigners" in general and Muslims in particular. For them, Islam is a hindrance to integration since it cannot be reconciled with Danishness, a concept that has only very rarely been defined.

The Danish People's Party has considerably influenced the political agenda and gained general respectability among politicians and the general population. Stereotypes about Islam and Muslims as well as the use of aggressive language are not only widespread among populist

---

[10] According to Baladas Ghoshal, today more than ten percent of the 445 Indonesian districts live under some form of Islamic inspired law. Baladas Ghoshal, "Islam in Malaysia and Indonesia. The Rise of Extremism," at **Qantara.de** May 2007, **www.qantara.de/webcom/show_article.php/_c-476/_nr-774/i.html**

politicians. Today, mainstream politicians and even a number of former left-wing politicians and intellectuals have adopted some the rhetoric.

Economic crisis and political oppression in Nigeria

Over the past thirty years, poverty in Africa has increased in rural as well as urban areas. In Nigeria, over seventy percent today live below the poverty line.[11] The country is plagued by insufficient access to social and economic services, limited opportunities for income generation activities and a lack of purchasing power. This has seriously affected people's lives, including the way in which different ethnic and religious groups relate to one another, especially in areas where one or more ethnic groups dominate the others.

General discontent with this situation, the failed development process in the country, lack of progress, years of misrule, massive corruption of politicians and others who should be role models and the unequal distribution of wealth and poverty have led to more and more people seeking refuge in their faith. Political leaders see political power as a way to obtain access to resources for their own consumption and resources have been distributed among family, friends, political patrons and supporters. As a result, politicians have lost all credibility. Since there seems to be no reason to believe in a better future or in the government's ability to solve their problems, people look for contentment in other ways.

Nigerian Muslims generally believe that for a long time the Christians in the South have controlled many sectors of the economy and administration. When Muslims gain more influence, Christians complain that they are losing such. In a country ravaged by deep economic crisis, there is a constant struggle over maintaining and gaining power and privileges.

Social and economic crisis in Indonesia

The economic crisis in Indonesia has been slightly less severe than in Nigeria. The social infrastructure is better organized and there is a strong

[11] According to the United Nations Development Program (UNDP).

emphasis on education at all levels for as many as possible. Education is the central precondition for economic growth and the subsequent reduction of poverty. More efficient political and administrative systems will still need to be developed.

The economic crisis affecting Indonesia since 1998 has been one of the main reasons for growing tensions and outbreaks of violence. The conflicts in Central Sulawesi and Maluku (pp. 55-62) have been a threat to national cohesion and previously existing peaceful coexistence. It has been feared for a long time that unless the distribution of wealth and economic resources between the central and local governments is regulated, Indonesia will disintegrate.

Since 1998, many people have lost their livelihood and lifetime savings, and public discontent has grown as a result of economic hardship. An estimated fifteen percent unemployment and rising inflation have affected especially the urban poor and middle class. The growing gap between rich and poor has contributed to hatred and mistrust of others. At the same time, many have turned to their faith, and their religious identity has become more important to them.

Socioeconomic developments in Denmark

The arrival of the first labor migrants in the 1960s was welcomed and looked upon as a necessity in order to ensure continued economic growth. At a time of full employment, immigrants were therefore not regarded as competitors to the native Danish labor force.

In the early 1970s, the social welfare system suddenly and quite unexpectedly came under heavy pressure and unemployment increased. Gradually the Danes' attitude to immigrants changed; they became afraid that something might be taken away from them. The immigrants' ethnic, religious and cultural "otherness" gradually became an increasingly important issue in the public debate. Culture and religion came to be regarded as problems and a hostile image of Islam and Muslims was slowly beginning to dominate the public debate.

More and more Danes began to listen to populist agitation, according to which the high rate of unemployment among immigrants and their continued growing numbers represent an economic burden and threat to the existing welfare system. Today this view is reinforced by the Danish People's Party, according to which Muslim immigration is one of the most important threats to Denmark's future, also in economic terms. According to them the country's welfare system can only be rescued if immigration is stopped.[12]

Escalation of conflicts

In all three countries, political transition resulted in an escalation of religious tensions and conflicts between Christian and Muslims. Since the 1970s, there have been over seventy major eruptions in Nigeria, mostly in urban centers. At first mainly spontaneous, they developed into well-prepared attacks—often armed and supported from outside.[13] In Indonesia, the conflicts have been more localized and not on the same scale nor as significant as in Nigeria. Tensions simmered below the surface and have only rarely boiled over. However, when they did, as in Maluku and Central Sulawesi, they were violent and brutal.

One of the reasons for this is that the tensions are not fuelled by national divisions like in the case of Nigeria, and debates about secularism and Sharî'a not so contentious. Added to this is what Dr M. Abdullah Amin has called a common "cultural capital," a strong integrative force, binding people together as Indonesians by helping them to relate to one another and creating basic standards for conduct.[14] "Cultural capital" is understood

[12] The member of the European Parliament, Mogens Camre (Danish People's Party), has gone so far as to say that the birthrate among Danes is going down because Danes have neither time nor the energy to have children because of the economic burden they have to carry due to the immigrant population.

[13] On the conflicts, see Sati U. Fwatshak, "A Comparative Analysis of the 19th and 21st Century Religious Conflicts on the Jos Plateau, Central Nigeria," in *Swedish Missiological Themes*, vol. 94, no. 3 (2006), pp. 259-280.

[14] Prof. Dr M. Amin Abdullah, rector of State Institute of Islamic Studies (IAIN), was part of the LWF study team. During our visits to Denmark and Indonesia, he repeatedly came back to this concept of cultural capital as a foundation of coexistence in Indonesia. This was in many ways confirmed during our stay in the country.

The term "cultural capital" was first articulated by the French sociologist, Pierre Bourdieu, as one of three types of capital: economic, social and cultural. Capital acts, according to Bourdieu, as a "social relation within a system of exchange." It comprises three subtypes: embodied, objectified and institutionalized cultural capital. In the context of our studies in Indonesia, cultural capital is used in the sense of embodied cultural capital—knowledge and attitudes, a way of thinking, speaking, relating that which is inherited and acquired by the individual Indonesian.

here as a cultural surplus of shared values and ideas. It is seen as a cultural framework and a way of constructively dealing with very heterogeneous and sometime tense situations nationally as well as locally.

In Nigeria and Indonesia, the immediate cause of conflict varies from place to place. Nonetheless, the remote causes of conflict are in many cases similar as is their course. Often minor incidents, fuelled by rumors, sparked off the riots. Several stages of escalation followed during which each side claimed that the atrocities were committed in retaliation or self-defense.

In Denmark, there have been no actual major outbreaks of physical two-way violence. Like in most other European societies, one-way violence and threats have taken the form of racially motivated harassment, threats via SMS or e-mails, violence against taxi drivers, vandalism against shops and desecration of Muslim graveyards. The conflicts took the form of verbal abuse and aggression, sweeping generalizations, hate speeches, extremism, etc.

As in Nigeria and Indonesia, the conflicts were triggered by certain incidents, statements by politicians, media or by some Muslim individual (often referred to as "imam"). The events of 9/11, the murder of the Dutch film director Theo Van Gogh, the freedom prize awarded to the Dutch politician Ayaan Hirsi Ali, the murder of an Italian tourist committed by three youngsters of Turkish background, the bombings in London, arrests of young Muslims under suspicion for complicity in the terrorist attacks in Sarajevo, and more recently the caricatures of the Prophet in a Danish newspaper, are some of the incidents that have forced Muslims into a defensive position. However, these incidents did not provoke any violent actions among Muslims. Their reaction has taken the form of radicalization, isolation, resignation and anger against Danish society.[15]

Pierre Bourdieu and Jean Claude Passeron, "Cultural Reproduction and Social Reproduction," in Richard K. Brown (ed.), *Knowledge, Education and Cultural Change* (London: Tavistock, 1973); Pierre Bourdieu, "The Forms of Capital," in J. G. Richardson, *Handbook for Theory and Research for the Sociology of Education* (New York: Greenwood, 1986), pp. 241-258; Pierre Bourdieu, *The State Nobility. Elite Schools in the Field of Power* (Chicago: Stanford University Press, 1996). Reference can also be made to Robert W. Hefner's use of the term "cultural quality" and "social capital." Hefner, *op. cit.* (note 9), p. 10.

[15] In April 2007, a twenty-five-year-old Muslim of Palestinian background, Asmaa Abdol-Hamid, wearing a head scarf and refusing to shake hands with men declared her candidacy for parliament as member of a small political party, the Unity Party. This created a strong reaction among some Members of Parliament from the Danish People's Party who took turns explaining why

In the next section we shall examine the causes of the escalation of conflicts with the aid of three concrete case studies which will help us to understand the mechanisms behind the walls that have been built between Christians and Muslims. This knowledge and understanding is needed so that our efforts to overcome violence, improve relationships and build bridges will be relevant and constructive.

---

she was not fit for the assembly, and the former pastor, Søren Krarup, publicly and in parliament compared Muslims and their scarves to Nazis and their swastikas. He saw the head scarf as a totalitarian symbol. Mogens Camre from the same party and member of the European Parliament added that because of her wearing the head scarf she had been brainwashed and needed psychiatric treatment. These statements gave rise to a heated debate.

Wall Structures
Stories of Conflict

The Danish Cartoon Crisis

Mogens Mogensen

In February 2006, Denmark experienced its worst crisis in terms of international politics since World War II. The crisis had been brewing for months before it exploded. On 30 September 2005, Denmark's largest newspaper, *Jyllands-Posten*, published twelve cartoons of the Prophet Muhammad. One showed the Prophet wearing a turban in the shape of a bomb with a burning fuse, another depicted him wielding a cutlass and a third had him saying that paradise was running short of virgins for suicide bombers.[1] The images, considered blasphemous under Islam, drew intense criticism from across the Muslim minority in Denmark and the Muslim world at large.

Growing anti-immigrant and anti-Muslim sentiments in Denmark

The Muhammad cartoons did not come out of the blue. They were published amid growing anti-immigrant sentiments in Denmark, reflected in the rise of the far-right Danish People's Party. The party, which held thirteen percent of the seats in the Danish parliament, had helped to push through the toughest anti-immigration laws on the continent, including one preventing Danish citizens aged twenty-four or younger from bringing in spouses from outside Denmark. Søren Krarup, a retired pastor and leading voice in the party, said the Muslim response to the cartoons showed that Islam was not compatible with Danish customs. He said, "Muslims who come here reject our culture [...] Muslim immigration is a way for Muslims to conquer us, just as they have done for the past 1,400 years."[2]

[1] Flemming Rose, "Muhammeds ansigt" [The face of Muhammad], in *Jyllands-Posten*, 30 September 2006. The drawings are available on the internet, among others at **http://epaper.jp.dk/30-09-2005/demo/JP_04-03.html 21-06-07**. Some of the drawings, however, made fun, not of Muhammad, but of those who they perceived were anti-Muslim, including *Jyllands-Posten's* editors and the head of the Danish People's Party.

[2] Dan Bilefsky, "Denmark is Unlikely Front in Islam-West Culture War," in *The New York Times*, 8 January 2006, at **www.nytimes.com/2006/01/08/international/europe/08denmark.ready.html?ex=1294376400&en=bc5d2cb7b5c7df14&ei=5090&partner=rssuserland&emc=rss**, 29-06-2006.

From its inception in 2001, the Liberal-Conservative government, led by Anders Fogh Rasmussen, depended on the Danish People's Party for its majority in parliament. The Danish People's Party, with the two pastors Søren Krarup and Jesper Langballe (see p. 96) had clearly managed to influence developments in immigration and integration policies and also the political rhetoric concerning Muslims. Politicians from the Danish People's Party referred to Islam as "a fascist ideology," "religious Nazism," "an ideology of evil," "a plague," "the greatest threat to world peace since the fall of Communism," "a terror organization," and they called for all Muslims to be repatriated.[3] Politicians and newspapers critical of the government objected to the aggressive anti-Muslim rhetoric, and international commissions and committees criticized the way in which Muslims and other immigrants were treated and talked about. The government rejected this critique.

On 25 September 2005, at the annual meeting of the Conservative Party, the Minister for Cultural Affairs, Brian Mikkelsen, called for a new offensive in the culture wars. He specifically directed his remarks against Muslim immigrants who allegedly would not recognize Danish culture and European norms, but have developed a parallel society based on medieval standards and undemocratic ways of thinking. Mikkelsen claimed that freedom of expression was threatened, because a Danish stand-up comedian had not dared to urinate on the Qur'ân and illustrators had not dared to put their name under drawings of Muhammad in a children's book.[4]

The publication of the Muhammad cartoons in Jyllands-Posten

Little surprise then that it was *Jyllands-Posten* that decided to publish such cartoons of Muhammad. It was the culmination of a yearlong anti-Muslim campaign. In the late 1980s, *Ekstra Bladet* initiated a campaign against immigrants and Muslims, in which Søren Krarup was allowed to write over 200 articles. Later, *Jyllands-Posten* became the most im-

[3] Tøger Seidenfaden & Rune Engelbreth Larsen, *Karikaturkrisen. En undersøgelse af baggrund og ansvar* [The cartoon crisis. An examination of the background and responsibility] (Copenhagen: Gyldendal, 2006), pp. 26f.

[4] George Blecher, "Politics Dressed up as Principle," in *Eurozine*, 6 March 2007, at **www.eurozine.com/articles/2006-03-06-blecher-en.html#**, 20-06-06.

portant newspaper in terms of aggressively anti-Muslim sentiments in letters to the editor, editorials and some of its articles.[5]

On 30 September 2005, *Jyllands-Posten* published the series of cartoons of Muhammad drawn by twelve Danish illustrators. In the accompanying article, "The Face of Muhammad," the cultural editor, Flemming Rose, picked up issues raised by the minister in an article on self-censorship and freedom of speech. Rose wrote that he decided to commission the cartoons for *Jyllands-Posten* after he had heard that Danish cartoonists were too scared of Muslim fundamentalists to illustrate a new children's biography of Muhammad. Annoyed at the self-censorship he claimed had overtaken Europe, he stated:

> The modern, secular society is rejected by some Muslims. They demand a special position, insisting on special consideration of their own religious feelings. It is incompatible with contemporary democracy and freedom of speech, where you must be ready to put up with insults, mockery and ridicule. It is certainly not always attractive and nice to look at, and it does not mean that religious feelings should be made fun of at any price, but that is of minor importance in the present context. [...] We are on our way to a slippery slope where no one can tell how the self-censorship will end. That is why *Morgenavisen Jyllands-Posten* has invited members of the Danish editorial cartoonists union to draw Muhammad as they see him.[6]

Rose defended his decision referring to the murder of the Dutch filmmaker Theo van Gogh. "The cartoons did nothing that transcends the cultural norms of secular Denmark and this was not a provocation to insult Muslims," said Rose. "But if we talk of freedom of speech, even if it was a provocation, that does not make our right to do it any less legitimate before the law." [7] In an article in the *Washington Post*, Rose justified the commissioning and publication of the cartoons, stating that

---

[5] At the same time, *Jyllands-Posten* also publish articles that are much more nuanced and sensitive to Muslims, e.g., by one of their senior journalists, Orla Borg, who received the EU's anti-discrimination prize for his journalism, *Journalisten*, no. 8 (2005).

[6] Rose, *op. cit.* (note 1). English translation at **www.answers.com/topic/jyllands-posten-muhammad-cartoons-controversy#wp-_note-3**, 20-06-06.

[7] Bilefsky, *op. cit.* (note 2).

> The cartoonists treated Islam the same way they treat Christianity, Buddhism, Hinduism and other religions. And by treating Muslims in Denmark as equals they made a point: We are integrating you into the Danish tradition of satire because you are part of our society, not strangers. The cartoons are including, rather than excluding, Muslims.[8]

Initial reactions

Many Muslims were offended by the cartoons and protested in many different ways. A few days after their publication, eleven Muslim organizations led by Islamisk Trossamfund wrote a letter to the ambassadors of eleven Muslim countries asking them to alert their governments with a view to issuing an official protest. In a press release, they expressed their criticism of *Jyllands-Posten*, stating that normally there were limits to the freedom of expression when it comes to anti-Semitism and scorning the Danish flag, and that they demanded that *Jyllands-Posten* express its regret for its action. Furthermore, they wrote to the Minister for Cultural Affairs asking for dialogue with the media, politicians and other key persons in society to prevent negative reactions to and consequences from this arrogant attitude toward a minority. Three thousand five hundred Muslims demonstrated peacefully in Copenhagen against the cartoons.

Other major Danish newspapers chose not to publish the cartoons. While emphasizing the importance of freedom of expression, most of them dissociated themselves from *Jyllands-Posten's* decision to print the cartoons, deeming them to be an unnecessary insult to Muslims.

Within a couple of weeks, the cartoons captured international attention. On 11 October 2005, Imam Sheikh Raed Hlayhel, Århus, was interviewed on Al Jazeera TV where he protested against the publication of the cartoons. Soon afterwards, other mass media in the Muslim world began to report on the issue.

In their letter to the Danish Prime Minister on 12 October 2005, ambassadors from eleven Muslim countries tried to draw the Primer Minister's attention to an "ongoing smear campaign in public circles and the media

[8] Flemming Rose, "Why I Published those Cartoons," in the *Washington Post*, 19 February 2006, at **www.washingtonpost.com/wp-dyn/content/article/2006/02/17/AR2006021702499.html**, 30-06-06.

against Islam and Muslims." Apart from public statements made by a minister and a parliamentarian, they protested in particular against the publication of the cartoons, all of which are against the spirit of Danish values of tolerance, civil society, and which "can also cause reactions in Muslim countries and among Muslim communities in Europe." Therefore they urged the government to "take all those responsible to task under the law of the land and in the interest of interfaith harmony, better integration and Denmark's overall relations with the Muslim world."[9]

The ambassadors asked for a meeting with Prime Minister Anders Fogh Rasmussen. This was declined nine days later. In his letter, Rasmussen stated that he would not intervene in the affair on the grounds of freedom of expression, but said the diplomats were free to undertake legal proceedings.[10] The Social Democratic Party and the Socialist People's Party (SF) advised the Prime Minister to meet with the ambassadors, but he still declined. Later, twenty-two former Danish ambassadors and high ranking diplomats criticized the Prime Minister for not accepting to meet the eleven ambassadors, a criticism for which the former Foreign Minister, Uffe Ellemann Jensen (Liberal Party), expressed his full support.[11]

[9] **www.rogerbuch.dk/jpabrev.pdf**, 29-06-06. The ambassadors represented Turkey, Saudi-Arabia, Iran, Pakistan, Egypt, Indonesia, Algeria, Bosnia-Herzegovina, Libya, Morocco and Palestine.

[10] **www.rogerbuch.dk/jpfoghssvar.doc**, 29-06-06. "Det danske samfund hviler på respekt for ytringsfrihed, religiøs tolerance og ens normer for alle religioner.Ytringsfriheden er selve fundamentet for det danske samfund. Ytringsfriheden har stort spillerum, og den danske regering råder ikke over midler til at øve indflydelse på pressen. Dansk lovgivning forbyder imidlertid handlinger eller udtryk, der er af blasfemisk eller diskriminerende art. Den krænkede part kan bringe sådanne handlinger eller udtryk for en domstol, og det er så op til domstolene at behandle den enkelte sag." [Danish society is based on respect for the freedom of expression, religious tolerance and the equality of all religions. Freedom of expression is the foundation of Danish society. There is a wide scope for freedom of expression, and the Danish government has no means to exert influence on the press. Danish legislation, however, forbids acts or expressions of a blasphemous or discriminatory nature. The offended part can take such actions or expressions to court, and then it is up the courts to deal with each individual case.].

[11] **http://politiken.dk/VisArtikel.iasp?PageID=425732**, 29-06-06 " Såvel religionsfriheden som ytringsfriheden er blandt de grundlovssikrede friheder, men det har aldrig været foreneligt med danske holdninger at udnytte friheden til bevidst at såre et mindretal på deres tro. [...] Det ville have klædt det demokratiske Danmark, om statsministeren havde imødekommet den anmodning om en samtale, som blev fremsat af elleve fremmede ambassadører fra muslimske lande." [Freedom of religion as well as freedom of expression are among the constitutional freedoms. Nonetheless, this freedom has never been used consciously to hurt a minority concerning their faith. [...] It would have been very becoming for the democratic Denmark if the Prime Minister had complied with the ambassadors' request for a meeting].

From the middle of October, the crisis spread to many parts of the Muslim world through the intervention of Muslim organizations such as the Organization of Islamic Conference (OIC), Islamic Educational, Scientific and Cultural Organization (ISESCO) and the Arab League.[12] One example is the OIC's general secretary, representing more than one billion Muslims in fifty-seven Muslim countries, who in a letter to the Prime Minister warned him that the conflict might escalate unless the Danish government unequivocally took a stance regarding the cartoons and took all the necessary measures.[13] "This has trespassed all limits of objective criticism into insults and contempt of the religious beliefs of more than one billion Muslims around the world, including thousands in Denmark," so Al-Azhar's Islamic Research Academy in a statement issued on 10 December.[14]

Non-Muslim organizations also began to criticize the publication of the cartoons. Louise Arbour, the High Commissioner for Human Rights, said she was "alarmed" by such an "unacceptable disregard for the beliefs of others." Similar condemnations came from the European Commission and the Council of Europe. But neither the editors of *Jyllands-Posten* nor the Danish government wanted to accept the criticism, which according to them would lead to an undermining of the principle of freedom of expression.

In December, Muslim organizations in Denmark sent two representatives to present their case to the media, politicians and Muslim leaders in the Middle East. The Danish Muslims felt that their complaints had not been properly responded to by the Danish authorities or media and therefore chose to seek support from Muslim friends abroad. The delegations had compiled a file of the cartoons, other drawings and articles which they thought to be insulting to Muslims. Later, two interrelated issues about the journeys of these two delegations were hotly debated in the Danish media and among politicians. Were these Muslim delegations guilty of spreading misinformation about the situation of Muslims in Denmark? Second, was the subsequent crisis entailing a boycott of Danish goods, demonstrations, burning of embassies, etc, primarily the result of this

[12] Larsen & Seidenfaden, *op. cit.* (note 3), pp. 64-72.

[13] *Ibid.*, p. 65.

[14] Adel Abdel Halim, "Al-Azhar Takes Anti-Prophet Danish Cartoons to UN," at IslamOnline.net, 11 December 2006, **www.islam-online.net/English/News/2005-12/11/article04.shtml**, 29-06-06.

misinformation? There were a few examples of incorrect information on file—a fact that some of the Muslim leaders later accepted. There are however clear indications that the subsequent crisis was not primarily a result of activities or mistakes made by these delegations.

The Prime Minister tried to defuse the row mostly by ignoring it. After having rejected a request for a meeting with eleven ambassadors from Islamic countries, he was attacked by twenty-two former Danish ambassadors to Muslim countries, who deplored his neglect of diplomatic niceties. After some hesitation, the Prime Minister tried to tackle the matter in his New Year's address, in the last section of which he dealt with the cartoon crisis, albeit without directly commenting on the Muhammad drawings published in *Jyllands-Posten*. While strongly affirming that freedom of speech in Denmark is absolute and non-negotiable, he condemned "any expression, action or indication that attempt to demonize groups of people on the basis of their religious or ethnic backgrounds." While some found the tone of the debate too shrill and unpleasant, he concluded that, bar a few exceptions, the debate was civilized, fair and peaceful. "However, we are all responsible for administering freedom of speech in such a manner that we do not incite to hatred and do not cause fragmentation of the community that is one of Denmark's strengths."[15]

On the international scene, these statements were used to persuade Muslim leaders that the Danish government dissociated itself from the cartoons and to underline its respect for other religions. On the domestic political scene, they were used to emphasize the government's strong position concerning freedom of expression.

The Prime Minister's statements were positively received by some of the ambassadors from Muslim countries, and the Foreign Minister, Per Stig Møller, succeeded in reaching an agreement with the general secretary of the Arab League. This decision was based on a common understanding of mutual respect between religions and non-interference of politicians in the affairs of private media.

---

[15] Prime Minister Anders Fogh Rasmussen's New Year's Address, 2006, at **www.stm.dk/Index/dokumenter.asp?o=6&n=0&d=2468&s=2&str=stor**, 27-06-2006.

The cartoon crisis—an international crisis

In early January 2006, the cartoon crisis was generally assumed to be over. However, in mid-January, the crisis gathered new momentum, climaxing in the last days of January and early February.

On 10 January, a conservative Christian magazine in Norway published the twelve Muhammad cartoons. *Jyllands-Posten* had previously declined requests to give other mass media permission to publish the cartoons, but now changed its policy and allowed the cartoons to be spread all over the world.[16] In this way the Muslim world's attention was again directed towards the cartoons. The OIC condemned the republication of the cartoons, and the grand mufti of Saudi Arabia demanded an apology from *Jyllands-Posten*. On 25 January, Saudi Arabia was the first of a number of Muslim countries to withdraw its ambassador from Denmark. In the following days, a boycott against Danish products spread throughout the Middle East and beyond. On 29 January, the Danish flag was burned in Gaza, and shortly afterwards Danish flags were burned in many Muslim countries during mass demonstrations.

The crisis had now reached such dimensions that the Prime Minister had to act. For the first time since the publication of the cartoons four months earlier, Anders Fogh Rasmussen publicly expressed an opinion regarding the cartoons on 30 January. Without committing his government, he personally dissociated himself from the cartoons. "Personally I have such a respect for people's religious convictions that I would never represent Muhammad, Jesus or any other religious figure in a way that might offend other people," he said on the TV2 News. However, he underlined the freedom of the press in Denmark, stating that since the media were free and independent they can decide which cartoons they want to publish.

On the same day, *Jyllands-Posten* published an apology to the Muslim world.

[16] Later also a number of other media in the West (and a few in the Middle East!) decided to publish the cartoons.

> In our opinion, the twelve drawings were sober. They were not intended to be offensive, nor were they at variance with Danish law, but they have indisputably offended many Muslims for which we apologize.[17]

Jyllands-Posten did not apologize for the publication of the cartoons, but only for the offence that the publication of the cartoons had caused involuntarily. Subsequently, twenty-five Muslim organizations in Denmark demanded a new, unreserved apology from *Jyllands-Posten* before they would contribute to solving the boycott.[18]

A few days later, Anders Fogh Rasmussen was interviewed on the Arabic TV station Al Arabiya, where he repeated his previous statements.

> The Danish people have defended freedom of expression and religious freedom for generations. We deeply respect all religions including Islam and it is important for me to tell you that the Danish people have no intention of offending Muslims. On the contrary we will do our utmost to continue our historic tradition of dialogue and mutual respect. And therefore I am deeply distressed that many Muslims have seen the drawings in a Danish newspaper as a defamation of the Prophet Muhammad.[19]

The following day, meeting with seventy-six ambassadors, the Prime Minister repeated his previous statements and concluded by expressing the hope that they might now return to a constructive dialogue. However, the Prime Minister did not issue an official apology for the cartoons—neither in Al Arabiya, nor at the diplomatic meeting. This did not contribute significantly to solving the crisis.

Mass demonstrations took place in a number of Muslim countries. Many of the demonstrations turned violent. Danish (and other Western) flags were burned, property was destroyed, the Danish embassies in Damascus, Beirut and Teheran attacked and dozens of people were killed in clashes with the police as ranging from Afghanistan to Nigeria.

---

[17] "Honorable Fellow Citizens of the Muslim World," in *Jyllands-Posten*, 30 January 2006, at **www.jp.dk/meninger/ncartikel:aid=3527646**, 01-07-06.

[18] Britta Søndergaard, "Imamer kræver en ny undskyldning" [Imams demand a new apology], in *Kristeligt Dagblad*, 1 February 2006, p. 2.

[19] Statsministeriet, "Prime Minister Anders Fogh Rasmussen's interview with Al Arabiya," at **www.stm.dk/Index/dokumenter.asp?o=2&n=0&h=2&t=18&d=2508&s=1&str=stor**, 01-06-06.

Apparently governments and local political and religious groups took advantage of the public anger over the cartoons to mobilize the masses for their own political or religious purposes.

The international community condemned the attacks on the embassies and the threats against Danes, often coupled with a criticism of the cartoons published in *Jyllands-Posten*. Denmark's allies in NATO and the EU supported Denmark: violence was completely unacceptable. However, some of them also dissociated themselves from the publication of the cartoons.

Jyllands-Posten also received support. On 1 March, an international group of intellectuals issued a manifesto in the French satirical weekly, *Charlie Hebdo*, stating that the cartoon crisis was part of a struggle between Islamism and democracy. This was immediately published in *Jyllands-Posten*.

> After having overcome fascism, Nazism, and Stalinism, the world now faces a new totalitarian global threat: Islamism. We, writers, journalists, intellectuals, call for resistance to religious totalitarianism and for the promotion of freedom, equal opportunity and secular values for all. The recent events, which occurred after the publication of drawings of Muhammed in European newspapers, have revealed the necessity of the struggle for these universal values. [20]

In Denmark, Muslims did not protest violently against the cartoons. At a later date, a police intelligence officer informed the public that they had worked closely with a number of Danish imams before and during the crisis. He believed that the imams had significantly contributed to

---

[20] "Manifesto: Together Facing the new Totalitarianism," at **http://news.bbc.co.uk/2/hi/europe/4764730.stm**. Among the initial twelve signatories were Salman Rushdie, Ayan Hirsi Ali and Bernard Henri Lévy. A number of media people, however, were concerned about the newspapers' printing of the manifesto. See *The Editors Weblog*: "From October 2005 to February 2006, all newspapers could agree on solidarity with a newspaper under attack, a newspaper afforded the right - or the duty - to inform its readers. This 1st of March manifesto is totally different because it reintroduces a left-right divide. Some right-wing newspapers will consider that they agree with the manifesto and they will promote it, the left-wing newspapers will be worried by a threefold risk:

- firstly, the always easy assimilation between Islam and Islamism
- secondly, the threat the manifesto makes to the possibility of beginning a real dialogue with the Muslim world after the Mohammed cartoons controversy
- thirdly, the risk to fall into the "clash of civilizations" trap and the "World War IV" assertion.

In other words, the Salman Rushdie/Taslima Nasreen manifesto (among others) could add fuel to the fire." At **www.editorsweblog.org/print_newspapers/2006/03/jyllands_posten_reprints_manifesto_fight.php**, 03/08/06.

maintaining peace by calling on the Muslim community not to resort to violence, but only to use democratic means.[21]

Diplomacy and dialogue

Throughout the cartoon crisis there were private and official attempts to promote dialogue and reconciliation. In mid-February, a Danish church delegation, headed by two bishops, went to Egypt in an attempt to reduce the tensions between Muslims and Christians in Denmark and the Middle East. In the Middle East, the visit was perceived as expressing an understanding of the frustration in the Muslim world, and evidence that there were groups in Denmark who wanted dialogue with Muslims and distanced themselves from the publication of the cartoons.[22]

Towards the end of February, the United Nations (UN), OIC and a number of Arab countries called for restraint and dialogue. At the opening of a meeting in Qatar for the Alliance of Civilizations, UN General Secretary, Kofi Annan, tried to contribute to reconciliation by stating that

> [i]n truth, the present conflicts and misunderstandings probably have more to do with proximity than with distance. The offensive caricatures of the Prophet Muhammad were first published in a European country which has recently acquired a significant Muslim population, and is not yet sure how to adjust to it. And some of the strongest reactions—perhaps especially the more violent ones—have been seen in Muslim countries where many people feel themselves the victims of excessive Western influence or interference.[23]

---

[21] Larsen & Seidenfaden *op. cit.* (note 3), p. 183.

[22] Det Mellemkirkelige Råd, "Danske udtalelser overbragt under delegationsrejse i Egypten" [Danish statements delivered during the visit of the delegation to Egypt], at **www.interchurch.dk/mkrdan/aktuelt.php?key=1409&mt=0**, 05-09-06. Allan Sørensen, "Stor presseinteresse for danske biskoppers besøg i Egypten" [Great interest of the press for the visit of Danish bishops to Egypt], in *Kristeligt Dagblad*, 20 February 2006. The visit was arranged by the Danish Interchurch Council and Danmission. The delegation met with the leader of Al-Az-har, Sheik Muhammad Sayyed Tantawy and the grand mufti, Dr Aly Gomaá, and presented the public statements made by *Jyllands-Posten* and the Danish Prime Minister.

[23] Doha, Qatar, 26 February 2006, "Statement by the Secretary-General at the Opening Session of the Second Meeting of the High-level Group for the Alliance of Civilizations," at **www.un.org/apps/sg/sgstats.asp?nid=1936**, 05-09-06.

On February 26, the Danish ambassador returned to Damascus and normal diplomatic activities were resumed in the Middle East. The following day, foreign ministers of the EU agreed on a statement in which they emphasized the principle of freedom of expression while regretting any harm that the cartoons might have caused the feelings of Muslims. They stated that freedom of expression must be used responsibly, and strongly condemned the violent reactions in a number of countries. With this statement, the EU countries set the stage for a number of initiatives geared towards strengthening the dialogue between Europe and the Muslim world.[24]

Towards the end of March, a delegation of Muslim leaders from Denmark left for Bahrain to attend a conference of about 300 Muslim leaders from around the world in order to end the trade boycott against Denmark, or at to least to restrict it. Their initiative, however, was not successful and the conference communiqué called for the boycott to continue.[25]

In April, the cartoon crisis waned and during the summer months other international issues began to make the headlines.

Legal responses

The Muhammad cartoons were also dealt with by the Danish judicial system. On 29 October 2005, eleven Danish Muslim organizations filed a complaint with the police, claiming that *Jyllands-Posten* had violated the laws against blasphemy and racial discrimination. The spokeswoman, Asmaa Abdol-Hamid, emphasized that while they supported freedom of expression, they called for decency in expression. "What we notice is the article accompanying the publication of the cartoons. As we read it, it is evident that the intention of the newspaper has been to scorn and mock."[26]

In January 2006, the regional public prosecutor in Viborg rejected the complaint. The ruling was appealed, and the public prosecutor confirmed the previous decision on 15 March 2006. Interestingly, the prosecutor commented that the freedom of expression in Denmark is not without limit.

---

[24] Maria Lindeberg og Christian Lindhardt, "Dansk glæde over Muhammed-erklæring" [Danish joy at Muhammad statement], in *Kristeligt Dagblad*, 28 February 2006.

[25] Larsen & Seidenfaden, *op. cit.* (note 3), pp. 181-182.

[26] *Jyllands-Posten*, 29 October 2006. Quoted from *ibid.*, p. 244.

> Although there is no basis for instituting criminal proceedings in this case, it should be noted that both provisions of the Danish criminal code—and also other penal provisions, e.g. about defamation of character—contain a restriction of the freedom of expression. Section 140 of the Danish criminal code protects religious feelings against mockery and scorn and section 266 b protects groups of persons against scorn and degradation on account of i.e., their religion. To the extent publicly made expressions fall within the scope of these rules there is, therefore, no free and unrestricted right to express opinions about religious subjects. It is thus not a correct description of existing law when the article in *Jyllands-Posten* states that it is incompatible with the right to freedom of expression to demand special consideration for religious feelings and that one has to be ready to put up with "scorn, mockery and ridicule."[27]

In March 2006, seven Muslim organizations led by Islamisk Trossamfund started legal proceedings action against *Jyllands-Posten's* editor-in-chief, Carsten Juste, and the cultural editor, Flemming Rose, for having violated paragraphs 267 and 268 of the Danish penal code concerning defamation and slander of Muslims in Denmark by having published the twelve cartoons. In October, the editors of *Jyllands-Posten* were acquitted by the court in Århus. In his ruling, the judge stated that it could not be ruled out that the cartoons might have offended the honor of some of Muslims, but that there was no basis for assuming that the purpose of the cartoons had been to offend or slander Muslims.[28]

Political responses

The cartoon crisis became occasion for Naser Khader, a Muslim immigrant from Syria and Member of Parliament for Det Radikale Venstre, the Social-Liberal Party, to launch a political initiative. While initially critical of the cartoons, he decided on 4 February, following the escalation of the cartoon crisis, to form a network of moderate Muslims called Demokratiske Muslimer

[27] Possible criminal proceedings in the case of *Jyllands-Posten*'s article, "The Face of Muhammad," 15 March 2006, at **http://66.249.93.104/search?q=cache:-iHh1LUOyAgJ:www.rigsadvokaten.dk/ref.aspx%3Fid%3D890+%22Decision+on+possible+criminal+proceedings%22&hl=da&gl=dk&ct=clnk&cd=1**, 30-06-06.

[28] "Jyllands-Posten frifundet" [*Jyllands-Posten* acquitted], in *Jyllands-Posten*, 26 October 2006.

(Democratic Muslims). This was in opposition to Islamisk Trossamfund and all the imams who had actively protested against the cartoons both in Denmark and in the Middle East. The network, which soon counted 1,500 Muslim members and 6,000 non-Muslim supporters, was warmly welcomed by the government as well as other political parties. While the Prime Minister had been very hesitant to meet with Danish Muslim religious leaders, he already on 13 February invited representatives of this new network to a meeting. The result was a polarization in the Muslim community between a more radical Muslim group around Imam Abu Laban and Islamisk Trossamfund, and a secular Muslim group around Naser Khader and Demokratiske Muslimer.[29] Most Muslims however did not feel that either of the two groups represented their position or their interests.[30]

From the beginning, the Danish government held that the cartoon crisis was about the freedom of expression. The government chose to interpret the letter from the Islamic ambassadors, which asked for a meeting with the Prime Minister, as if they had asked the government to interfere with the free press and to curb the freedom of expression. When the government was criticized for its handling of the cartoon crisis and its unwillingness effectively to dissociate itself from *Jyllands-Posten's* publication of the cartoons, Prime Minister Anders Fogh Rasmussen, in an interview with the conservative daily, *Berlingske Tidende*, on 26 February, went on the offensive and attacked representatives of the media, intellectuals and business people for betraying the principles of free speech. Like US President George W. Bush had said when referring to the fight against terrorism after 9/11, "You're either with us or against us in the fight against terror," Fogh Rasmussen stated that it was time to separate the sheep from the goats. Either you are for free speech or against.

The Prime Minister's polarizing statement was strongly criticized by former Foreign Minister, Uffe Ellemann Jensen, some politicians from the government and the opposition as well as some industrial leaders. However, he received considerable support from The Danish People's Party and most politicians from the parties in government.

---

[29] Larsen & Seidenfaden, *op. cit.* (note 3), pp. 113ff.

[30] Leif Vestergaard, Safet Bektovic & Mogens S. Mogensen, *Rapport fra en lytterunde blandt muslimske organisationer og moskeer* [Report from a listening round among Muslim organizations and mosques] (Århus: Folkekirke og Religionsmøde, 2006).

Christian responses

From the beginning, it was very clear that the cartoon crisis was not a religious conflict between Muslims and Christians but rather a conflict between people with religious sensitivities and people with secularist views. While defending the freedom of expression (at the legal level), many Christian groups expressed their condemnation of the printing of the cartoons (at an ethical level).

> We should treat Muslims in Denmark in the same way that we would like to be treated. When I do not like to see my own religion smeared, I should not smear theirs either. I am not of the opinion that we should stop drawing Muhammad but we should not make drawings of him in situations that are offending.[31]

Other Christians, however, were of the opinion that Muslims had to accept scorn and ridicule just as Christians have been used to doing in a secular society.

When the international crisis erupted at the beginning of February, the bishop of Copenhagen called on both Muslims and Christians to keep cool. "We have to dissociate ourselves both from the cartoons and from the burning of the Danish flag with the white cross. And then it is extremely important that we continue to talk to each other."[32]

On 2 February, the board of the Committee for Church & Encounter with other Religions of the Evangelical Lutheran Church in Denmark (Stiftssamarbejdet "Folkekirke og Religionsmøde") issued a statement in which it said that

> freedom of speech does not exclude showing respect for the individual person's religious faith. On the contrary, the respect for the individual person is the presupposition for having freedom of speech in Denmark. With freedom of speech follows respect for others. [...] In the public

---

[31] Statement by Mogens S. Mogensen, in Bente Clausen, "Sund reaktion fra muslimer" [Healthy reactions from Muslims], in *Kristeligt Dagblad*, 12 October 2006.

[32] Karin Dahl Hansen, "Biskopper maner til besindighed" [Bishops call for circumspection], in *Kristeligt Dagblad*, 1 February 2006, p. 1.

> debate, an understanding of what is sacred and what can offend the individual person of which faith he or she may be is often missing. To provoke or offend another person's faith for the sake of provocation alone does not serve any purpose.

The committee therefore decided to work toward the creation of a dialogue forum where religious leaders could debate common issues.[33]

The following day, the Roman Catholic bishops in the Nordic countries issued a joint statement about the cartoons in which they stated that they

> deplored this attack on the religion and the unquestionable wounds that this has caused among our Muslim friends. For most people religion gives meaning to their life and its basic rules are the source of the traditions and rules, according to which they live. Again and again it appears that certain opinion leaders feel that they are totally free to say what they want without any respect for the understanding and faith of others. We are adherents of a free and open discussion that seeks the truth but in a context and climate of mutual respect and knowledge of what you talk about.[34]

Already in November 2005, Danmission, the largest Lutheran mission society in Denmark, had "dissociated itself from these drawings, which are rightfully perceived as offending to the religious feelings of all people in the Islamic world. As Christians we also feel repulsed by these drawings." On 6 February, they issued a statement addressed to its partners in which they declared that

> Being the second largest Christian NGO in Denmark and one that has been working to build up dialogue between Muslims and Christians for the last 27 years, Danmission looks with a worried mind upon the present agitated situation that has followed up on the drawings. Therefore,

---

[33] Stiftssamarbejdet, Folkekirke og Religionsmøde, *Press Release: Freedom of Speech and Respect*, 2 February 2006, at **www.religionsmoede.dk/index.php?indl_id=2813&id=5822**, 01-07-06.

[34] William Kenney, "Den nordiske bispekonference beklager offentliggørelsen af tegninger af Profeten Muhammad" [The Nordic Episcopal Conference regrets the publication of the drawings of the Prophet Muhammad], at **www.katolsk.dk/2164/**, 03/08/06

> Danmission asks that all good forces pursue dialogue rather than conflict as Danmission will continue to build up dialogue.[35]

In February 2006, Christian groups in collaboration with Muslim groups arranged prayers and demonstrations for peace and reconciliation in Copenhagen and Århus.[36]

As a follow-up to the statement by the board of the Committee for Church and Encounter with other Religions of the Evangelical Lutheran Church in Denmark, this committee initiated a listening round, in which a team of two Christians and one Muslim visited twenty-two Muslim organizations and mosques in order to establish more and better contacts and relations between the church and the Muslim community. The report, published in June, states that the vast majority of the Muslim leaders interviewed were very positive towards the establishment of a Christian-Muslim or interreligious forum.[37] In August, a conference was held between fifteen Muslim and fifteen Christian leaders. At this first dialogue conference between national leaders from the Muslim and Christian communities it was agreed to carry on with this dialogue process.[38]

A the end of April, seven Danish bishops went on a study tour to Leicester, UK, to learn from the Anglican Church how to relate to Muslim and other religious communities. One of the conclusions was that a forum for Christians and Muslims (and representatives of other religious groups) should be set up in Denmark.

Probably in reaction to this initiative, a group of pastors from the Evangelical Lutheran Church in May established the Islamkritisk Netværk (Islam Critical Network). Many of the more than one hundred pastors belong to the theological group Tidehverv, and some of them are also

---

[35] "Statement Addressed to Its Partners," in *Netværk*, no. 2 (April–May 2006), p. 5, at **www.danmission.dk/files/Bibliotek/Netvaerk/Netvrk06-2.AprMaj-web.pdf**.

[36] Anne Ehlers, "Lad ikke vore hjerter fordærves," at **www.religion.dk/nyheder/artikel:aid=280832** 04/08/06; Lissi Rasmussen, "Islamisk-Kristent Studiecenter (IKS) Årsberetning 2005-6" [Islamic-Christian Study Centre (IKS) Annual Report 2005-6], at **www.ikstudiecenter.dk/%C5rsberetning_2005-6.doc**, 04/08/06.

[37] Vestergaard, Bektovic & Mogensen, *op. cit.* (note 30).

[38] "Historisk møde mellem kristne og muslimer" [Historic meeting between Christians and Muslims]. Press statement issued at the end of the conference, at **www.religionsmoede.dk/index.php?indl_id=3731&id=5822,** 05-09-06.

related to the Dansk Folkeparti (Danish People's Party). Instead of dialogue with Muslims they call for mission, understood as the verbal proclamation of the gospel. The two pastors who took the initiative to establish the network dissociate themselves from the idea of an inter-religious council. "[...] Why should we have this, if we do not share the same faith, and why should we give the imams a platform to speak from? It is not the task of the *folkekirken* (folk church) to give them this, but to proclaim Jesus as Christ."[39]

A new cartoon crisis

On 6 October, *Nyhedsavisen*, a small daily, published photos from video footage taken in early August at a summer camp of the Dansk Folkeparti's youth organization. The video clips, later also to be seen in other media, showed young politicians competing as to who could draw or present Muhammad in the most ludicrous and degrading way. Muslims all over the world protested against the new Danish cartoons.

This time, the Danish government reacted promptly to prevent the situation from escalating. Already two days after the publication of the video footage, Prime Minister Anders Fogh Rasmussen dissociated himself from the actions of the young politicians.

> I strongly condemn the behavior of members of the youth wing of the Danish Peoples' Party during their summer camp. It is unacceptable behavior of a small group of young people. Their tasteless behavior in no way represents the way the Danish people or young Danish people view Muslims or Islam. I have noted with great satisfaction that a broad spectrum of the youth wings of the political parties, including the Liberal Party, have jointly expressed their strong condemnation of the behavior.[40]

---

[39] Katrine Winkel Holm & Torben Reinholdt Rasmussen, "Kristendom er modsigelse" [Christianity is a contradiction], in *Kristeligt Dagblad*, 23 May 2006.

[40] "Private video clips during a summer camp of the Danish People's Party's youth organization," Udenrigsministeriet, 9 October 2006, at **www.ambteheran.um.dk/da/menu/Eksportraadgivning/Markedsmuligheder/SidsteNyt/PrivateVideoClipsDuringASummerCampOfThe-DanishPeoplesPartysYouthOrganisation.htm**

This time, ambassadors of all Muslim countries represented in Denmark were called for a meeting with the director of the Foreign Ministry at which they were briefed about the Danish government's position. The Foreign Secretary, Per Stig Møller, held a number of meetings with representatives from Muslim countries, and Danish embassies worked hard to contain the crisis. The Muslim Brotherhood in Egypt called for a trade boycott of goods from countries that allowed such actions. The government of Indonesia officially condemned the insults against the Prophet. There were demonstrations in front of Danish embassies, but the situation never developed into a serious crisis.

What was the cartoon crisis all about?

The cartoon crisis started with the publication of the Muhammad cartoons in *Jyllands-Posten*, 30 September 2005, escalated into an international crisis in February 2006 and had slowly faded away by June 2006. From February onwards, the cartoon crisis brought Denmark into the international limelight. As Prime Minister Fogh Rasmussen stated, it was Denmark's most serious political crisis since World War II. Danish exports to Muslim countries (albeit only a very small percentage of total exports) suffered losses amounting to hundreds of millions of Danish crowns. Moreover, the crisis seems to have contributed to a polarization in the Muslim community and to a certain extent in Danish political life. What was the crisis really about? At least three interpretations may be offered.

Was it a matter of freedom of expression? This was the position taken by *Jyllands-Posten*. The reason for publishing the Muhammad cartoons was to overcome an increasing self-censorship in Denmark regarding material possibly offensive to Muslims. Therefore, *Jyllands-Posten* could not make an apology for having published the cartoons but only for any unintended offense to the feelings of Muslims. The Danish government took the same position. It decided to defend this freedom, and would therefore not comment on what the press had written or apologize for it.

Was the cartoon crisis an indication of a clash of civilizations? Was it basically a clash between a democratic West and an undemocratic Muslim world? It was of course tempting to combine the cartoon conflicts with the fight against terrorism, which in most people's minds is a battle against

Islamism. Furthermore, for many it does not make sense to distinguish between Islam and Islamism. Some of the statements by other politicians in the Danish People's Party clearly point in that direction.[41]

A possible third interpretation is that the cartoon crisis has to do with the recognition or lack thereof of a religious minority. In retrospect, the Danish authorities' refusal to enter into dialogue with Muslim representatives in Denmark and abroad who felt offended by the cartoons led to an escalation of the crisis. The Minister of Cultural Affairs refused to meet with Danish Muslims, and no minister took the time to receive the 16,000 signatures gathered in protest against the cartoons. Most important was the Prime Minister's refusal to meet with the eleven ambassadors. In an official analysis of the so-called "Arab Initiative," conducted by Danish scholars it is stated that

> [...] it was the absence of the recognition that there are individuals who have another view on the freedom of expression than *Jyllands-Posten* and the Danish government that caused the cartoon issue to escalate as much as it did. By completely dismissing that there might be other points of view than the unlimited freedom of expression, the dialogue was blocked. This was perhaps the real offence (or insult) in the cartoon issue: Not that the prophet was scorned, but the lack of recognition of the offence of the scorn of the prophet. Would the recognition that somebody might feel offended have led to a restriction of e.g. the right of *Jyllands-Posten* to print the cartoons? Not the least, but it might have opened up for a real dialogue much earlier in the course of events.[42]

The development of immigration and integration policies and growing anti-immigrant and anti-Muslim sentiments in Denmark over the last few years speak in favor of this interpretation. The cartoon crisis, however, is still too much with us to allow us to draw any final conclusion now.

---

[41] Larsen & Seidenfaden, *op. cit.* (note 3), pp. 305-313.

[42] "Betingelser for dialog: Civilisationskonflikt eller anerkendelse" [Conditions for dialogue: civilizational conflict or recognition], cited at **www.modernetider.dk/Default.asp?m=93&a=452**; "Analyse af det arabiske initiativ og anbefalinger til næste fase" [Analysis of the Arab initiative and recommendations for a next phase], May 2006, at **www.um.dk/NR/rdonlyres/0A10F382-378B-4295-90BE-67E5AE36B6E4/0/helanalyse.pdf**, 01-07-06.

The Cycle of Violence in Plateau State

Ingo Wulfhorst and Nafisat Lawal Musa

The 7 September 2001 riots in Jos, Nigeria, the capital of Plateau State,[1] were triggered when a young Christian woman crossed a roadblock in front of a mosque in downtown Jos. However, a number of incidents had led up to what became the most violent riots ever to erupt in Jos.[2] Some months earlier, such questions as why Muslims block roads on Fridays from 1 p.m. to 2.30 p.m. during *Juma'at* (Friday) prayers and whether they should be allowed to do so had been debated in the press. Religious leaders became increasingly involved in this discussion. Since the Muslims had refused to stop blockading, the Christians too had started to block roads all day on Sundays.

Three weeks prior to the riots, strong rumors had circulated according to which the "war" was going to begin on a Friday. Therefore *ulamâ* (Sunni Muslim scholars) had instructed the imams in Jos to focus on the need for peaceful coexistence in their *khutbas* (Friday sermons). However, on that particular Friday, Rhoda Nyam, a young Christian woman whose parents' house was next to a blockage, decided to pass in front of a crowd of Muslim worshippers who as usual had spilled over from the mosque onto the street. They slapped her, which provoked Christians to retaliate by burning the mosque.

There are different versions of this story such as for instance, that Rhoda Nyam went home only to return shortly afterwards with armed youths who threw stones and used bows, arrows and sticks to attack Muslims in the mosque. This was followed by the burning of the mosque and the adjoining houses. The arson, looting and killing escalated and spread to other parts of

[1] The city of Jos was founded in 1915 as a tin transportation camp and has today about 800,000 (greater Jos), predominately Christian inhabitants. It is located in what can be referred to as the "Middle Belt" of Northern Nigeria.

[2] This story is partly based on the coauthor, Nafisat Lawal Musa's (she is a citizen of Jos and was present in Jos during the crisis) own observations, interviews and experiences of the study team in Jos and in Gusau (March 2005), on reports published in different books and pamphlets and on research and conclusions by the 143 representatives from 54 ethnic groups and other stakeholders at the Plateau Peace Conference, 18 August–21 September 2004.

Jos and violence continued for six days. Over 1,000 people were killed, and thousands of people displaced. Property worth millions of Naira, including places of worship, schools, homes and businesses were destroyed.

Another immediate cause was the appointment of Muhammed Muktar Usman, a Hausa-Fulani, as coordinator of the National Poverty Eradication Program (NAPEP) for Jos North Local Government Area. The indigenous people, the predominantly Christian Birom, Anaguta and Afizere (or Afisare), did not accept this appointment because Usman was considered a settler.[3] Furthermore, according to Umar Danfulani and Sati Fwatshak, Muhammed Muktar Usman was "indicted by a court ruling, which in 1994 removed him from office for, among other offences, falsification of birth records, perjury and falsehood."[4]

Hausa-Fulani youth (also known as Jasawa[5]) distributed anonymous incendiary leaflets, some of which read, "The seat is dearer to us than our lives. In that case, do you have a monopoly on violence?" "Death is the best friend of Hamas. Rest assured that we will do it better." Youths from the three ethnic groups and some others from Plateau State also distributed anonymous pamphlets threatening violence and retribution (blood for blood).

The government intervened by calling together the elders of the Hausa-Fulani and the non-Muslim ethnic groups. Representatives of these groups stressed that they would only concede if there were a substitute for Muhammed Muktar Usman. Hausa-Fulani representatives disagreed arguing that an appointment made by the President of the Federal Republic could not be contested. No decision was reached, but Muhammed Muktar Usman was never allowed to assume office, as there were death threats against him.

The Yelwa-Shendam crisis

By early 2002, the previously contained violent conflict spread from Jos city across the state, resulting in loss of life and material resources

[3] Isa Abdusalami, "Armed Soldiers Deployed to Restore Peace to Jos," in the *Guardian*, 9 September 2001.

[4] Umar Habila Dadem Danfulani and Sati U. Fwatshak, "Briefing: The September 2001 Events in Jos, Nigeria," in *African Affairs 101* (2002), p. 248.

[5] A term that means "owners of Jos."

on a scale never before experienced in Plateau State. Fighting became very intense, especially in Yelwa-Shendam. [6] Most Yelwa residents are Muslim, predominantly Jarawa, i.e., from a local ethnic group akin to the Afizere (in Jos and Bauchi). They had come from the town of Bauchi before colonization, speak the same language and are fully integrated. Nevertheless, they are Muslims and therefore identified by the local Gomai and other Christian groups with the Hausa-Fulani.

The people in Yelwa, who saw themselves as indigenes, felt dispossessed by the Hausa-Fulani in political as well as economic terms. They saw the Hausa as the cause of all their problems. The youth especially felt marginalized and looked down on the Hausa with contempt and disrespect, suspecting that the government was favoring the Hausa. They furthermore accused the Hausa of insulting their chief by calling him *sarkin arna* (chief of the pagans) and *kafirai* (infidel).[7] These youths were very active in the fighting.

In February 2004, Hausa-Fulani fighters killed seventy-five ethnic Taroks (Christians), at least forty-eight of them inside a church compound in Tarok village outside Yelwa. The reason for the violence was a prolonged conflict between Taroks and Fulanis over land use, the status of indigenousness, as well as political control over the town. A previous violent conflict in June 2002 had led to the division of the town into a Tarok-Christian and a Fulani-Muslim area.

On 2-3 May 2004, hundreds of heavily armed Christians retaliated by surrounding Yelwa and killing around 700 Hausa-Fulani. Thousands of inhabitants were displaced, taking refuge in the neighboring local government area and other states.[8] Mosques, churches, petrol stations, schools, market places, residential buildings and vehicles were destroyed. In March 2005, people from Yelwa told the study team that the sporadic attacks and killings were continuing.[9]

---

[6] Yelwa is a market town located 200 kilometers southeast of Jos. Yelwa is administered by the Shendam Local Government Area headquartered in the town of Shendam, twenty kilometers away. Shendam is a predominantly Christian town, and residents in the surrounding villages are also predominantly Christian.

[7] Nafisat Lawal Musa was on the Peace Committee that investigated the incidents.

[8] "Nigeria: Religious Violence Fuelled by Impunity," in *Human Rights Watch* (23 May 2005).

[9] Interview with two Muslim leaders from Yelwa, 22 March 2005.

The devastating conflict in May 2004 not only threatened the state's social fabric but also had implications for the entire nation. On 18 May 2004, President Olusegun Obasanjo declared a state of emergency in Plateau State. He suspended the state governor, Joshua Dariye, and nominated Major General M. C. Alli as interim state administrator in order to stop the incessant violent riots, restore confidence and unite the people of the state. Justifying his decisions he said, "Plateau State is blessed with all good things of life and only needs the right leadership to unleash the creative energies of the people for sustainable growth and development."[10] The state of emergency was lifted six months later.

Religious community responses

The federal government tried to resolve the crisis by putting in place different judicial commissions to inquire into communal conflicts as well as a Presidential Peace Initiatives Committee on Plateau State, headed by the Emir of Zaria, Alhaji Shehu Idris. Representatives at the Plateau Peace Conference gathering in 2004 in Jos were very critical in their report.

> At best, these efforts have seemed more palliative than making any appreciable impact since recommendations of the reports have not yet been released nor implemented. The result has been the creation of further trauma for certain victims, despair, hopelessness, frustration, bitterness and unforgiveness. Others have used the government's inaction and seeming failure to protect citizens as an excuse to seek vengeance through taking the laws into their hands and/or in the name of self-defense.[11]

Muslim and Christian communities lost many members; others were injured or displaced and religious groups had to provide succor by way of treatment, shelter, feeding and to organize emergency burials during the first few weeks of the crisis. Noteworthy was the magnanimity of religiously based refugee camps in accommodating people of different

[10] "Plateau Resolves: Report of the Plateau Peace Conference (18 August–21 September 2004)," in *Main Report*, no. 2, vol. 9 (Jos: Government Printer, Plateau State of Nigeria Gazette, 2004), p. 3.

[11] *Ibid.*

faiths until it was safe to return home, as were the pains taken to hand people over to their own people.

Everyone we interviewed assured us that during the crisis people had reached out to one another and helped one another. Numerous families were saved by their neighbors, who despite the problems they could have encountered, helped regardless of whether they were Christian or Muslim. The Lutheran Guest House, Dogon Dutse, assisted people who were injured and displaced, whether they were Christians or Muslims.[12]

It is worth noting that in Jos it is Lutherans and Catholics who are most active in interfaith dialogue and cooperation. On the Muslim side there is no consensus as to whether one should take part in dialogue activities, but it is left to the discretion of the individual organization or person. Apart from the more polemic debates, the Yan Izala Movement[13] for instance, does not want to engage in interfaith activities, whereas Jama'atu Nasril Islam (JNI)[14] and the National Council of Muslim Youth Organizations (NACOMYO),[15] have cooperated with the Catholic Relief Services and are active in the Association of Christian-Muslim Mutual Relations in Nigeria (see pp. 163-70).

From peaceful coexistence to conflict

The inhabitants of Plateau State unanimously affirm that a multiplicity of ethnic groups were living peacefully together before and after the creation of the Plateau State in 1967. This new state attracted people from many different ethnic groups and regions of Nigeria. Jos quickly turned into a cosmopolitan city, home to residents from different parts of Nigeria. Natives and new settlers interacted freely and even jointly participated in public life. The peaceful coexistence between indigenous

[12] Interview with Dick Mbodwam, LCCN, Dogon Dutse, Jos, March 2005.

[13] Jamâ'at izâlat al-bid'a wa-iqâmat as-sunna (The Society for the Eradication of Innovation and the Establishment of the Sunna) was founded in 1978 by Abubakar Gumi on the basis of Saudi Wahhabism.

[14] Jama'at Nasr al-Islami (The Association for the Victory of Islam) was established in 1962 by Ahmadu Bello, the late Sardauna of Sokoto and Premier of Northern Nigeria to coordinate Islamization efforts in Nigeria, and to unite all Muslim currents in the country.

[15] NACOMYO was established in 1986 and is headquartered in Jos.

ethnic groups, settlers and many Europeans (because of its climate, Jos has the second largest European population in Nigeria after Lagos) was such that the state prided itself as the "home of peace and tourism."

In the beginning of the 1990s, mounting tensions between Hausa-Fulani and the three traditional ethnic groups Anaguta, Afizere and Birom became more and more evident in the Jos area. The traditional groups claimed to be indigenous to the area, insisting that the land belongs to them, and that the Hausa-Fulani who had settled later in Jos should not have the same rights.

While Muslims argued that some Hausa and Fulani had founded Jos over a century and a half ago, and that therefore they were indigenous owners of Jos, the traditional ethnic groups increasingly felt manipulated and politically pushed to the margins by the Hausa-Fulani. In addition to the question of land ownership this became increasingly obvious during the 1990s, when traditional tribes and Hausa and Fulani supported or fought against certain government policies and appointments to political positions in Jos. Two particular governmental decisions had sparked off the violent riots in 1994. The mounting tensions between indigenous peoples and Hausa and Fulani culminated with the 2001 conflict in Jos.

Deeper causes of violence

The causes of the cycle of violence are highly complex. Many people we met in Nigeria confirmed that the tensions leading to the 2001 confrontation were largely related to ethnicity, religion, ownership of land and access to public office. Ethnicity and religion are used in connection with political candidates, not only in Plateau State but in the whole country, in order to get access to power and economic resources.

Different ethnic groups are trying to get as large a part of the "national cake" as possible. In this struggle, the differentiation between indigene and settler becomes an issue. Some ethnic groups claim that they arrived earlier than others and complain that one ethnic group has the upper hand over the others, who consequently are marginalized. Even some of the major ethnic groups complain of marginalization. Cases in point include the fighting between Tiv and Jukun in Taraba State, Ife and Modakeke in Oyo State, Bassa and Ibira in Nasarawa State.

The Peace Conference listed thirteen major causes of the conflicts that have erupted in Jos since the 1990s.[16] One important factor was "the bastardization" of the role of traditional institutions (e.g., traditional rulers) as custodians of culture, customs and traditional values.[17]

The conference participants believed the disrespect for traditional institutions to be linked to factors such as corruption, intolerance and marginalization. Due to the "low economic activity and subsequent poverty," a large segment of the population had been "dependent on the civil service" and had received neither salaries nor financial support.[18] Extremely high unemployment levels, particularly among youth, also led to violent actions by people who were paid to participate in the violence.

Moreover, armed militias came to Jos from other states with the sole purpose of participating in the violent conflicts. As a result, youth and ethnic militias emerged in order to protect their own communities in the conflict area. Discrimination against women—no equality in terms of education, resources and employment—was mentioned as a further cause of conflict, as was the fact that some media had publicized inciting reports and propagated their own interests.[19]

Indigeneship and settlership

The representatives of fifty-four ethnic groups at the 2004 Plateau Peace Conference, led by the state administrator, not only identified the so-called indigeneship-settlership issue as one of the principal causes of the conflicts but also decided that the term "settler," as applied to Nigerians, was offensive. Therefore only the term "residents" should be used.[20] Thereafter they used the term "citizenship," as clearly defined in the 1999 Constitution: "every person born in Nigeria on or

[16] The question of land use/ownership linked with the indigeneship-settlership syndrome, traditional matters, security issues, social, religious, political factors and economic factors, farmer/grazer factors, the role of the media, youth matters, women's issues, lack of release and implementation of previous reports of administrative and judicial commissions of inquiry into conflicts in Plateau State. See *Plateau Resolves*, *op. cit.* (note 10), pp. 23–145.

[17] *Ibid.*, p. 37 (interview).

[18] *Ibid.*, p. 108.

[19] *Ibid.*, pp. 89f; 127, 130, 137.

[20] *Ibid.*, p. 34.

before the date of independence, either of whose parents or any of whose grand parents belongs or belonged to any community indigenous to Nigeria."[21]

Since the term "indigenous" is not clearly defined in the Constitution, the conference decided on the following definition:

> Indigeneship should be peculiar to a people who are the first to have settled permanently [!] in a particular area and who are often considered as "natives." Such people have the rights to their lands, their traditions and culture.[22]

According to this definition, only the Afizere, Anaguta and Berom ethnic groups are to be regarded as "indigenes" of Jos, whereas the Hausa-Fulani people are only "citizens" of Jos.

The Hausa and Fulani (and Jarawa) from Jos and Yelwa appealed to the conference to be included as indigenes, because they had lived in Jos and Yelwa for a long time, had contributed to the socioeconomic and political life and did not know any home other than Plateau State. The Peace Conference, however, decided that the Hausa should not be treated differently from other ethnic groups, such as the Yoruba, Igbo and Urhobo who had settled in Jos at the same time as the Hausa, or even earlier.

The conference clearly recommended "that lands that were known as historical boundaries should be maintained and other ethnic groups should not lay claim to these lands" and that "non-indigenes should desist from making frivolous demands on issues that are not their heritage."[23] This conclusion elicited considerable controversy and the Plateau State government later claimed to have accepted the report and its conclusions as a legitimate guidance for state policy with regard to these tensions.

Talking to many people in March 2005 in Jos, we got the impression that the distinction between indigenes and settlers is still a factor causing much hatred and mistrust. The 2001 crisis is still being discussed and as long as the distinction is officially recognized, the potential for conflict remains. However, we also saw the beginning of a long and difficult process of reconciliation in Plateau State and the hope that the different ethnic groups, Christian and Muslim, will be able to coexist in peace.

---

[21] Constitution of the Federal Republic of Nigeria, Section 25.1 (a).

[22] *Plateau Resolves*, *op. cit.* (note 10), pp. 30f.

[23] *Ibid.*, pp. 33f.

Intercommunal Fighting in Sulawesi

Syafa'atun Almirzanah

In 1998, President Suharto had to step down in the midst of economic and political upheaval. Already in 1996, a harbinger of things to come, allegedly religiously motivated violence had rocked the country. Politics and religion had become closely intertwined during the long Suharto years and independent investigators soon ascertained that the burning of churches, such as those in the east Javanese town of Situbondo, had not been carried out by angry religious zealots, but the result of careful planning that had involved the military. To prevent political reform and in a last attempt to hold on to power, the regime tried to destabilize the country. When it fell, conflicts erupted, the root cause being a confluence of economic, political, ethnic and religious tensions. In many of the conflicts, competition over jobs and political position, the distribution of wealth and ethnic differences are seen as recurring factors.

Poso, Sulawesi and Ambon, Maluku

The conflict discussed here occurred in Poso, a town in Central Sulawesi. Between December 1998 and 2001, Muslims and Christians were pitted against each other in one of the most violent and persistent conflicts the nation has ever witnessed. After a peace deal was brokered in 2001, the violence diminished but continued sporadically. In September 2006, three Catholic men, Fabianus Tibo, Dominggus Da Silva and Marinus Riwu were executed for initiating the violence. By 2007, the fragile balance seemed to have been restored sufficiently for President Yudhoyono to embark on a visit to inaugurate the rebuilding of several Islamic and Christian schools and houses of worship.[1] Those whose lives had been torn apart by the conflicts observed that two conditions had changed:

[1] "Yudhoyono to get a Look at Rebuilding Efforts in Poso," in the *Jakarta Post*, 30 April 2007.

political power struggles in the local administrations had resulted in a new balance of power and the radical Muslim group, Laskar Jihad, whose arrival in 2001 had escalated the violence, disbanded in October 2002 in the aftermath of 9/11.[2]

This conflict did not stand on its own: violence erupted all over Indonesia. Following the 1998 violence in Sulawesi, severe riots erupted in January 1999 among inhabitants of the spice island of Ambon, Maluku. Many of those who analyzed the conflict saw similarities between the way in which the violence developed in Poso and Ambon, and many wonder how relatively minor incidents could have spun out of control to such an extent and lead to a cycle of recurring attacks. The other question is why they were so severe in those two areas, even though many other regions in Indonesia suffer from similar economic, political and ethnic tensions.

Both conflicts were triggered by minor incidents. In Poso, the 1998 violence started on the eve of Christmas and Ramadan with a street brawl involving two young men, a Protestant and a Muslim. In Ambon, a predominantly Christian area, an argument between a Muslim and a Christian over the price of public transport sparked off the bloody events. What initially were private conflicts transformed into communal violence involving hundreds of Muslims and Christians and resulting in death and the destruction of homes, villages, schools and houses of worship on both sides. In Ambon, the conflict raged until 2002. In Poso, it calmed down after four years but recently started to erupt again. All in all, the fighting has cost more than 7,000 lives and displaced a total of 1.3 million people.[3]

Poso—the running sore

Sulawesi is one of Indonesia's 17,513 islands. Until the 1970s, the coastal areas of Central Sulawesi were mostly inhabited by Muslims, while predominantly Protestant Christians lived in the mountainous highlands.

[2] See "Context, Causes, and Laskar Jihad," in *Human Rights Watch*, III, part 1, at **www.hrw.org/reports/2002/indonesia/indonesia1102-03.htm#P119_15133** .

[3] "What Happened in Poso?," in the *Jakarta Post*, 14 October 2003.

Poso is located about 220 km south of Central Sulawesi's provincial capital, Palu. The town's approximately 420,000 residents are divided more or less equally between Christians and Muslims.

By the 1970s, the government in Jakarta had designated the area for transmigration (migration within the nation) which brought in Muslims from South and North Sulawesi, Java, Bali and Nusa Tenggara. The influx of migrants transformed the area from a traditional into a modern community, with wide-ranging consequences for the balance of political and economic power. Local traditional governmental institutions were replaced by national bureaucracies in which modernist Muslims were given high ranking military positions and community and religious leaders were replaced by military "territorial" officers. Christian leaders were sidelined in local governments and the Suharto government repossessed schools and hospitals originally set up by Christians.

At the time the violence flared up, the *bupati* (Muslim district leader) was up for election and local Christians had high hopes for replacing him with one of their own candidates. For both Muslims and Christians it was vital to have their own candidate in power, because of the impending regional autonomy when the power over natural resources was to shift from the national to the local government.

The anthropologist Lorraine Aragon has written several detailed accounts of the Poso violence and its aftermath. Until the December 2001 Malino Peace Declaration, she divides the conflict into five stages.[4] When latent religious tensions exploded for the first time, it resulted in one week of full-blown violence. After that week, Christian resentment increased considerably since only Christians were being jailed and prosecuted for the violence. The second phase was similar with two weeks of fighting and led to the third phase when Christian militia massacred over one hundred Muslims. During the fourth phase, heavily armed radical Islamist Laskar Jihad fighters were brought in who, in the fifth phase, took revenge by killing around the same number of Christians. After the 2001 Malino Peace Declaration was signed by Christian and Muslim leaders, the violence diminished. However, the agreement was

[4] Lorraine V. Aragon, "Waiting for Peace in Poso. Why has this Muslim-Christian Conflict Continued for Three Years?" originally published in *Inside Indonesia* (April-June 2002), at **www.serve.com/inside/edit70/Poso1.htm**

not satisfactory, since it failed to address the underlying issues of power sharing between Christians and Muslims.

Groups from outside Poso not only exacerbated the conflict but turned the town into an incubator for terrorism. For example, several of those implicated in the 9 September 2004 bombing in front of the Australian embassy in Jakarta were Poso veterans.

What is mystifying is why local authorities did not interfere when they could have and why perpetrators on both sides were not punished. The events of 9/11 brought Laskar Jihad's actions into a new light and put pressure on the Indonesian government to address the group's violent actions and underlying agenda. Its leader, Ja'far Umar Thalib, has returned to Yogyakarta where he leads an Islamic boarding school without having to account for his actions. Although his "Jihad Army" has officially dissolved, he continues to harass local groups. For example, in summer 2006, his followers tried to disrupt an interreligious event organized by the Center for the Study of Religion of the Christian Duta Wacana University, a center that the LWF study team visited in 2004.

The conflict was multilayered and did not erupt out of nowhere. It was the result of local processes that had evolved over thirty years and were brought to the surface because of the reconfiguration of political power structures. Two elements were pivotal: the decentralization program that granted autonomy to Indonesia's districts and Laskar Jihad's role and agenda.

Pemekaran in Mamasa District

The conflict in Mamasa, a remote area of West Sulawesi, is an example of an administrative conflict, primarily rooted in local officials' desire for personal gain. This got out of hand, and on 24 April 2005 five people were killed and five houses burned. Since Mamasa is a predominantly Christian area and the opposition was initially concentrated in twenty-six predominantly Muslim villages, it was generally perceived that it was a communal struggle, which had attracted the attention of Muslim radicals from outside the immediate area.[5]

[5] The Indonesian government clearly recognized the danger of this polarization along religious lines and quickly made arrests and sent additional security forces to the area. If communal conflict is to be prevented, the underlying administrative dispute needs to be addressed urgently.

The roots of the Mamasa conflict lie in the decentralization program, known as *pemekaran*, a process of administrative fragmentation whereby new provinces and districts are created by dividing existing ones. The Mamasa district was formed in 2002 out of the district of Polewali-Mamasa (Polmas). This was but one of over 100 such divisions that have taken place in Indonesia since 1999 through which the total number of provinces and districts in the country has increased by roughly fifty percent.

During the campaign, which began in 1999, several villages in subdistricts opposed their inclusion. The most persistent opposition came from twenty-six (of thirty-eight) villages of the Aralle, Tabulahan and Mambi subdistricts, collectively known as ATM. Supporters of incorporation in these subdistricts were given the nickname "pro," opponents "kontra." [6]

When the national parliament passed a law to form Mamasa, it disregarded the compromise reached at the local level which allowed for the exclusion of these twenty-six villages. As a result, a system of parallel governments emerged. Opponents were supported by the government of the "mother" district, Polmas, which continued to pay the salaries of civil servants who refused to work for the Mamasa government and maintained an administrative structure in the three subdistricts. Mamasa established its own government structure in the subdistricts; consequently, many places had two subdistrict heads and often two village heads. Children were forced to go to schools based on their parents' political affiliation.

The tensions associated with the "pro-kontra" divide, combined with local land disputes that in late September 2003 had led to three murders, resulted in major displacement. No effective action was taken to resolve the conflict, however, and three more people died in October 2004 following another clash. By the time the central government had sent an independent team to evaluate the district boundaries, issues of displacement, segregation and justice loomed large and the conflict had become much more than an administrative dispute.

Mamasa thus became an example of what can happen when there is not a clear procedure to resolve disputes during the *pemekaran* process. A cycle of violence can emerge when the wishes of those involved are

[6] These were divided roughly along ethnic and religious lines with the Christian Torajan as the "pro-area" and the Muslim Mandar as the "kontra-area". International Crisis Group, "Decentralisation and Conflict in Indonesia: The Mamasa Case," in *Asia Briefing*, no. 37 (3 May 2005).

ignored and the law is not promptly and transparently enforced. The deaths underline the dangers of allowing low level conflict to fester. The costs can be disastrous if militants decide that the conflict is now ripe for exploitation.

The role of religion

Although religion was not the main factor causing the conflicts, people often framed their political interests and identity in terms of religious symbols, values and ideals. This can be seen specifically in Maluku and Poso, where Laskar Kristus and Laskar Jihad were battling against each other.[7]

Ja'far Umar Thalib is the central strategist and leader of the Laskar Jihad movement. Of Arab heritage, Thalib entered military training with the support of his father, a Muslim missionary from Yemen. His study at a *pesantren* (Islamic boarding school) up to university level molded him into a representative of a radical interpretation of Islam. He was a soldier in Afghanistan, where he met Osama bin Laden. Instead of joining Bin Laden, he preferred to join a puritanical Islamist organization, Jama'at al-Da'wa ila al-Qur'ân wa Ahl-I Hadith, that is based in Saudi Arabia and well known for ordering its followers to overthrow governments that do not implement Islamic law.

Thalib believes that an international conspiracy is out to destroy the Islamic community in Maluku. In his attempts to incite Muslims to engage in *jihâd*, he uses religious sentiments to spread hatred within religious communities. He considers Christians as "the others" and "the enemy." Regina Schwartz has identified such a tactic as violent behavior. In her book, *The Curse of Cain: The Violent Legacy of Monotheism*, Schwartz shows that by creating a type of "shadow identity," a group separates itself from the other, thus forming and promoting an (imagined) impression of

[7] Robert Hefner, "Civil Pluralism Denied? The New Media and Jihadi Violence in Indonesia," unpublished article (2002), p. 6; Robert W. Hefner calls the Laskar Jihad a fundamentalist movement or neo-*Salafi*, as it stresses an extremist political view. One of its foci is the belief that America and Israel both conspire to destroy Islam, and that the Muslims' response to this conspiracy should be *jihâd*.

the other.[8] In the case of Laskar Jihad, waging war on Christians under the banner of Islam, is preceded by conceptualizing them as "the others," as *kâfir dhimmî* (non-Muslim unbeliever) *kâfir harbî*, (unbeliever who should be waged war against) and other such stereotypes.

Analysts of the conflicts have observed that Laskar Jihad's involvement was not haphazard. Both Central Sulawesi and Maluku were of strategic interest to the larger network which Jemaah Islamiyah (JI) belongs to.[9] Both areas were possible footholds from which to strengthen their bases in East and Central Java and the southern Sumatran province of Lampung. Moreover, JI leaders believed that through its agricultural wealth and the boom in cacao and other commodities, "Poso had the potential to replace Singapore and Malaysia as the income generating area for the organization."[10]

Conflict prevention and conflict resolution

The first reconciliatory meeting to end the conflict in Poso took place on 26 December 1998, in Tagalu. The peace agreement was breached the day after it was signed. The 2001 Malino Peace Declaration was signed after the violence had raged for several years and thus had run its course. It consists of ten items and was the result of a two-day meeting. Twenty-five Muslims and twenty-three Christian representatives of groups involved in the conflict agreed to end all violence by signing the agreement. They also promised to respect one another's religion in accordance with the prevailing rules.

Furthermore, the declaration mentioned that both parties reject the state of emergency, as well as intervention by third parties. Both parties also agreed to restore their rights and property. Refugees could return to their place of origin and together with the government both parties

[8] See Regina Schwartz, *The Curse of Cain: The Violent Legacy of Monotheism* (Chicago: University of Chicago Press, 1997).

[9] Jemaah Islamiyah is a Southeast Asian Islamist network blamed for a series of bomb attacks across Indonesia.

[10] International Crisis Group, "Jihadism in Indonesia: Poso on the Edge," in *Asia Report*, no. 127 (24 January 2007), p. 5. According to the report, the governments of Malaysia and Singapore had by this time defeated their respective JI structures.

promised to rebuild the economic infrastructure. In 2004, Lorraine Aragon checked on the reconstruction efforts and observed that many of those who had fled their homes had not been able to return yet, and that funds for rebuilding had disappeared due to mismanagement and corruption. According to her analysis, this condition contributed to the continued low levels of violence: "This endemic corruption, fuelled by poorly regulated aid and military funding, makes the region conducive for criminal operations and their unholy alliances with ideological extremists."[1] Those who had initially failed to protect the citizens of Poso, now were not only failing to apply the peace agreement, but were also hindering people from rebuilding their lives.

The government solved the conflict without taking into account the root problems. Efforts made to resolve the conflict were not serious enough since they failed to address significant issues such as strengthening the social and economic foundations of society and addressing inequalities in access to political power, resources and wealth. Interference from the outside continues, also in the form of military intervention and outsiders taking charge of the funds to rebuild Poso. NGOs are trying to break the deadlock by facilitating discussions among the various parties involved and organizing Muslim-Christian dialogues. Furthermore they work on empowering the local population to claim their rights without reverting to violence.

[1] Lorraine V. Aragon, "Profiting from Displacement. In Search of Honest, Well-Designed Aid for People Displaced by the Poso Conflict," in *Inside Indonesia* (January-March 2004, at **www.serve.com/inside/edit77/p14-15aragon.html**.

Beyond the Stories

Lissi Rasmussen

In all three countries, conflicts have escalated over the past twenty-five years, especially since the mid-1990s. This escalation is partly due to the cumulative effects of many years of cultivated grievances. Indonesia and Nigeria have a long history of Christians and Muslims living together. Religion permeates daily life, is a natural part of society and religious plurality has been a positive experience. In Denmark, religion plays a much lesser role in people's daily lives, and the presence of inhabitants from different cultural and religious backgrounds is a much more recent phenomenon, dating back to the 1960s. Islam continues to be perceived as a foreign religion, and for most Danes coexistence remains something to be learned and fought for rather than natural or based on tradition. Nonetheless, relations have not only been problematic, and good relationships are a part of daily reality, especially among youth.

The case stories show examples of three different types of conflict. They mirror the fact that while the situation in the three countries is very different, some mechanisms and developments resemble one another since they share some of the same background.

The "Us vs Them" syndrome

The stories show how, in three different contexts, distinctions between human beings have resulted in uncontrollable situations. The two stories from Indonesia and Nigeria point to unemployment, poverty, corruption and uneven development as the major factors leading to these developments. In both countries, there has been an increasing social and economic polarization, with especially youth lacking opportunities.

Connected to this economic inequality is an "Us vs Them" discourse. In all three stories, the dichotomy between indigenes and settlers, hosts and foreigners, has played a crucial role. Whereas in Nigeria and Indonesia this relates primarily to the prevalent socioeconomic conditions, in Denmark it reflects questions of identity and recognition at the psychological and symbolic levels. The attitude to the difference between "Us and Them" constitutes the problem rather than diversity itself. In all three countries, discussions have focused on the questions of who belongs, who fits the description of a "true" citizen and how allegiance is expressed. Moreover, both in Nigeria and Denmark, the dichotomy and the associated enemy images have been used by political leaders for populist purposes.

The socioeconomic dimension

The fear of losing or being excluded from ancestral land has turned the "indigenous" people in many parts of Northern Nigeria, including Plateau State, against those who arrived later, namely the Hausa-Fulani, whom the indigenous wanted to exclude from land, offices and economic resources.

In Jos area, the economy has been largely dominated by commercial trading activities that are mainly in the hands of "newcomers" such as the Igbo, Yoruba and Hausa-Fulani. Therefore, most of the conflicts in this and several other areas revolved around economic issues, and the indigene-settler disputes concerned access to farmland, fishing ponds, markets and the opportunity to engage in economic activities. The indigenes insisted that the Hausa-Fulani had no claim to land in their community, while the Hausa-Fulani argued that since they were born in this community and had lived there all their lives they had equal rights.[2]

Various conflicts in Sulawesi, the Maluku islands and other parts of Indonesia, for instance Central Java[3] and Sumatra, grew out of economic issues such as unemployment, poverty and economic inequality. Social and economic frustration and jealousy on the part of those who are economically disadvantaged have resulted in making a scapegoat of

[2] According to the Plateau Peace Conference Report pressure on land occurs as "a result of growing human and livestock population, mining activities as well as the activities of vast land speculators." "Plateau Resolves: Report of the Plateau Peace Conference 2004: Main Report," in *Plateau State of Nigeria Gazette*, no. 2, vol. 9 (Jos: Government Printer, Plateau State of Nigeria Gazette, 2004), p. 114. The resolution therefore implied that people "should make a better effort to engage in dialogue to settle land matters rather than resorting to the use of violence."

[3] At the Conference at Stain, 12 June 2004, Rev. Joseph Hehanusa spoke about the conflict in 1998 in Surakarta (Solo) in Central Java (some 65 km northeast of Yogyakarta) and the economic impact of inflation and unemployment. He stated that these deplorable economic conditions created further tensions between ethnic and religious groups, especially among young people who are in need of role models.

others and a lack of confidence in what the future might hold. This has created mutual suspicion and communal discord, sometimes falling in line with ethnic and/or religious divides.[4]

Disputed land ownership has often been at the heart of conflict.[5] In certain areas, such as the Mamasa district in Sulawesi and in north Maluku, *pemekaran* (process of decentralization, see pp. 58f), has led to fears of new conflicts over land, mineral wealth and boundaries and to local politicians manipulating tensions for personal gain. The introduction of new boundaries has often resulted in disputes over the exact location and ownership of land and led to accusations of land grabbing or land "vanishing." For instance, the question of the legal status of *adat* (traditional) land and the final authority over it became uncertain.[6] When no efficient action was taken to resolve these disputes, they escalated into violent conflicts, and sometimes the parties involved ended up identifying themselves and their opponents as Muslims and Christians.

Economic conditions have not been a decisive factor in the development of tensions in Denmark. However, there are some economic inequalities between ethnic minorities and the majority population, caused by difference in job opportunities.[7] Research has shown that people from ethnic minorities experience direct or indirect forms of

---

[4] Rev. T. Simamora of Huria Kristen Indonesia (HKI), the Indonesian Christian Church, confirmed this during the visit of the LWF study team to Medan, 5 June 2004, by saying that economic problems are often considered much more important than religion. Socioeconomic issues were also mentioned in the two Malino Declarations in Poso and the Maluku Islands.

[5] During the study team's meeting with Majelis Ulama Indonesia in North Sumatra, 7 June 2004, Mr Burhan N. noted that the roots of the conflicts, e.g., in Mandaling Natal, South Tapanuti, lie in the problems of ownership of land. Also in Ambon, there have been Christian Muslim tensions over land and control over local business.

In some instances, such as the Tentena market bombing in May 2005, violence was linked to corruption. Tentena is located 60 km south of Poso town, on the shores of Poso lake. It is the main Christian stronghold in Poso district where the Central Sulawesi Christian Church (GKST) is headquartered. The bombing was allegedly organized by certain local officials to disrupt the ongoing investigation into corruption in Poso and to protect powerful individuals from prosecution. See, "Weakening Indonesia's Mujahedin Networks: Lessons from Maluku and Poso," in International Crisis Group, *Asia Report*, no. 103 (13 October 2005), pp. 10 and 12.

[6] "Indonesia: Overcoming Murder and Chaos in Maluku," in International Crisis Group, *Asia Report*, no. 10 (2000).

[7] According to 2003 statistics, the employment rate among citizens of non-Western origin is forty-seven percent, whereas the corresponding figure for Danes is seventy-seven percent. The Danish Ministry of Refugees, Immigration and Integration, *Årbog om Udlændinge i Danmark* [Foreigners in Denmark Yearbook], (2004).

discriminatory treatment on the labor market. A number of cases have been publicized of Muslim women who wear head scarves accusing their employers of discrimination.

There is no doubt that economic jealousy on the side of ethnic Danes plays an important role in the development of xenophobic sentiments. For instance, a considerable number of ethnic Danes believe that the majority of those who are granted asylum are not real refugees but have come to exploit the Danish public welfare system.[8]

The present liberal government considers immigrants and refugees an economic burden on Danish society. The restriction of immigration and limiting welfare are connected. Therefore, according to the government, the country has to stop immigration from so-called less developed countries such as Somalia, Iran, Iraq, and Lebanon and only accept immigrants who can benefit Denmark, i.e., those who are educated and skilled.

The high rate of unemployment among Muslims has had the unfortunate effect that ethnic Danish workers do not often meet Muslims on the factory floor. According to a June 2006 opinion poll, almost fifty percent of ethnic Danes have no contact with anyone from an ethnic minority.[9] This has contributed to a lack of knowledge of "the other" on both sides.

The role of the youth

Young people played a major role in the violent riots during the Jos crisis. According to the Plateau Peace Conference Report, youths had been sponsored and armed to foment trouble.[10] Due to the high unemployment

---

[8] This transpired when thousands of Danish citizens, predominantly of Lebanese-Palestinian background, were evacuated from Lebanon in July 2006 during the Israeli attack on the country. The Danish People's Party suggested that the social authorities take advantage of the opportunity to check these people—many of them having undergone traumatic experiences—whether they had been cheating the social service system by having traveled to Lebanon without having informed the social authorities. The party claimed that a great number of Danes had contacted them wondering how so many people were able to go on vacation to Lebanon, since many of them were unemployed.

[9] Gallup opinion poll for the daily, *Berlingske Tidende*, 7 June 2006. Every fifth person has Muslim friends while almost one third has Muslim colleagues, especially among children and youth.

[10] *Plateau Resolves, op. cit.* (note 1), p. 130. Youth organizations were involved in the conflict such as the Hausa-Fulani youths (under twenty-five) and the (Christian) Plateau State Youths. See "Jos: A City Torn Apart," in *Human Rights Watch Report*, vol. 13, no. 9 (December 2001), pp. 5-6.

rate among youths from poor families and the resulting poverty and despair, the promise of money meant that they were easily persuaded to participate in acts of violence. The report therefore suggested that youths should be encouraged to engage in useful ventures, to "take up vocational training" and "become investment generators rather than consumers."[11] Moreover, measures should be taken to train youths and provide employment for them at the local, state and federal government levels through investment in the school system, vocational centers, small industries, agriculture and private industry.

In Maluku and Poso, youth were involved in mujâhedîn networks[12] which continued to cause security problems, even after the intercommunal fighting had ceased. Members of these networks were mostly men in their twenties and thirties who were motivated by revenge rather than ideology, as had been the earlier generation of Indonesian jihadists who had gone to Saudi Arabia and Afghanistan for training. Their *jihâds* were local and situational, and they had fewer connections to the Middle East and South Asia.[13]

The youths had contacts in different areas and often commuted between them. In the 2004 Mamasa conflict in West Sulawesi, as well as in Poso, there were indications that youths came from outside the area to take part in the conflict. In this way, they contributed to spreading the conflicts. Recommendations were made to include these youths and to implement reintegration programs through which they would be introduced to new social contacts, while being given viable alternatives to violence.

In Denmark, unemployment prevalent among ethnic minorities especially distresses those youths born and raised in Denmark. They see themselves as Danes and want to have equal opportunities. They want to be a part of society, whereas their parents, who came for a limited time, were less aware of their rights. Since the early 1990s, many of these young

[11] *Plateau Resolves*, *op. cit.* (note 1), p. 109.

[12] Mujahedin is a kind of network of two groups: 1) Laskar Jihad established in 2000 to defend Muslims in the communal conflict in the Maluku Islands. They depict their struggle and obligation as a fight to defend the Indonesian state and integrity from Christian separatists and 2) smaller groups who are more militant and committed to establishing an Islamic state in Indonesia. Some are attracted by the *salafi* jihadist ideology of Osama bin Laden, collectively known as Laskar Mujahedin, including Jemaah Islamiyah and different factions and splinter groups of the Darul Islam movement. Also Mujahedin Kompak belongs to this category. *Asia Report*, *op. cit.* (note 5), p. 2.

[13] *Ibid.*, p. 19.

people have become increasingly active in society and politics in order to contribute to the well-being of society. Frequently, they do not feel recognized and listened to as individual citizens, but rather viewed as part of a generalized group, in terms of their culture and religion. This feeling has been intensified over the past decade to the extent that the publication of the cartoons was perceived as an attack on their identity.

The three stories show how important it is to include young people in the communities and to take their needs, wishes and contributions seriously. This is done by integrating them into the labor market as well as by taking them seriously as human beings whose contribution is valued.

Indigenousness and settlership

In Denmark and Nigeria, the categories of indigene/native and settler/newcomer have been used in undesirable ways to mobilize people's negative feelings and have hindered the development of harmonious coexistence. This has led to a deep sense of alienation among many people, Christians and Muslims alike. In some areas of Nigeria it has resulted in confrontation over access to local power and economic resources, whereas in Denmark the consequences have often been polarization, verbal abuse, negative self-image and despair.

In Denmark, many immigrants or descendants of immigrants have found it difficult to be recognized as Danes. This was highlighted by the cartoon incident. Many ethnic Danes see the Danish nation as a culturally homogenous community of people who should be given certain and special rights in the state.

Some Muslim ethnic minorities are speaking in terms of "Us vs Them" and some, especially from socially weak families, have been using these categories to designate others as "decadent" or "infidels." This has led to problems in some government schools in Copenhagen, where some Muslim children have been bullying other children or committed criminal offenses.

The drawings of the Prophet were published at a time when many Muslims in Denmark felt degraded and stereotyped as a category that "does not belong." The cartoons were seen as the final straw. When their concerns about the drawings of the Prophet were categorically rejected by the government and much of the press, some could not contain their frustration within Denmark but thought it necessary to look for support from their co-believers in foreign embassies and Muslim countries (see p. 32). This did not help the situation, proving to many Danes that the imams still saw themselves as foreigners, although most of them had lived in Denmark for decades.

At the same time, reactions in Muslim countries increased the fear of Islam and Muslims. For a long time the Danish population had been fed political statements about a "culture struggle" between "Us vs Them," been exposed to negative stories and stereotypes about Islam and Muslims and had had no personal experiences with Muslims. Thus they were unable to counter this negative image.

The indigenous-settler dichotomy is at the root of most intercommunal conflicts and political quarrels in Nigeria, particularly in the North. It has diluted the real meaning of Nigerian citizenship. One is not really regarded as a citizen of Nigeria but only as a citizen of the place to which one is indigenous. Moreover, there is no real way for non-indigenous to become indigenous, regardless of how hard and how long they have struggled to integrate in and identify with the community they live in.

Nowhere have the clashes between indigenous and settlers developed more violently than in Plateau State, where historically the segregation between indigenes and settlers has been upheld, especially during the colonial system of indirect rule where "natives" and "immigrants" (in mining camps) were not treated as one entity. Hausa settlements were dealt with separately (with the creation of Jos Plateau Province in 1926) and maintained separate identities with a different religion and culture.[14] They have been denied opportunities for educational advancement and civil service jobs. This is why the appointment of a Hausa politician to a statewide post in a federal poverty eradication program sparked such clashes.

Today, Plateau State government and other state governments all over Nigeria issue "certificates of indigenousness" which serve as documentary proof that the bearer is a "native" of the area concerned. Those not granted a certificate are treated as non-indigenous in their formal interaction with all levels of government. They experience dis-

---

[14] The settler economy among the Igbo, Yoruba and Hausa-Fulani was dominated largely by commercial/tracking activities, whereas indigenes were preoccupied with farming on the outskirts of the cities Birom, Afizere, Basa and Anaguta.

crimination in terms of higher school fees, lack of access to positions in the federal civil service, military or police force, fewer employment opportunities and limited access to resources such as land. As a result of these ever more stringent discriminatory policies, levels of poverty and unemployment have increased.

All this is happening despite the fact that the 1999 Constitution states that "No citizen of Nigeria shall be subjected to any disability or deprivation merely by reason of the circumstances of his birth."[15] In the 1979 Constitution (which forms basis for the 1999 Constitution currently in force) the principle of "federal character" was introduced as a quasi quota system to ensure that all ethnic or other groups have equal access to education, public sector employment opportunities and resources at the federal, state and local levels. While the aim was to create national unity, in practice the principle has created a polarization between "indigenes" and other residents of a state. One of the reasons was that through the "indigenousness clause" the federal character principle was explicitly linked to indigeneity— determined by ancestry—as a legitimate basis on which to make political claims and assert entitlement to certain benefits.

In this way, the concepts "indigenous" and "non-indigenous" were constitutionally legitimized and discrimination justified against those whose ancestors may have migrated from other states. This has been exploited by various groups in order to further their own interests. Various human rights organizations have therefore suggested that all references to indigenousness should be removed from the Constitution and replaced by residency as the criterion for appointment.[16]

In Indonesia, the "Us vs Them" rhetoric between different groups is less explicit at a national level. There is a stronger awareness of being a nation than in Nigeria, and there are not the same cultural and religious obstacles. While Indonesian culture has been able to absorb various imported cultures, there is nonetheless an imbalance of resources, and an indigene-settler dichotomy has developed in certain areas such as Sumatra, Sulawesi and Central Java. Tensions between locals and set-

[15] Fundamental Rights Section of the Nigerian Constitution (1999). Section 42: Right to Freedom from Discrimination.

[16] For example, "Nigeria's Faltering Federal Experiment," in International Crisis Group, *Africa Report*, no. 119 (15 October 2006).

tlers (or transmigrants) have sometimes even lead to fighting, because locals envy the economically more successful migrants, who have often fared better than the local farmers and were better informed about new types of crops and methods of cultivation.[17]

The main reason for the indigene-settler conflicts in Indonesia has been a transformation in the demographic composition of certain provinces due to the government's huge transmigration program. Between 1969 and 1995, eight million people were resettled, for which the World Bank paid over half a billion dollars. In these areas, the local communities were often predominantly Christian. During the 1990s, this was the case in Ambon, Sampit, Poso and Mamasa, where with the arrival of immigrants the composition changed and the confessional balance tipped in favor of the Muslims. This shift was accompanied by a rise in the political and economic fortunes of individual Muslims. Power and bureaucratic weight shifted from Christians to Muslims, as did money and opportunity.[18]

In some of these situations, the decentralization process added to the tensions or created new ones between indigenes and migrants. This happened because of a new influx of migrants and new opportunities for some communities to gain access to political power provided under the program.[19] Furthermore, extremist groups, connected to Saudi Arabia, who came from outside and had no interest in local areas contributed to the maintenance of this dichotomy between "Us vs Them."

---

[17] This was for instance the case in Luwu, South Sulawesi in the 1970s and 1980s. There was, however, also fighting between individual villages.

[18] "Indonesia: Overcoming Murder and Chaos in Maluku," in *Asia Report*, *op. cit.* (note 5). The 2001 conflicts between the local Dayak community (mainly Christians) and the newcomers, the Madurese (mainly Muslims) in Sampit, Central Kalimantan (Borneo), are an example of this development. After a massacre of about 500 Madurese, almost the entire Madurese community fled. The main reason for this was the dislocation of the Dayak community. Due to immigration from other provinces many Dayaks were forced to leave land they had previously used. Consequently, they felt marginalized in the province, looked down upon by other communities as backward and uncivilized. See "Communal Violence in Indonesia: Lessons from Kalimantan," in International Crisis Group, *Asia Report*, no. 18 (27 June 2001), pp. 4ff. Furthermore, they felt that their interests were being neglected by the central government (p. 20).

Most Christians have been in Maluku for a long time, while a significant minority of Muslims have migrated in the last thirty years. They are seen as more aggressive and commercially more adept than the locals. Towards the end of the Suharto years, Muslims also dominated the bureaucracy. This led to conflict in the area, especially between the native Kao, who were mostly Christians, and the Makianese migrants who were mostly Muslims. See "Indonesia's Maluku Crisis: The Issues," International Crisis Group, *Indonesia Briefing* (19 July 2000), p. 4.

[19] The Mamasa conflict was probably the clearest example of this development (see pp. 58f).

For instance, tensions have also developed between local Javanese and the Chinese élite. Chinese middle-class entrepreneurs have been made scapegoats for the economic and political troubles in the area. They are mostly Christians, more advantaged and members of relatively affluent churches. It must be added that there has always been a power struggle between Java and the outer islands. Over all, there is a feeling that Java dominates and receives most of the resources.

Enemy images and mutual fear

We have seen the development of enemy images in all three countries. Even in majority populations, such as in the predominantly Christian Denmark, Muslim Indonesia and Muslim Northern Nigeria, a substantial percentage of the majority feel discriminated against by those whom they see as a threatening enemy.

Thus in certain areas of Indonesia, Christians have in recent years increasingly been associated with the imperialist West, and a fear of "creeping Christianization" has developed among many Muslims. In Poso and Maluku, members of jihadist organizations such as Jemaah Islamiyah (JI), descendants of Darul Islam and Mujahidin Kompak, regard Christians as infidels and "enemies of Islam," who pose a threat to the local Muslim community.

Many Indonesian Christians feel unsafe, and some see Islam as a coercive, terrifying and unfriendly religion. This for instance was the case in the Medan area in Sumatra. During a meeting with church leaders in Medan, Rev. Simatupang (GKPA) commented on how the attitude in the area has changed:

> I have lived in a Muslim environment most of my life. We never thought that there were differences among religions. If our Muslim friends invited us for Islamic events we came, as for instance during the Idul Fitri celebration. We joined them in the celebrations. But over time, more Muslim scholars stressed difference and gave rise to conflicts. Differences started to occur. The tradition of visiting each other changed; Islamic teaching changed; the idea of *najis* (impure) started to come up.[20]

[20] 5 June 2004. Gereja Kristen Protestan Angkola (GKPA) is the Christian Protestant Angkola Church.

Rev. Wilson Siahaan from the HKBP in Medan added:

> In daily life we have good relations with those who are of other religions. But after a *fatwâ* (a legal opinion or decree handed down by an Islamic religious leader) that Muslims cannot wish Christians Merry Christmas, things changed. For example, suddenly Christians who wanted to visit a Muslim friend were no longer welcome [...] . Last night I heard about a *becak* (rickshaw) driver who refused to take a Christian to the church. This does not occur often but it happens. Religion has also become a means to get promoted; especially in the field of education. This has happened in Medan, but also in other places. [21]

Some church members regard the willingness of provincial heads and governors to implement parts of Sharî'a as an attempt to strengthen their political standing. In their eyes, this could divide the nation and lead to a loss of its local cultural roots and traditions due to Islamic-Arab cultural imperialism.[22] Some Christians in Nigeria share this fear.

In Denmark, some political leaders and other opinion makers have expressed the fear that Muslims will grow in number and take over the country, introducing an Islamic state. Mogens Camre of the Danish People's Party and member of the EU-Parliament goes further: "All Western countries are infiltrated by Muslims. Some of them speak to us in a nice way while they are waiting to be sufficient in number to kill us."[23] This rings true for many Danes who look at the future with great anxiety. On the side of the minorities, enemy images of the West and Danish society and its decadence have developed and some feel that all Danes are against them.

In Nigeria, many Christians are afraid of Muslim dominance, and Muslims see Christianity as part and parcel of Western imperialism and aggression. They fear being excluded from national power and control and therefore many in the North regard Sharî'a as a solution guaranteeing that this will not happen. In general, ethnic self-assertion has become a threat

[21] Medan, 5 June 2004. Huria Kristen Batak Protestant (HKBP) is one of the main Lutheran churches in Indonesia.

[22] Rev. Andreas Yewangoe in "Sharî'a Complaints," interviewed by Patung, 26 October 2006, at **www.indonesiamatters.com/772/Sharî a-complaints/**

[23] Annual meeting of the Danish People's Party, 16 September 2001.

to national coherence and created mistrust and fear among people. When one part gains more influence, the other worries about losing control.

"Us vs Them" in Denmark

In Denmark, a rhetoric of a protective and positively defined "We" versus a threatening and negatively defined "They" has become more and more common among ethnic minorities as well as ethnic Danes. This became manifest during the cartoon affair. Since 2001, leading politicians have emphasized that Danes have to lead a culture war against those who still "adhere to medieval values." They argue as follows: "We" [Danes] have to defend our values, our freedom of speech and our civilization's achievements against "Them," [Muslims] who do not understand us. We have to stand firm in this struggle and not surrender.

In 2001, Members of Parliament such as the former Minister of Integration (currently Minister of Education and Ecclesiastic Affairs), Bertel Haarder (Liberal Party), and Søren Krarup (Danish People's Party), have gone as far as to say that Denmark must be defended against those who come from outside. They draw a parallel between the Danish resistance movement against the German soldiers during World War II and today's fight against Muslims.[24]

According to the government, Western tolerance and liberalism must draw the line when they come under threat. In this way, liberalism is at the same time claimed and denied. This ambivalence was clearly shown in Prime Minister Anders Fogh Rasmussen's 2003 New Year's address, in which he claimed that Danes had been foolishly kind for too long and that they had not dared to say that some values are better and more valuable than others. This must happen now, and Danes must speak out against "fundamentalist imams" and prevent medieval forces and political fanaticism from taking root in Denmark. One quarter of his speech

[24] *Jyllands-Posten*, 27 May 2001. Søren Krarup stated in parliament on 18 April 2007 that the Muslim head scarf is a symbol of a totalitarian ideology and as such comparable to the swastika. This statement came in the wake of a debate on Asmaa Abdol-Hamid who is running as candidate for parliament for a small left-wing party. She declared that she intends to wear her head scarf in the parliament if she is elected. The EU-Parliament member, Mogens Camre, added that either Asmaa Abdol-Hamid should leave the country or undergo psychiatric treatment.

was devoted to this issue. Many Muslims were offended, feeling that their Prime Minister did not speak to them but about them.

It is striking that this speech resembled a speech given by another political leader, the Governor of Plateau State, Joshua Chibi Dariye, himself a Christian, in an interview with the *Daily Champion* in March 2004:

> From the onset, let me say it again, as I have before that Jos, capital of Plateau State, is owned by the natives [...]. Simple. Every Hausa-man in Jos is a settler whether he likes it or not. In the past, we might not have told them the home truth, but now we have [...]. They are here with us, we are in one state but that does not change the landlord/settler equation, no matter how much we cherish peace [...]. Our problem here today is that the tenant is becoming very unruly. But the natural law here is simple: if your tenant is unruly, you serve him a quit notice! [...] This unruly group must know that we are no longer willing to tolerate the rubbish they give us. The days of "over tolerance" are gone forever. All of us must accept this home truth.[25]

These comments were made when indigene-settler tensions erupted around Yelwa and were widely condemned by people within and from outside the state as being irresponsible and inflammatory. It underlines how important it is that political leaders, especially in tense situations, act as leaders for the whole the population and do not protect their own ethnic group to the detriment of others.

In Denmark, public and parliamentary debate repeatedly revolves around such issues as forced marriage, parallel societies, the repression of women, punitive laws and "failed integration." In these discussions, the "guests" are often pressurized to tone down their visible cultural and religious differences and to become like their "hosts." According to many Danes, integration is incompatible with Islamic values. Therefore the minorities have to choose sides, to be Muslim with or without Islam. There is a reluctance to acknowledge "difference" and a tendency to suppress disagreement.

Also among certain Muslim groups a strong "Us vs Them" rhetoric is widespread. One example is the growing number of Muslim youths moving around in safe, formalistic circles, focused on code of conduct, *harâm* (not

[25] The *Saturday Champion*, 20 March 2004, p. 9. Cited in "They do not Own this Place. Government Discrimination Against 'Non-Indigenes'," in *Human Rights Watch*, vol. 18, no. 3 (25 April 2006), p. 45.

lawful according to Islam), *halâl* (permissible) and Muslim rituals. They are not active in wider society, mix only with one another and confirm each other in their Muslim identity in opposition to the Western world. Instead of reading modern books about Islam or consulting modern Muslim intellectuals, they consult each other and compete with one another as to who is the most learned person, meaning who has studied the most traditional books and scholars. This provides them with an identity of a strong and uniform sense of "Us," over and against "Them," the ungodly and unprincipled others.

Global perspectives

We have seen how outside fighters have adopted local agendas as their own and have helped to plan and implement attacks in Indonesia and Nigeria. Many of those found guilty of the massacres and violence perpetrated were outsiders who had come to the area to gain power. Also in Denmark, "outsiders" were blamed for the crisis in connection with the caricatures of the Prophet. The Muslim ambassadors who protested and the imams who traveled to the Middle East to gain support for their case were accused of manifesting their "foreignness." They were not regarded as Danes but as outsiders and by some even as traitors. Groups and individuals, especially in the Arab world, used the situation politically in their own interests. Enemy images and mutual fears were exacerbated by both Christians and Muslims and used nationally and globally.

All this shows the global aspect of the "Us vs Them" frustration. The conflicts in all three countries, especially in Denmark, were stimulated by the asymmetry in the global perspective and the lack of democracy at a global level. Incidents and fears at a global level, given prominence in the Internet, radio and television, fueled the anger of Christians and Muslims in Nigeria and Indonesia. Ironically, along with the increasing movement and mixing of people, globalization has contributed to an ideology of fear based on the unequal distribution of wealth and power. This has exacerbated the "Us vs Them" syndrome.[26]

[26] On the "Us vs Them" syndrome at the global level, see Amartya Sen, *Identity and Violence: The Illusion of Destiny (Issues of our Time)* (New York: W. W. Norton, 2006).

During Friday prayers at Mecca during the cartoon crisis, an imam stated, "Now we cannot be ignored anymore. We have been despised, humiliated. Now we will be heard."[27] This statement reveals what was at stake for many in the Muslim world. They interpreted the cartoons as an offence and a sign of contempt of the West vis-à-vis the Islamic world. The fact that it issued from a tiny country such as Denmark was even more provoking. Denmark became the scapegoat for a long-established collective discourse or trauma regarding the Islamic self versus the imperialist "others."

Reactions in Nigeria and Indonesia were similar. The issue was associated with the unequal distribution of wealth and power and the Muslim world feeling part of a civilization that has been in constant decline since the Middle Ages. At the same time, the reactions indicated the need of many in the Muslim world to stand together united in collective feelings of indignation and anger against the West and its double standards and domination.

Political leadership and the mass media

One of the reasons for the escalation of the conflicts was the governments' lack of credibility. Especially during the cartoon crisis, there was insufficient trust in the ability of political leaders to control the situation. However, there have been positive actions and initiatives in which political leaders, sometimes in collaboration with religious leaders and organizations, have attempted to restore peace and order.

In Denmark, social and political factors have been pivotal in the development of the conflict. The media have played a crucial role, and a vicious circle has developed between political leadership, the media and the population, a cycle that is difficult to break.

Negative and positive experiences of leadership

The people we spoke to in the three countries frequently cited poor governance or a lack of political leadership as reasons for the crises.

[27] A Danish journalist who understands Arabic was present in the mosque and referred to the *khutba* (sermon) in a Danish TV-program.

It was generally agreed that political leaders at different levels did only little to diffuse the situation, and therefore did not live up to their responsibility. They did not grasp the dangerous polarization that had taken place. When the conflicts developed they did not get at the root of the problem, as many NGOs were able to do.

In Indonesia, the problems were localized, whereas in Nigeria there was a correlation between tensions and conflicts at the national and local levels. In both countries, the injustices suffered under many years of authoritarian rule (see pp. 18f) were now remembered. In Denmark, tensions were primarily at the national level, while localized problems could often be solved without further complication.

In Nigeria and Indonesia, instability and insecurity in the areas of conflict were regarded as the main reasons for the clashes. Land disputes were not effectively managed and local governments unable to mitigate the conflicts. According to many citizens, the government did not take effective action to solve the conflicts.

In Denmark, an expert report, ordered and published by the Ministry for Foreign Affairs and written by eighteen Middle East researchers, concluded that the Danish government's attitude was a much greater offence to Muslims around the world than the twelve cartoons. The government's unwillingness to dialogue was responsible for the development of the crisis.[28] Especially in the Arab world, the Danish government's attitude of "we have nothing to learn" and the complete lack of self-critique were interpreted as Western cultural arrogance. From the beginning, this attitude affected how the crisis developed. Even after the incident exploded outside Denmark, the government's position still reflected the national political situation, populist considerations and its dependence on the Danish People's Party, while the crisis took its own course according to the different political interests in various Muslim countries.

According to many people, the Plateau State government had failed to guarantee every citizen access to basic resources and fundamental rights. The leaders were thought to be incapable of maintaining law and order. This neglect of responsibility and resolution led to the suspension

[28] Tøger Seidenfaden & Rune Engelbreth Larsen, *Karikaturkrisen. En undersøgelse af baggrund og ansvar* [The cartoon crisis. An examination of the background and responsibility] (Copenhagen: Gyldendal, 2006), p. 8.

of the Plateau state house (assembly) as the formal legislative body of the state.[29] Because the government was not firm during the early stages of the conflict and for various political interests, a peaceful solution could not be found. President Obasanjo was criticized from many sides. For instance, Yakubu Pam, chairman of Christian Association of Nigeria's (CAN) State Chapter of Plateau State,[30] accused him of being one-sided in declaring a state of emergency[31] when Muslims were victimized in Yelwa.[32]

Nevertheless, there have also been positive experiences of political leadership. For instance in the Birom area, outside Jos, some village districts, despite tensions, did not experience violence due to the good efforts of their leaders and elders. One of the villages the LWF study team visited, Korot, in the Forum area,[33] is such an example. During the

---

[29] According to the Plateau Peace Conference Report, political leadership/governance in Plateau State 1999-2004 was seen as "a key to creating disenchantment, unhealthy rivalry, struggle for control of power and resources which culminated in the crises." *Plateau Resolves, op. cit.* (note 1), p. 71.

[30] CAN was formed in 1976 to serve three main objectives: "Firstly, it was meant to serve as a basis for the unity of Christians in Nigeria. Secondly, it was to be a medium for all Christians in the country in executing a united action. Thirdly, it was meant to propagate the Gospel of Christ and promote understanding among the various groups of people in the country." P. L. Udoma, *The Cross and the Crescent. A Christian Response to two Decades of Islamic Affirmation in Nigeria* (London: St Austin Press, 2002), p. 27.

[31] Nankin Bagudu, *Recrudescent Civil Disturbances and Human Rights: The Jos and Statewide Crises 2004* (Jos: League for Human Rights, 2004), p. 85.

[32] Also in Adamawa, where the Lutheran church (initiated by the Danish Branch of the Sudan United Mission in 1913) has its stronghold, conflicts have been caused or prolonged by politicians trying to acquire power by all means and in this way enrich themselves (Meeting with people from the Lutheran church, Yola, 7 March 2005). Thus, on 8–10 June 2004, some Bachama youths attacked Muslim youths in Yola when they were trying to rebuild a mosque destroyed in 2003. It was considered too close to the house of one of the prominent Christian community leaders and the Lutheran cathedral. The state government deposed the traditional ruler and accused him of delaying a security meeting to end the clashes on two occasions. He was, according to the state government, demonstrating indifference, insensitivity and reluctance to solve the conflict.

[33] Interview in Korot, 10 March 2005. Korot is also called Sabon Gidan Forum (the new part of the local government area, Forum) which indicates that the settlement is newer than the rest of the villages in the Forum area. The village is situated in predominantly Christian surroundings, the Birom area outside Jos. It has an almost equal number of Christians and Muslims. The author did research in the village from 1977 to 1979. See Lissi Rasmussen, *Christian-Muslim Relations in Africa. The Cases of Northern Nigeria and Tanzania Compared* (London: I. B. Tauris, British Academic Press, 1993), pp. 75-79. Many families in Korot still have adherents of both religions, all living under one roof, working together and participating in each other's celebrations. In some of the neighboring villages and areas such as Riyom acts of violence occurred.

crisis, when rumors about attacks and killing were spreading, some of the young people were ready to take up stones and start fighting. The supreme chief traveled around the villages and convinced people of the benefits of peaceful coexistence and patience. There was constant contact with district heads, *ardos* (Fulani leaders) and Christian and Muslim leaders in order to warn each other about élites inciting people to take up weapons. They managed to stay calm throughout the crisis.[34]

In Indonesia, there was strong critique of the national government for not taking sufficient action in the conflicts in Sulawesi and the Maluku Islands. Furthermore, the success or failure of the *pemekaran* process to prevent or limit conflict depended "in large part on the capacity, commitment and connections of the *bupati* (district head) concerned."[35] In North Luwu, South Sulawesi, the *pemekaran* process helped reduce conflicts, thanks primarily to an effective partnership between a strong *bupati* and district council leader and his deputy, who all belong to the same prominent *adat*, clan, with a strong local leadership tradition.[36]

Attempts at brokering peace

A number of initiatives were taken by the national and local governments in Nigeria and Indonesia in order to resolve the violent conflicts and create peace between the warring factions. From 2001 to 2004, ten judicial commissions of inquiry were set up by the state and federal governments in Plateau State, and in Central Sulawesi four peace agreements were signed by warring factions between 1998 and 2001.

Most of these efforts failed because of a lack of mutual trust and the government's unwillingness to get at the root of the problems (i.e., grievances over the control of economic resources and political posi-

[34] Interview, *ibid.*

[35] "Indonesia: Managing Decentralization and Conflict in South Sulawesi," International Crisis Group, *Asia Report*, no. 60 (8 July 2003), p. 1.

[36] The opposite happened in the Mamasa District (see pp. 58f) because there were no such strong leaders or local institutions to resolve disputes. As a result, conflict erupted. Also in Maluku the government authorities—at the national and regional levels—have been largely ineffective in containing the violence, let alone in dealing with the underlying causes. "Indonesia: Overcoming Murder and Chaos in Maluku," in *Asia Report*, *op. cit.* (note 5), p. iii.

tions) and to arrest and charge the culprits. Too many exceptions were made and too many personal interests involved. Furthermore, most of the reports and recommendations submitted were never published.

The situation gradually deteriorated and finally spiraled out of control, or as President Obasanjo said, it came "close to mutual genocide" (700 people were killed in Yelwa in two days). In both Nigeria and Indonesia, the presidents declared a state of emergency (2004 in Plateau State and 2000 in Poso). The conflict in Poso continues while Plateau State has remained relatively calm with only sporadic outbreaks of violence. The state governor, Joshua Chibi Dariye, was suspended, together with his deputy and the state house of assembly.[37]

Often the police and military, sent to provide security for the unarmed victims, stood on the sidelines as violence raged. Some units even became a part of the problem, selling weapons to the combatants or even participating in fighting. In Maluku, soldiers sided with Muslims, while police paramilitary personnel sometimes sided with Christians.[38]

A fifth peace declaration was signed in December 2001 in Malino, seventy kilometers southeast of South Sulawesi's capital, Makassar. The meeting between the two warring factions from Poso was sponsored by the Indonesian government and mediated by the Coordinating Minister for People's Welfare, Jusuf Kalla. A second Malino peace agreement was brokered in February 2002 between opposing factions from the Maluku province. In June 2004, following the crisis in Plateau State, a peace committee was set up in Jos to initiate a peace and reconciliation process.

---

[37] Governor Joshua Chibi Dariye was reinstalled after six months but in September 2004, the London Metropolitan Police arrested him for alleged money laundering. He skipped UK bail and returned to Nigeria where legislators impeached him for the same charges in November 2006. A high court later nullified his sacking and ordered his reinstatement. This was later confirmed by the Supreme Court, and on 29 April 2007 Dariye returned to the state after having formally resumed office until the newly elected governor was to take over by the end of May 2007. This created tensions and worries in Jos.

[38] Another problem in both countries was that the federal agencies were not equipped to check the influx of aliens to the areas of conflict. For instance, in Maluku and Poso there was no attempt to stop Laskar Jihad's passage from Java, despite specific instruction from President Wahid to do so. "Indonesia's Maluku Crisis," in *Indonesia Briefing*, *op. cit.* (note 18), p. 3.

The Danish "pollocracy"[39]

One of the main reasons for growing anti-Muslim sentiments among the Danish population since the mid-1980s, and especially after 9/11, is that among most Danish politicians voters' support seems to have become the only criterion of success. Opinion polls, often commissioned by newspapers, have replaced the development of ideas, formation of attitudes and visions for the future development of society. Therefore a journalist from the daily *Information* stated that Denmark was no longer a democracy but rather a "pollocracy."[40] Politics and political statements are formed by sentiments in the population.

This means that often laws have been suggested and even implemented as a result of isolated incidents that have scandalized the population. Immigrants, especially Muslims, seem to be good media material to cause such scandal so that politicians feel called to react by making speedy pronouncements or to suggest new legislation that may provide increased voters' support. Politics today is the struggle for parliamentary seats, and not so much about principles and securing certain values for the future.[41] This populist tendency is not new, but has become much more widespread than before.

As a result, no concrete attempts have been made politically to eliminate or reduce the increasing fear and mistrust between the majority and

[39] Pollocracy is a term coined for the first time in a letter to the editor published on 4 May 1990 in the *Ann Arbor News*, Michigan, USA. It is defined as the power of the polls. This political phenomenon can be both a useful tool and a detrimental tool to democracy.

[40] Georg Metz, 10–11 September 2005.

[41] Therefore it was also difficult to find political parties during the cartoon crisis that wanted to go against the firmness of the Prime Minister who saw the crisis exclusively as a matter of freedom of speech instead of looking inwards critically. At some point, two blaming possibilities existed, an "imam-school" and an "ambassador-school." One either blamed the imams in the delegation that traveled to the Middle East (see pp. 36, 40 and 44), or the ambassadors from the Muslim countries who brought the issue out of Denmark. The government's attitude was that the others are to blame. When we Danes are criticized, it is because we are misunderstood. All critique that has come from outside of Denmark, as for instance from Alvaro Gil-Robles, Commissioner in the European Council, who encouraged the government to respect minorities, was rejected and sometimes even ridiculed. According to Gil-Robles, Danish integration politics is built on fear—the fear of losing national identity. This places people in a moral ghetto which is bound to generate confrontation, *Politiken* and *Kristeligt Dagblad*, 17 January 2006. Earlier human rights committees and centers under the UN, the EU and the European Council have criticized the Danish Aliens Law for being too strict and as only just conforming to human rights conventions. All these critical voices were rejected by the government and the Danish People's Party.

Muslim minorities. Rather, responsible political leaders have used this fear to garner votes and to achieve or remain in power. Instead of giving signals of inclusion and promoting cultural pluralism, they have further contributed to the tensions by legitimizing anti-Muslim sentiments.

The government and its supporting party have viewed the presence of Islam in the country primarily as a problem, albeit not one of the major problems facing Denmark. According to the government, the solution to the "Muslim problem" has been the implementation of stricter laws, speaking out against medieval traditions and controlling the imams, most of whom, according to the then Minister of Integration, Bertel Haarder, are "strongly conservative," "an impediment to integration" and "indeed hopeless."[42]

A number of restrictive immigration measures have been introduced. This includes making it easier to reject asylum seekers and applications for Danish citizenship, tighter regulations for permanent residence and family reunion, reduced levels of social benefits, etc. These measures are at the very limit (or over the limit, according to some human rights organizations) of what is compatible with human rights.

In the political debate, the rhetoric in relation to Islam and Muslims has become increasingly harsh. The then Danish People's Party's Member of Parliament, Per Dalgaard, whom the LWF team met in October 2003, stated in *Jyllands-Posten*:

> This is not the Middle East. This is not the jungle, and it is not a Balkan society of thieves where only the strong person has the right to life. We wish our old Denmark back. We try with all our might to have these wild and uncontrollable people sent home. Home to the conditions they want a society to consist of: chaos, violence, murder, robbery and pure anarchy. Here in this country they only give us trouble and are of no use.[43]

It seems that today many ethnic Danes no longer take the same interest in negative statements and stories about Islam and Muslims. According

[42] The *Information*, 20 January 2003.

[43] *Jyllands-Posten*, 3 January 2003, and again in *Jyllands-Posten*, 26 May 2004: "Everything they get freely. And the rewards are robberies and assaults. And free us from the statement that this is only a minor group [...]. We will not accept that an old book, the Qur'ân should be above our laws [...] a throughout intolerant religion/culture. Those who do not put up with our democracy, our 100-year-old model of society built with the help of hard labor, must leave. They are useless here."

to the EU Commission's research in early 2007, two out of three ethnic Danes complain that discrimination has become more common in Denmark over the past five years. Most think that ethnic minorities are treated too negatively in Denmark and that immigration policies are too tight. Many Danes, including a number of politicians and parliamentarians, are calling for decent conditions for Iraqis seeking asylum in Denmark.[44]

Another indication is that the New Alliance, a new social liberal political party, has gained overwhelming support among the population. Within a few hours of its establishment in May 2007, thousands of people, including politicians and parliamentarians from various other parties, joined the party, one of whose main goals is to restrict the influence of the Danish People's Party. For many of the supporters, this was the main reason for their membership since they are tired of the xenophobic rhetoric.

Lack of acknowledgement

Two national meetings in Nigeria and Denmark show what is at stake when it comes to the ex- or inclusion of Muslim leaders in societal development by the political leadership. On 30 November 2004, Prime Minister Anders Fogh Rasmussen invited representatives of ethnic minorities to a meeting in Copenhagen in order to discuss the problem of integration. The Prime Minister wanted to meet with people who had made an effort to improve integration, but deliberately avoided imams and other practicing Muslims. "It is not a religious meeting. I am a politician," he said. Since he often spoken out against "fundamentalist" imams, this was seen as a sign that the Prime Minister found it useless to speak to religious Muslims, and only wished to talk to secular Muslims. At the same time, he and other Members of Parliament have stated that imams have a responsibility in relation to integration and radicalization of Muslims in the country.[45]

[44] Around 600 Iraqi asylum seekers have stayed in refugee camps in Denmark for up to eight years under hopeless conditions, especially for children.

[45] This was later legitimized by the Minister of Integration who encouraged politicians to boycott the imams. She would not discuss integration issues with them in the future. Generally the influence of imams in Denmark has been exaggerated. According to a survey, two out of three Muslims do not attend mosque. Thirteen percent regularly attend Friday prayer and thirty-one percent never pray. Rambøll Management for *Jyllands-Posten*, 11 May 2006.

On 14 March 2005, President Obasanjo invited delegates from all over Nigeria to a National Political Reform Conference (CONFAB) to discuss constitutional change. This was met with skepticism. One of the points of critique was that the composition of the delegates was biased and regarded as an insult to the Muslims in the country. Out of 393 delegates, 233 were Christians. Muslim leaders felt excluded and accused the President of having rejected those whom he thought too radical.[46]

In both cases, the sidelining of certain Muslim figures was seen as an indication that the political leadership does not recognize the importance of religion and pursues an exclusive policy. Obasanjo as well as Fogh Rasmussen did not recognize that the religious character matters and must be reflected in the appointment of candidates for an important meeting. Since there are people, in this case Muslims, who feel politically marginalized, these two political leaders' acts were counterproductive.

Responses to the cartoon crisis in Nigeria and Indonesia

In Northern Nigeria and Indonesia, like in many other predominantly Muslim countries, there were demonstrations against the publication of the Danish cartoons. These took place especially in larger cities such as Jakarta, Medan and Surabaya in Indonesia, and Maiduguri, Kano and Bauchi in Northern Nigeria. In Jakarta, smaller youth organizations such as Front Pembela Islam (FPI) organized riots and demonstrations, and 300 Muslims stormed the Danish and Norwegian embassies on 3 February 2006. They saw the cartoons as being a part of the Western (Christian and Jewish) conspiracy against Islam and were convinced that the cartoons were deliberately designed to destroy Islamic civilization. In an attempt to calm down the situation, President Susilo Bambang Yudhoyono and many other high ranking officials condemned the publication of the cartoons as well as the violent reactions.[47]

---

[46] Alabi Wilson, "Regionalism: Tales from the Good Old Days," in the *Guardian*, March 13, 2005, p. 39; Pini Jason, "CONFAB: 'Who will Speak for Nigeria?'," in *Vanguard* 11 February 2005; "Nigeria: National Conference on Constitutional Change Meets with Skepticism," at **Irinnews.org**, 20 February 2005.

[47] Arndt Graf, "Debates on the Danish Cartoon Affair in Islamic South East Asia," in *ASIEN* 101 (October 2006), pp. 66-67.

Reactions in Nigeria were much stronger in certain places, In the North it came to violent riots and actual killings. The 19 February 2006 riots in Maiduguri can be directly related to the cartoon issue. Danish flags were burnt, churches destroyed and around fifty people (mainly Christians) were killed. Demonstration also took place in Kano, and Danish commodities were boycotted.

In Bauchi, Muslims set fire to a number of churches and more than a hundred people died during four days of violence. The immediate cause was an alleged act of blasphemy but the riots must also be seen as part of the avalanche that was set in motion by reactions to the cartoon issue.[48]

All this led to acts of retaliation against Muslims in Onitsha, a predominantly Christian city in the South, where a number of Muslims were killed and mosques were burned. Also in southeastern Enugu, Christian youths attacked Muslims and burned a mosque.

It never came to violence in Indonesia and, unlike Nigeria, preexisting conflicts were not revived. There were some misunderstandings and confusion between Christians and Muslims in certain areas, but these did not escalate. The government reacted by revising the rules for issuing licenses to build houses of worship.

The Indonesian government stated that freedom of expression could not be used as an argument to condone the Danish mass media's insult of or attack on a religious symbol.[49] This was affirmed by a number of representatives from all major religions in Indonesia who met on 18 February 2007 to discuss the issue. They agreed on a joint message, stating that reactions to the cartoons should not fuel a global conflict. While condemning their publication by *Jyllands-Posten* and subsequent reprinting in some European newspapers, they expressed their support of the free press, stressing that the freedom of speech should not be used to violate religious sensitivities.[50]

The news of the video made by members of the Danish People's Party's youth organization came as a great disappointment. Both Nahdlatul

[48] Also in the northern town of Kontagora, people were killed, churches torched and in northeastern Potiskum, churches and houses belonging to Christians were burned by Muslim youths.

[49] *ANTARA News*, 2 February 2006. The publication of the cartoons was forbidden in Indonesia and one person who put them on a Web site was jailed. The publishers and the editor in chief of *Peta* were tried for having published some of the cartoons. See Graf, *op. cit.* (note 47), p. 66.

[50] *Opinion News*, 20 February 2006.

Ulama (NU) and Muhammadiya saw this as a serious insult, aggravated by the fact that it was the second time, this time as Muslims all over the world were observing Ramadan.[51]

The publication of the cartoons was discussed in the electronic as well as printed media. The critique was mainly directed against the newspapers that had published the cartoons for having manipulated and abused the principle of freedom of speech. Furthermore, it was regretted that this case had strengthened the mistrust that exists between the Muslim and the Western world. Most people rejected conspiracy theories or the claim that this was a deliberate insult against Islam as such, but rather saw the cartoons as symptoms of carelessness and insensitivity.

In Nigeria, the crises developed a logic of its own. The violence that had occurred may have been triggered off or reinforced by the cartoons, but the underlying reason for unrest had to do with political leadership. In Bauchi, Maiduguri and Katsina uncertainty over the political future, in particular President Obasanjo's plans for the future, had been very evident.

Maiduguri and Katsina were hosting a public hearing on constitutional reform. Many Nigerians believed that this was geared toward furthering the so-called "third term agenda" and thereby to maintain the status quo. This existing Constitution barred Obasanjo from seeking a third term. To allow him to do so, the Constitution needed to be amended. This created a bad political atmosphere within the whole country, because the transition from military rule to a multiparty democracy was at stake. Especially in the North, unemployed Muslim youth were strongly opposed to the third term agenda believing that the presidency should go to one of their own, not to a Christian Southerner.

The North felt left behind since the South, in addition to its dominant economic role, held the political leadership. In this way, the cartoons were used to mobilize supporters. Another means was the attempt by a Christian group, the Save Nigeria Movement, to mobilize Nigerians to pray in mosques and churches across the country for divine intervention in order to abort the President's third term project.[52] This seemed

---

[51] Muhammadiya's chairman, Din Syamsuddin, accused Western people and media of double standards. "They claim themselves to be democratic and pluralist but their attitude shows otherwise," in the *Jakarta Post*, 9 October, 2006, at **www.thejakartapost.com/misc**

[52] **www.orjikalu.com**, 27 February 2006.

to work since the Senate rejected the bill in June 2006, and the People's Democratic Party, the President's party, accepted this decision.[53]

The role of the mass media

In all three countries, the "Us vs Them" dichotomy is fundamental to the media's approach to conflict and tension. The media capitalize on people's differences and thereby reinforce polarization. This is especially so in Denmark, where the mass media play a central role in relation to the image of Islam and Muslims among the majority population, and certainly in relation to how politicians act or react in terms of their integration policies. This was also the case during the cartoon crisis.

In Indonesia and Nigeria, the media are playing an increasingly important role. Since the media do not have as dominant a position as in Denmark, and Christians and Muslims meet on a regular basis and are culturally not as far removed from one another, the media's impact is not as pronounced as in Denmark and some other European countries.

The media have contributed to the deepening of the crisis in Nigeria through false or biased reporting. Moreover, they were used by political leaders to garner support for the conflicts through "selective reporting, prejudicial stereotypes, attributing individual statements to collective causes, stating unconfirmed rumors as facts and blowing interpersonal or intergroup conflicts out of their original contexts."[54] In Plateau State, the state media helped fuel the conflict, but we cannot conclude that they were partly responsible for the conflict.

The national media were divided. The Southern media perceived the crises primarily as a religious vendetta against all Muslims, whereas the Northern media promoted a Northern Muslim agenda. Foreign media were only allowed to cover the crisis, provided they were not biased, otherwise reporters were transferred outside the state. At one stage, there was only one agency left in the state, namely *Media Trust*.[55]

---

[53] **http//today.reuters.com**, 22 February 2006.

[54] "Advocacy for Peace in Kaduna and Plateau States, Nigeria," in *Inter-Gender* (Jos, 2004), p. 37.

[55] Information given by Nafisat Lawal Musa.

During the peacemaking process, the mass media played a more important role in the positive as well as in the negative sense. The media were used as an important instrument for peace building and to prevent conflict from recurring, but also as a means to attract political support. As the director of the Peace Program under the Mennonite Central Committee, Rev. Gopar Barnabas Topkida, told the LWF study team: "The process of reconciliation and peace building has been stolen by politicians and the media from the people who are suffering. It must be given back to the grass roots," who work with community groups and organizations to build bridges of understanding and develop peace building skills, especially in and around Jos. Peace conferences were shown on television, all starting and ending with a Christian and a Muslim prayer, and politicians embraced each other. According to Topkida, it was merely done for show, a way for politicians to promote themselves and there was no real interest in promoting a process.[56]

The fact that daily many Indonesians are able to watch demonstrations, rioting and conflict on national television undoubtedly emboldened people, especially local youth gangs, to participate in the fighting. Like the Danish and Nigerian media, the Indonesian media tend to portray any conflict involving different ethnic groups as a communal conflict with implied Christian-Muslim divides. The overall bias is with the majority religion and the focus primarily on long-standing ethnic and religious tensions as the cause of conflict, rather than on land disputes, social problems, weak institutions and the inadequate enforcement of the law. In this way, the media contribute to creating a major difference between local and national perceptions of the conflicts.[57]

Sensationalism and essentialism of the media

The mass media have significantly influenced public opinion in Denmark. In much of the Danish media, Islamic culture is perceived as monolithic,

---

[56] Interview in Jos, 11 March 2005.

[57] The use of impudent language about non-Muslims is forbidden in the written media in Indonesia. It only occurs in the publications of radical or extremist groups which are readily and cheaply available. It also happens during *khutbas* but seldom on television.

static and the cause of all problems related to immigrants. Discrimination and marginalization are only rarely mentioned. The media are marked by essentialism and culturalism in their portrayal of Muslim minorities. The individual Muslim represents Islam; that is Islam in the eyes of the media.

This is especially problematic when the way in which the media portray Muslim minorities in Denmark has become fixated on unpleasant news and when Islam is equated with Islamism.[58] Stories are often exaggerated, skewed, sensationalized and dramatized. When this occurs almost daily, with only little personal experience to rectify this one-sided and negative image, a feeling of general hopelessness arises, not only among ethnic minorities but also among the general population.

Instead of conveying in-depth information and attempting to go beyond actual stories, newspapers bombard their readers with opinion polls that confirm certain prejudices.[59] Positive events and statements expressing solidarity, innovation and progress do not make the headlines.

Like in many other countries, the media are generally no longer driven by lofty ideals, convictions or ethical considerations. Sales forecasts determine content. Furthermore, the media take over more and more functions in society and are not only detector and informer but also prosecutor, judge, pillory, expert and arbiter of taste.

One could say that the majority of the Danish media and the public debate have constructed a meta-discourse living a life of its own and devising its own reality. This discourse has also influenced Muslims. The media have quasi not only stolen a process of real dialogue and understanding from the grass roots, but have also achieved a formative impact on the Muslims' Islamic discourse. This obstructs dialogue.

Muslims themselves are partly responsibly for this development. They are divided and have been unable to organize themselves into overall Muslim organization. They have also not established educational institutions to prepare representatives to speak on their behalves and provide the public with a more nuanced and positive picture. Only very few Muslim scholars

[58] Media studies carried out by universities, journalists and ethnic minority organizations have shown that nearly seventy percent of all media coverage of foreigners in Denmark focus either on crime or social problems.

[59] An example is a front-page article in *Berlingske Tidende*, 14 June 2006, about an opinion poll where the following question was asked: Are Muslims of advantage to Denmark? Fifty-seven percent answered no.

are able to reflect upon and explain the meaning of Islam to Muslims, the media and the Danish public. Furthermore, most imams are "imported." Since they are only allowed to stay in the country for up to four years they never learn Danish or acquire sufficient knowledge of Danish society, let alone develop the ability to reflect contextually on Islam and its traditions.

At the same time, some politicians and others from a Muslim background have used Islam for their own self-promotion. They have drawn attention to themselves by degrading others from a similar background by depicting them as being Islamists and antidemocratic. This contributes considerably to the negative image of Islam and Muslims both within and outside their own communities.

The role of religion and religious leaders

We have seen that in all three conflict stories the causes are multiple and complex and cannot be reduced to religion. Some of the conflicts may have been triggered by events related to religion, but the real reasons are not religious but socioeconomic, ethnic and political. Almost everyone we talked to during our field studies in Nigeria and Indonesia affirmed this.

Religious leaders, institutions and organizations have played constructive as well as destructive roles. Extremist tendencies, the implementation of certain parts of Sharî'a and the stubbornness of some religious leaders have been destructive, while peace and dialogue initiatives, interfaith committees, seminars, conferences and delegations are constructive strategies. The communities have become more polarized but at the same time there is an increased awareness that inclusive thinking and dialogue are necessary.

The religious component of the conflicts

Similarities in the development of the conflicts and their underlying causes in Nigeria and Indonesia are striking. In both countries, the conflicts occurred in the context of economic decline and the struggle for political power. Over the years, tensions and rivalries had accumulated over access to political power and economic resources, especially over land. Religion and ethnicities became vehicles for certain interests, and what was initially a political and economic conflict assumed ethnic and religious dimensions. Since the political actors have different religious affiliations and ethnic backgrounds, the conflicts were connected to these differences. Christians and Muslims started to attack one another, hundreds of people were killed and churches and mosques, as tangible symbols of the enemy, became targets. This widened the conflict, also in geographical terms. Rumors about certain religious groups or buildings being under attack spread and the conflict spilled over to other areas.

During the conflicts, religion and religious feelings were increasingly being used and manipulated to deepen divisions. Religion was used to inflame passions and mobilize large numbers of people. Political leaders played on the population's religious affiliation in order to influence people so as to win their support and to divert their attention from the real problems or from the underlying agendas. They exploited differences in order to achieve their own ends. As a result, Muslims and Christians turned against each other and rivalries were stirred up between various ethnic groups. Seeds of distrust were sown often leading to fear of one another. It seemed impossible to undo the damage and restore confidence.

Since the state governments were fairly passive in relation to the conflicts, and the regional governments, local military and police were largely ineffective in containing the violence, violent militias could easily penetrate the area. Thus, well-organized Muslim militias arrived in Maluku and Poso, and local *jihâd* groups and smaller Christian militant groups began to form. A cycle of retribution escalated out of control.[60] In Plateau State, outside ethnic militias came in.

In Sulawesi, Maluku, Jos and Yelwa offense and violations of "the other's" dignity also played important roles. This was so in the Danish cartoon conflict. The conflict and the reactions to it were quickly reduced to a religious crisis (inside as well as outside Denmark) in order to make

[60] Robert W. Hefner has indicated that while in East Java during the *minja* killing in 1998 the Nahdlatul Ujama (NU) leadership were quick to mobilize anti-violence teams, this was not the case in Maluku a year later. There was no NU or any other well-established NGO to contain the violence. "Disintegration or Democratization? Muslim-Christian Violence and the Future of Indonesia," in Olle Tørnquist (ed.), *Political Violence: Indonesia and India in Comparative Perspective. SUM Report 9* (University of Oslo, 2000), pp. 47f. In the same article, Hefner maintains that the real author of the first wave of conflict in Maluku were the "hard-line elements" of the Suharto regime intent on "exploiting tensions in society so as to create major obstacles to democratic reform," while trying to demonstrate that "only a firm non-civilian hand is capable of governing Indonesia," pp. 47-48.

it more conceivable and manageable and to provide an excuse for not relating ethically and self-critically to the issue at hand. Many people, including certain politicians, media and opinion makers, believed that the Muslims were being oversensitive and medieval in their attitude.

In reality, however, the controversy in Denmark was not so much about blasphemy and the depiction of the Prophet. Instead, it was about social marginalization and the failure to recognize the offence to the Muslim minorities in Denmark. It was not about self-censorship in relation to Islam and Muslims or about limiting the freedom of speech. There was no evidence that freedom of speech was under pressure in Denmark.

Even Muslims who do not take much interest in Islam felt insulted and offended by the depiction of the Prophet. However, had the Muslims generally felt recognized and respected by Danish society, they probably would have ignored the drawings and not reacted with anger and despair. This was the case in Norway, where the drawings were published a few weeks later in a Norwegian newspaper. The Muslims expressed their disappointment but did not go any further. In Denmark, the cartoons became a symbol for the struggle of many, especially youth, to be recognized as Danish Muslims.

Constructive roles of religion during the crises in Nigeria and Indonesia

Many dialogue initiatives and other forms of cooperation have developed out of the three conflicts. Religious leaders and organizations have contributed to peace declarations and processes.

In both Indonesia and Nigeria, some religious leaders on both sides defended only the interest of their own religious group and blamed the other side for the conflict. Totally lacking self-critique, they were interested in framing the conflict as religious, sometimes using scriptural language. Muslims led a campaign about "Christianization," and there were rumors about forced conversions and attacks on local people as well as migrants. Christians on the other hand depicted the conflicts as an Islamic "holy war" against Christians, an attempt by Muslims to take over the country and to turn it into an Islamic state.

Other religious leaders played a significant role in peace building with some successfully appealing to people to stay calm. Christian and Muslim leaders also cooperated with each other to avert widespread violence. In both countries, it is customary for political leaders to call upon religious leaders and to engage in face-to-face communication. For instance, religious leaders in Poso met with local security authorities to issue a joint communiqué calling for a halt to the conflict, which both sides ignored.[61] There are many testimonies to the courage and integrity of both Christians and Muslims who saved others from the onslaught of members of their own faith.

The two most important interreligious meetings were the first conference in Malino, 2001 (Sulawesi) and the peace conference in Jos, 2004, which included dialogue between religious, ethnic and community leaders. In Jos, the government initiated a six-month program comprising different committees, including one consisting of religious leaders, to restore peace in the area. Documents from these committees were the basis for a peace conference in August 2004 (see p. 50). Many Muslims criticized the conference for being unbalanced. The commission consisted of five Christians and two Muslims, whereas 155 Christians and twenty Muslims participated in the conference.

In Sulawesi, a government sponsored meeting was held to end the conflict in Poso. It resulted in the Malino Declaration (pp. 57f).[62] Both conferences involved Muslim and Christian groups who agreed to work together and to end all conflicts. They were partly successful in mitigating further conflict, especially in Jos. Until today, violence continues to erupt sporadically in Poso.[63]

On the whole, many NGOs took peace initiatives during the crisis. Community groups were established in Nigeria many of which had women at the forefront.[64] Also youth organizations were involved, such

---

[61] Badri Djawara, the *Jakarta Post*, 4 December 2001.

[62] Another meeting was held in February 2002 in Malino (Malino II) between the opposing factions from Maluku province. It ended in an agreement to end the three-year bloodshed and to work together to maintain peace in Maluku.

[63] For instance, in October 2006, a Christian pastor was shot dead in Palu, and the Communion of Churches in Indonesia (PGI), the country's leading Protestant umbrella organization, urged the government thoroughly to investigate the murder and called on religious leaders in Central Sulawesi to avoid pitting religious groups against each other, at **www.Indahnesia.com**, 16 October 2006. In the same year, a team was set up by the government to tackle the violence in Sulawesi. Measures are now taken to avoid escalation of violence in the area.

[64] For instance, the National Council for Women Societies, NCWS, Plateau State Chapter, organized a march in conjunction with other women NGOs and groups, be they ethnic, religious or profes-

as the Council Plateau Youth Council.[65] Furthermore, the International Center for Gender and Social Research, Inter-Gender, supported by the European Commission, launched a peace project.[66]

In 2002, the Institute for Strategic Study and Empowerment (LKSP) was established in Maluku. Its mission was to study the economy, politics and education and to bring about reconciliation between Maluku's segregated societies. The institute also helped internally displaced people. [67]

Christian and Muslim leaders and organizations during the cartoon conflict

There were different and sometimes conflicting attitudes and reactions to the cartoon incident in Denmark. Eleven Muslim organizations began a protest campaign against the publication of the cartoons and the delegation of imams[68] who went to Egypt and Lebanon. Undoubtedly this delegation contributed to the escalation of the conflict and influenced the Danes' reaction. Nonethe-

sional. The day is known as "Black Wednesday." All women came out in black signifying their grief over the violence. They visited the Gbong Gwom (Chief of Jos), the State House of Assembly and the governor of Plateau State. They walked about 150 km in the scorching sun and heavy rains. The central message was that the women were tired of violence. It had to be stopped.

The Federation of Muslim Women's Associations in Nigeria (FOMWAN), Plateau State, was involved in peace initiatives and peace education for youth. They own a school and a maternity and child welfare clinic in Jos (information given by Nafisat Lawal Musa, Jos). On FOMWAN, see Hussaina J. Abdullah, "Religious Revivalism, Human Rights Activism and the Struggle for Women's Rights in Nigeria," in Abdullahi A An-Naim (ed.), *Cultural Transformation and Human Rights in Africa* (London: Zed Books, 2002), pp. 163-171.

[65]" Advocacy for Peace in Kaduna and Plateau States, Nigeria," in *Inter-Gender Monograph Series* (Jos, 2004), p. 56.

[66] Inter-Gender, one of the most important organizations, launched peace projects in Jos and Kaduna. Other NGOs include the Center for Peace Initiative and Development (CEPID), Civil Liberties Organization (CLO), Community Action for Popular Participation (CAPP) and the Christian Foundation for Social Justice and Equality. Also the Nigeria Inter-Religious Council, NIREC played a role. In 1999, twenty-five Muslim and twenty-five Christian members, representing their respective groups under the joint chairmanship of the Sultan of Sokoto, President General of the Nigerian Supreme Council for Muslim Affairs, the Primate of the Methodist Church of Nigeria and the President of CAN, met on the Plateau.

[67] Alpha Amirrachman, "Hasbollah Toisuta: Removing the Seeds of the Conflict in Maluku," in the *Jakarta Post*, 13 February 2007.

[68] Five imams in the first delegation and four in the second, most of them from Palestinian and Lebanese backgrounds.

less, they were not the main reason for the global storm, as many people in Denmark wanted to believe. The main actors in the Arab countries knew what had happened before they arrived in the Middle East.

Two now retired Lutheran pastors and cousins, Søren Krarup and Jesper Langballe, played a crucial role in the prelude to the entire cartoon conflict. Both Members of Parliament belonged to a theological movement called Tidehverv, originally a backlash to Pietism and inspired by dialectic theology (see p. 43). Throughout Krarup's long leadership, the movement emphasized the Christian's obligation towards their nation and people, which led to a xenophobic and anti-EU attitude. The two pastors' polemic against Muslims and Islam has been extremely aggressive. The publication of the cartoons was inspired and legitimized by their odious rhetoric and its significant effect on public opinion.[69] However, many Christians in Denmark supported the Muslims in their critique of the publication of the cartoons.

In Nigeria, CAN's secretary general, Rev. Joseph John Hayab, said that the publication of the cartoons was totally uncalled for at a time when the world was looking for unity. Freedom of speech does not mean absence of responsibility for social and human consequences (locally and globally). The question is whether or not we want to share a world of peace.[70]

In Denmark, two Christian declarations were issued and joint Christian Muslim prayers together with demonstrations for peace were arranged together by Christians and Muslims, in Århus and Copenhagen. Two delegations were sent to the Middle East to repair the damage: a Christian delegation to Egypt in November 2005, and a Christian Muslim delegation to Damascus in June 2006.

Since bishops and pastors of the Evangelical Lutheran Church in Denmark cannot speak on behalf of the church there was no official declaration from the church as such. The church, like the population, was divided. Despite this, on 13 December 2005, three pastors took the initiative to send out a statement signed by forty-two pastors. Entitled "There is still no room in the inn," it protested against the restrictions that the

---

[69] During the crisis, Søren Krarup referred to imams participating in the delegation as traitors. They cannot be trusted, he said, and therefore they cannot be communicated with. Rather they should be deported from the country. *Jyllands-Posten*, 10 February 2006.

[70] *BBC News*, 3 February 2006.

government and the Danish People's Party had imposed on refugees and asylum seekers. At the same time, they criticized the "tone" of the public debate on "foreigners," especially Muslims. "If we cannot see refugees as human beings who should be protected and assisted but only as a burden that should be rejected at any price, our view on human beings is in danger. Indeed, our whole society is in danger," they stated.

A number of pastors joined the so-called "pastor initiative," with 130 pastors signing a letter of protest sent to the Minister of Integration on 16 December 2005. They furthermore encouraged pastors all over the country to focus on refugees in their Christmas sermon. The number increased to 200.[71]

A number of politicians, especially the two pastors in the Danish People's Party, felt provoked. Rev. Jesper Langballe called the protesting pastors "cows roaring in a herd" while Søren Krarup branded them as "false Christians." According to them, the pastors needed to be called to order by the bishops. "Pastors should not do politics; that is to make fun of Christianity. They should separate religion and politics," he said. Consequently, a prominent government politician left the Evangelical Lutheran Church in Denmark in protest against "politicizing pastors."

The pastors insisted that the church would lose its credibility if it were to keep silent when human dignity is at stake. Bishop Kjeld Holm, who had backed the initiative, maintained that this was an ethical question. Freedom of speech does not imply ruthlessness. The gospel guides the way in which we live our lives and has to be preached clearly.[72]

---

[71] In 2006, again at Christmas time, a group of eleven pastors in the city of Hillerød made a united protest calling on other Christians to join. They protested against the expulsion of 600 Iraqi asylum seekers who had stayed in refugee camps for up to eight years under hopeless conditions. A church service for the Iraqis was held at which also Muslims participated. Five hundred participated from different sectors of the church landscape, conservatives as well as liberals, and also from free churches. The protest and the service provoked a debate as to whether pastors of the Evangelical Lutheran Church in Denmark pastors should be allowed to take action critical of government politics.

[72] On 15 December 2005, twelve writers also stood up against the xenophobic debate and discrimination in Denmark. The government and the Danish People's Party were the main targets of their protest. They were followed by the board of the writers' organization and 252 of their members. For them, human and social recognition are very important. Later, fifty-four medical doctors and a number of psychologists joined the protest and eleven former ambassadors to Muslim countries expressed their critique of the way in which the crisis was being handled. The Prime Minister was blamed for not having accepted the Muslim ambassadors' invitation to dialogue. Later the various protest groups worked together and arranged a large hearing.

The Danish People's Party found only one explanation for all this: the critique had to do with the fact that all these people disliked their party.

Ambiguous effects

In all cases, the effects of the conflict were ambiguous. While giving rise to further antagonism and increasing polarization, mistrust and hatred among people, many people learned a lesson and became locally involved in different peace activities and processes. Many positive activities were initiated. In Nigeria and Indonesia, interfaith families and neighborhood ties have become stronger and the collaboration between religious leaders more confident.[73] In Denmark, Christians and Muslims came together to counteract the negative atmosphere prevalent in the country. Furthermore, the rhetoric became more muted, at least for a certain time.

In Nigeria, especially Lutherans and Roman Catholics have been active in interreligious cooperation following the crisis, and different interfaith groups have been established. The Mennonite Central Committee launched a peace program for institutional capacity building with TEKAN.[74] The program included peace building workshops and in 2004 resulted in the TEKAN Peace Program Strategy to increase the TEKAN churches' capacity for effective peace building and conflict intervention. After 2002, attempts were made to involve Muslim leaders.[75] The program sought "to strengthen a network of facilitators with shared values and understanding beyond denominational boundaries,"[76] to stand together, to create unity in diversity and thereby to help understand differences. Regular networking among member churches occurred and peace education introduced in TEKAN schools.[77]

[73] For instance, in Nigeria, during and after the Jos crisis, public events started and ended with Christian-Muslim prayers.

[74] TEKAN consists of twelve churches: The Church of the Brethren (EYN), the Lutheran Church of Christ in Nigeria (LCCN), the Church of Christ in Nigeria (COCIN), the Christian Reformed Church of Nigeria (CRCN), United Church of Christ in Nigeria (HEKAN), Evangelical Reformed Church of Christ (ERCC), United Methodist Church of Nigeria (UMCN), Mambila Baptist Convention of Nigeria (MBCN), Sudan Church of Christ among the Tiv (NKST) and Reformed Church of Christ in Nigeria (RCCN). Interview, 11 March 2005, with Rev. Dr Caleb Ahima, Secretary General of TEKAN.

[75] Interview with Rev. Dr Caleb Ahima.

[76] *TEKAN Peace Program* (Jos, November 2004), p. 3.

[77] The time frame was as follows: 1) establishment of a peace office to coordinate the peace program in 2005; 2) creation of denominational peace teams by 2006; 3) establishment of at least five peace networks in each team at congregational levels by 2007; and 4) establishment of conflict monitoring and early warning signs and information systems throughout the peace

Also Muslims were politically active during and after the conflict and involved in peace building activities in the state. Jama'atu Nasril Islam (JNI) (Society for the Victory of Islam), the supervisory body for most of the Islamic organizations, was at the forefront of the dialogue between Muslims and Christians.[78] Furthermore, the Nigerian Council of Muslim Youth Organizations (NACOMYO), an umbrella organization of Muslim youth organizations established in 1987 to enhance unity of the *umma*, has been involved in peace activities and worked together with the Catholic Relief Services toward conflict resolution.[79]

In Indonesia, interreligious solidarity and networking have developed in areas of conflict. For instance, Muslim volunteers protected churches during Christmas and Easter celebrations.[80]

In April 2005, at least eighty Muslim and Christian leaders from Central Sulawesi met in Palu to establish a forum to ensure security and lasting peace in the conflict-torn Poso region. The forum, Alliance to Save Humanity, was arranged by the NU with the aim of promoting peace by conducting intensive dialogue among Christians and Muslims in the city.

In Denmark, new Muslim organizations were created or relaunched. Muslim leaders and organizations felt a need to profile themselves and to position themselves in relation to each other and the rest of the Muslim world. Reoccurring questions during and after the crisis were, Who presents Islam in Denmark? Who is Mr Islam? [81]

The group, Democratic Muslims, established during the crisis, became very popular in the government, media and among the non-Muslim population (see p. 40), but it helped further to polarize Muslims and the Danish population. The group had introduced itself as "the democratic voice"

---

teams in 2007, *ibid.* p. 18. Interview with Rev. Dr Caleb Ahima, 11 March 2005.

[78] Dennis Ityavyar & Zacharys Gundu, "Stakeholders in Peace and Conflicts. A Case of Ethno-Religious Conflicts in Plateau & Kaduna, Nigeria," in *Inter-Gender* (Jos, 2004), p. 22.

[79] Interview, Jos, 12 March 2005, and conversations with the chairman, Sani ibn Salihu.

[80] This also happened when churches in Medan were bombed between 2002 and 2004. Muslim youths helped guard the churches. Rev. Simatupang (GKPA), LWF study team meeting, 5 June 2004, Medan.

[81] A conference sponsored by the Foreign Ministry with the participation of a popular Muslim Egyptian TV-preacher, Amr Khaled, attracted much attention. It was aimed at calling on the Danish government to apologize for what the Muslim world called blasphemous caricatures of the Prophet and to suggest ways out of the crisis. Many Arab Muslim leaders strongly criticized Amr Khaled. Also in Denmark, the conference and the ensuing discussion contributed to the split between various Muslim groups.

giving the impression that Muslim democrats were something new, and that other Muslims, including those who had spoken out in public, were antidemocratic. This was underscored by the statement of the support committee's chair that membership in Democratic Muslims was a bonus when applying for jobs. "When they say that they have signed that they advocate for democracy and the rule of law, I believe that it is easier for them to be integrated into the labor market. It will work as an extra qualification of the applicants," he said.[82] A number of ethnic organizations and individuals were highly critical of this approach believing it to discredit imams and Muslims in general. During the months following the cartoon crisis, the organization became less and less visible because of internal controversies and the lack of organizational structures. Prominent people left the board, including its founder, Naser Khader.

In the wake of the cartoon crisis

In the wake of the crisis, many Muslims became more concerned about their future in Denmark. Some withdrew further and intensified their negative attitude toward society; others who had been active in the public debate withdrew. Nonetheless, a number of Muslim organizations, including some that had previously not related officially to Danish society, organized dialogue meetings during and after the conflict.[83] Organizations from the Muslim world and the US, in cooperation with Danish Muslim organizations and the Foreign Ministry organized conferences where young Danes and Arabs could meet and exchange views and experiences.[84] Youth exchange trips to Arab countries were arranged.

[82] The daily *B.T.*, 3 March 2006.

[83] For instance, one of the Shiite communities arranged two dialogue conferences in May 2006 in order to overcome prejudice and discrimination in Denmark.

[84] The conference, "Muslim Leaders of Tomorrow," was held in Copenhagen, 7–9 July 2006. It was arranged by the American Society for Muslim Advancement and the Cordoba Initiative, in order to come up with a strategy to recapture the monopoly of the extremists to speak on behalf of the Muslim world. The agenda included themes such as Muslim identity, marginalization and Islamic reaction to secularization. One hundred mainly young participants from sixteen Western countries represented a wide spectrum of Muslims.

The Foreign Ministry supported a festival, IslamExpo, on Christiansborg Palace Square. A number of Muslim organizations were asked to contribute in order to show a different aspect of Islam not so often shown in the Danish media. The festival was met by critique from the Danish People's Party.

A number of initiatives were taken by the Evangelical Lutheran Church in Denmark (pp. 43f), provoking a number of pastors to establish a new forum called the "Islam-Critical Network." Most of them related to Tidehverv with Søren Krarup's daughter at the helm. The network attempted to discredit colleagues, bishops and pastors who had supported dialogue between Christians and Muslims after the crisis.

One of the network's slogans was that Christians and Muslims do not believe in the same God and that therefore Islam must be met by mission: "The Muslim and the Christian tradition are like fire and water. We have to stand firm or vanish."[85] All those who look for consensus are trying to cover up opposites. This almost militant rhetoric about Islam and Muslims resembles some missionaries' slogans in Northern Nigeria during colonial rule. Christianity was presented as being intellectually superior to Islam, and Muslims had to reach a higher awareness and be civilized before they could convert to Christianity.[86]

A number of church leaders who had protested against the anti-Muslim tone and spoken in favor of cooperation felt that they had to defend themselves. They affirmed that they indeed stood for mission but that this could occur through dialogue. This created feelings of insecurity among those Muslims who were engaged in dialogue and cooperation with Christians.

Fundamentalist and extremist tendencies

In all three countries, radical religious groups contributed to and were a consequence of the conflicts. Especially in Nigeria and Indonesia, the radicalization and politicization of both Islam and Christianity have been on the rise in recent decades, with increasing economic and moral support coming from outside (particularly from the USA and Saudi Arabia). One of

[85] The *Christian Daily*, 15 May 2006. Tidehverv had never before taken any interest in mission.

[86] For instance, the letterhead of the Danish United Sudan Mission's (DFSM) from the early mission period reads: "DFSM wants to bring the Gospel to Sudan's millions of pagans before they are conquered by the advancing Muhammedanism. WHO WILL BE THE VICTOR? CHRIST OR MUHAMMED?" To "stem the tide of Islam" was another mission slogan. Rasmussen, *op. cit.* (note 33), p. 38. See also Isidore Uchechukwu Chibuzo Nwanaju, *Christian-Muslim Relations in Nigeria. A Historical-Theological Reflection Upon the Mutual Coexistence of Christians and Muslims* (Nijmegen: Brakkenstein 2004), p. 136.

the reasons for this is the commitment of radical groups, Christian as well as Muslim, to social and educational issues. Revivalism and radicalism have become tools to interpret and express dissatisfaction and political frustration over unemployment and poverty. Through these movements, people feel that they can become the subjects of their own lives.

Thus, Christianity and Islam have witnessed the proliferation of diverse religious movements whose preaching is revivalist and radical.[87] Generally, they use similar language in terms of literal interpretation, anti-secularism and exclusivism. In some cases, this has heightened conflicts; some of these movements have issued political statements that counteract peaceful coexistence. The Nigerian government has found it difficult to contend with these groups because of the sensitive nature of religion in the entire country.[88]

The radicalization among Muslims manifested itself in Indonesia in the various bombings that took place in Medan, 2000, Bali, 2002 and Jakarta, 2003. However, only small groups of Indonesian Muslims supported these actions.

In Poso and Maluku (especially in Ambon), *mujâhidîn* (radical groups) such as Laskar Jihad, were involved. While in these areas Muslims generally do not identify with these groups, they are simply grateful if they fend off Christian militias. When the fighting flared up in Poso in late 2001, it was reported that Laskar Jihad was leading the Muslim side in the conflict, and that JI was also involved. A paramilitary organization calling itself the Red Force emerged to retaliate on behalf of the Christian community. These groups were later included in the process of reconciliation and signed the peace accord in Malino, December 2001. As a result, violence and unrest declined.

---

[87] In Nigeria for instance the Islamic movements, Yan Izala and Muslim Student Society and Christian revivalist groups such as Scripture Union, Christian Union and Student Christian Movement. Members of CAN, Pentecostal Fellowship of Nigeria (a body that brings the Pentecostal/charismatic churches together) and the Fellowship of Christian Students share some of the influences of these exclusivist visions.

In Indonesia: JI, Front Pembela Islam (Islam Defenders' Front), Darul Islam Movement, Jamiat Kahir and al-Irshad and Christian movements such as Red Force, Laskar Jesus and Cowon Kristen (Christian Boys). The Christian groups in Indonesia, however, are not driven by an ideology or goal in the same way but are more like gangs, fragmented and focused on local goals of community protection and maintenance of land, ready to be mobilized if conflicts erupt. Therefore they are much less organized.

[88] Information given by Nafisat Lawal Musa, Jos.

In both conflicts, Christians blamed Laskar Jihad for much of the bloodshed.[89] There is no doubt that the fighting attracted Islamic militants. In August 2001, Laskar Jihad declared a *jihâd* in Poso; other extremist groups followed suit. In both places, people feared that Muslim radicals would ignite conflicts.[90]

Nigeria has a long tradition of revivalism.[91] Especially after the 1967-1970 civil war, the number of Islamist groups in Northern Nigeria and Christian revivalist and Pentecostal movements, initiated and sustained by Southerners, has significantly increased. These have especially appealed to youth. They have a decidedly negative attitude toward other religions and have nurtured each other throughout the 1980s and 1990s. During that time, Christian and Islamic radical groups became increasingly politicized addressing urban problems such as insecurity, violence, unemployment and poverty.[92]

Competition increased between Christian and Muslim radical groups over public space, dominance and access to the state's resources, with each group trying to undermine and eliminate the other. During the 1990s, the Pentecostal preachers' aggressive evangelism threatened Muslim leaders, while Christians felt vulnerable to the violent activities of radical Islamic groups.

Religious intolerance, the obstructing of public places of worship during prayer sessions (so-called street praying), the use of loudspeakers, incendiary preaching, the use and display of provocative posters—these were some of the activities of these groups that annoyed those of a different religious affiliation.

---

[89] *Cybercast News Service*, 12 December 2001.

[90] *Asia News*, 19 May 2005.

[91] Revivalism is in many ways consistent with the African worldview regarding the supernatural, evil spirits, divine healing, emotional/physical expression of worship and the special role of women in this tradition for instance.

[92] Mathews A. Ojo has pointed out that the Islamist groups have sought a centralization of the religious and social order because as he says, "Islam has always thrived on power and authority, which is often effective in a centralized political system." Conversely, revivalist and Pentecostal groups have favored a decentralization of the political and social order since "such centralization has in the past favored religious creativity which has stimulated rapid Christian growth. Decentralization is more suited to Pentecostalism, which with its emphasis on the personal empowerment of the Holy Spirit, has created alternative centers of power for solving human needs against the background of the failure of the centralized state." M. A. Ojo, "Pentecostal Movements, Islam and the Contest for Public Space in Northern Nigeria," in *Islam and Christian-Muslim Relations*, vol. 18, no. 2 (April 2007), p. 176.

In Denmark, strong secularist views were expressed during and after the cartoon crisis. Some people advocated the right to be free from religion.[93] The term freedom of speech was used in an almost fundamentalist way. The principle behind this hardcore atheism and secularism is that religion must be a private matter; freedom of speech is above religious concerns, and therefore Muslims should renounce Sharî'a. The Prime Minister also argued for a separation of religion and politics. After the crisis he said that there is too much religion in the public space.

The cartoon crisis showed that for many Danes secularism has become a strong principle, indeed the only decisive principle that Danes have to fight for in order to defend their values and identity. It is not just a preference but a criterion to which others, especially Muslims, are subjected in order to distinguish the "moderate" and "integratable" from the "fundamentalists."[94]

While a number of radical Muslim movements such as the Hizb ut-Tahrîr (HT) (Islamic Liberation Party) and certain *Salafi* groups[95] have increased their influence and membership in the country, they remain a small minority. Membership of these groups is often reactive, a way of tackling unrest and inner chaos and to put things right, and at the same time, they shut out interaction and discussion with people who live and think differently.

---

[93] For the first time, atheists in Denmark have organized themselves. Thus two organizations were established, the Atheistic Association in 2002 (Ateistisk Selskab: **www.ateist.dk**) and the Atheistic Forum (formally) in 2006 (Ateistisk Forum: **www.ateist.net**). Both emphasize the right to be free from religion and are against intervention by religious groups. The Atheistic Association has about 400 members. Its primary goal is to work for a separation of church and state and they have led a campaign for citizens to resign their membership of the Evangelical Lutheran Church in Denmark. The Atheistic Forum is basically an online association advocating a view of life that is founded on a scientific insight with human beings as the starting point for moral and individual right for freedom. Furthermore, they distance themselves from the idea that religion or religious people speak with a certain authority in relation to moral, ethical and humanistic issues.

[94] The Danish political scientist, Ole Wæver, has expressed this view, for instance in "Sekularisme er blevet Europas mission" (Secularism has become Europe's mission), in *Kristeligt Dagblad* 21 July 2007.

[95] *Salafi* covers many different groups, from traditional Sunnis with *Salafi*-elements to extreme *Salafis* who claim to be the only right (and thereby saved) sect (*firqa nâjiya*) within Islam. The term is used in this context for Muslims with a strong *Salafi*-identity (*najdi-salafis*), i.e., the more Saudi-oriented. They advocate a certain revival based on literal interpretation (*zâhiri*) of the Qur'ân and the tradition of Muhammad (*hadîth*). They have a strong consciousness of the universal *umma* and are often seen as isolationists who have turned against society and move in their own environment. *Salafism* is popular among militant Islamists all over the world. In Denmark it is especially attractive to converts.

Christian revivalist movements in Denmark do not express themselves politically but rather in individual socioeconomic terms marked by what is called "progress theology. "They are rather small groups living a more or less isolated existence. Tidehverv displays some of the characteristics of radicalism.[96] Under the leadership of Søren Krarup the movement has become highly politicized and anti-modern by reacting against what Krarup calls "worship" of development and progress that implies spiritual emptiness and irresponsibility. Human rights are opposed for allegçdly placing human beings instead of God at the center. Krarup has made Christianity an ideology just like HT or the other Islamist movements he rants against. He claims to have a monopoly on Danishness and Christianity, to posses the only truth. Therefore, he does not want to dialogue with others who think differently, especially Muslims. According to Krarup,

> [w]here Christianity rules it has to do with love for the things that are dear to you. Where Islam rules, there is on the contrary a high degree of self-righteousness which logically ends up being all-consuming hatred and an alarming urge to destroy other human beings.[97]

Common to all extremist groups and tendencies is the belief that reality is grounded in one principle (in a text, a political ideology, a scientific approach). They are searching for fundamental and absolute answers to all questions. This is done by a return to a common foundation, a premodern system of symbols. For religious movements, it is a matter of turning back to the past and reviving it, back to the original sources or cultural homogeneity. In addition, they have a high level of activism and willingness to struggle.

[96] Tidehverv was established in 1926 as an opposition to any kind of self-righteousness and the tendency at the time to idolize various types of leading figures in church circles. Christian faith was first of all to be faithful to the earth and to stick to the teaching of Martin Luther. "God is everything; I am nothing—and you are an idiot," was a saying about the movement, fathered in the 1930s by Johannes Nordentoft. Today Tidehverv is primarily attached to the circle around Søren Krarup and his family. It has changed to such a degree that many of its former members have left. It has, however, a strong political influence and indeed sets the political agenda. Krarup feels that he has been called to save Denmark from the floods of immigration. Denmark is an independent nation, and to be Danish is a privilege, he says.

[97] *Berlingske Tidende*, 2 February 2005. In Krarup's view the neighbor whom Jesus is telling you to love is the person close to you. One has to love the neighbor when one is stumbling over him/her and not, like in "an industry of charity" or in misunderstood solidarity, look for him/her.

Different developments of Hizb ut-Tahrîr

Hizb ut-Tahrîr (HT) is a Sunni Muslim party established in 1953 in Jerusalem by Sheikh Taqi al-Din al-Nabhani. It declared itself as a political party with Islam as its ideology. It is banned in the Middle East and in some European countries because of its extremist political views. The organization aims to implement Islamic law under the protection of a pan-Islamic *khilâfah* state in the Muslim world and to remove all Western influence. In this way they believe that the whole *umma* can be united, and its problems solved. Without the *khilâfah* state, Sharî'a cannot be implemented.

In the Nordic countries, HT only exists in Denmark, where it has a relatively strong presence. However, the considerable attention given to it in the Danish media is disproportionate to its size. Membership increased especially after 9/11 and is today around 500 members, including a number of sympathizers, many of whom are converts to Islam. Their members are primarily ordinary people but also university students. Currently they are recruiting members among young criminals, many of whom feel rootless and frustrated. They often feel excluded from society and have therefore lost interest in it or may even despise it.

Like similar radical movements, such as certain *Salafi*-groups, HT is a reactive way of finding security, personal identity and meaning in life in an unpredictable world. Their stereotypical black and white image of reality is not to be disturbed by any contextualization of Islam. Voting for elections is prohibited, since the only valid political action is to work for a *khilâfah* state. Their rhetoric is very anti-Western.

HT perceived the cartoons as yet another example of discrimination against and oppression of Islam by Danish society and the West as a whole. During and after the crisis they maintained that the government had encouraged *Jyllands-Posten* to publish the drawings and demanded an official apology.

In Indonesia, HT claims to have tens of thousands of members in twenty-six Indonesian provinces—mostly in larger cities—many of them intellectuals. They are much more pragmatic in their approach than their Danish counterparts, with a number of social themes on their agenda.[98] They

[98] In 2007, HT initiated a more extrovert and less confrontational course in relation to other Muslims and to society at large.

are involved in conservation and own an agricultural institute in Bogor. For them, voting in political elections is not forbidden *per se*, and they believe it to be possible to develop a political party in a secular society.[99]

HT developed in different ways in the two countries because the Danish arm of HT is a reaction phenomenon that provides a protest identity, while in Indonesia it has developed from within society; it is marked by Indonesian culture rather than in opposition to it. In Denmark, this protest identity is reduced to a single dimension, shut off from Danish society and other Muslims. They refuse to dialogue with those who do not share their opinion. In Indonesia, it is a much more open identity. Our interview with the spokesperson underlined this.

Furthermore, Indonesian religious leadership is much stronger.[100] Two huge Islamic movements, NU and Muhammadiya, have openly rejected radical teachings and have led campaigns to educate Indonesian Muslims about the inherent dangers of radicalism. Especially among women, there is strong opposition against what some have called the "Talibanization" of society. Recently they demonstrated against an anti-pornography bill that would make women suffer.

In Indonesia, there are many alternative communities to HT, whereas in Denmark it is one of a few movements that uses Danish and has a strong feeling of identity and fellowship. Furthermore, HT has become a way of becoming involved in political opposition to the West, democracy and US dominance. According to HT, Islam is compatible with modern technology but not modernity as a way of thinking.

The influence of Sharî'a[101]

The Nigerian and Indonesian central governments' granting of greater legal autonomy to local administrations (in states and provinces) in 1999/2000,

[99] Interview with the spokesperson, Muhammad Ismail Yusanto, 10 June 2004.

[100] A leadership survey conducted by the Islamic and Societal Research Center (PPIM), January–March 2007, revealed that Indonesians trusted their leaders more than any other individual or institution, including the President, and that the state institutions are weaker than religious ones. "We trust Clerics more than SBY [President Susilo Bambang Yudhoyono]," in the *Jakarta Post*, 16 May 2007.

[101] This section will deal with the influence of Sharî'a related to the conflicts mentioned whereas the following chapter will deal more broadly with Sharî'a in the three countries.

provided the opportunity to implement certain aspects of Sharî'a law at the local level. This occurred in twelve Northern Nigerian states and in twenty-two communities and districts in sixteen of the thirty-two Indonesian provinces. An increasing number of so-called bylaws with elements of Sharî'a have been passed in towns in West Sumatra, West and East Java and South Sulawesi.[102] Ambon, Maluku, has also implemented certain aspects of Sharî'a. Most of the laws introduced in Nigerian states and Indonesian provinces deal with individual moral behavior such as the wearing of head scarves, extramarital sex, drinking and the sale of alcohol and gambling.

Aceh is the only Indonesian province that has the legal right to apply the whole gamut of Sharî'a. As in Northern Nigeria, there is a historical precedent for Sharî'a, and Islamic courts have for a long time been handling cases of marriage, divorce and inheritance. In 1999 and again in 2001, special autonomy legislation was passed by the central government. This gave the courts the green light to extend their influence into criminal law.[103] This happened, not so much because of popular demand, but was the government's attempt to find a political solution to the conflict in Aceh and to keep the province as a part of Indonesia. Many if not all Acehnese (like many Northern Muslims in Nigeria), regarded the introduction of Sharî'a as a panacea that would eliminate social ills and bring about equality in society.

In Manokwari, a Christian-majority district in West Irian Jaya and the West Papuan capital, politicians have been working toward the introduction of a "Christian Sharî'a," an ordinance based on the Bible, despite protests from all sides, including from the Persekutuan Gereja-gereja di Indonesia (PGI) (Communion of Churches in Indonesia), in Jakarta.

The city of Manokwari has declared itself an "evangelical city." An article published in the *Jakarta Post* in June 2007, "Right on cue, Bible-based ordinances appear," states that

> [a]mong the hottest issues in the draft ordinance is a public ban on non-Christian religious clothing, a clause that has understandably provoked

[102] The districts of Pamekasan (East Java), Maros, Sinjai and Gowa (South Sulawesi), Cianjur, Garut and Indramayu (West Java) began to implement certain aspects.

[103] "Islamic Law and Criminal Justice in Aceh," in International Crisis Group, *Asia Report*, no. 117 (31 July 2006).

> anger from Muslim leaders. This reaction is particularly interesting because in other regions where Sharî'a based bylaws prevail, such as in Aceh and West Sumatra, non-Muslim women are tacitly required to wear Muslim dress for the sake of mutual respect.[104]

This act must be seen in relation to West-Papua's struggle to strengthen its autonomy vis-à-vis Jakarta. Jakarta's massive exploitation of their precious natural resources gives them a sense of being colonized.[105] There are fears, however, that the declaration in Manokwari could trigger civil conflict elsewhere (i.e., Ambon and Poso).

The Muslim Sharî'a based ordinances sparked protest by liberal Muslims as well as Christians in the two countries, who claimed that these would undermine national harmony. Many Christians felt that they were being reduced to second-class citizens. Church leaders complained of difficulties in obtaining land and accommodation and that Christians had been barred from some leadership positions. Christian businessmen and traders in Nigeria who depended on the sale of alcohol for a living also had difficulties.[106]

In various Nigerian states, this resulted in riots, especially in the city of Kaduna in 2000. These resulted in heavy loss of life. In Jos, the Sharî'a question arose during the 2001 crisis and reinforced tensions. Many Christians feared that Sharî'a laws would also be implemented in Plateau State. Some Christian leaders in Nigeria stated that it was unsafe for non-Muslims to live in the Sharî'a governed states in the North, and many Christians moved away. Several of them have come to Plateau State to find freedom there.

In Indonesia, opponents have included NGOs, particularly women's organizations, interreligious fora and broad sections of the Islamic community. The Sharî'a issue was not the actual cause of violence, but

---

[104] The *Jakarta Post*, 2 June 2007.

[105] Other local concerns related to *pemekaran*, to land rights, livelihoods, deforestation and ethnic identity in this province and in Papua as a whole are described in "Indonesian Papua: A Local Perspective on the Conflict," in International Crisis Group in *Asia Briefing*, no. 66 (Jakarta/Brussels, 19 July 2007). See also "Papua: Answers to Frequently Asked Questions," International Crisis Group in *Asia Briefing*, no. 53 (Jakarta/Brussels 5 September 2006).

[106] Interview with Rev. Jediel M. Nyenbensi, Bauchi, 9 March 2005. On Sharî'a in Nigeria, see Philip Ostien, Jamila M. Nasir and Franz Kogelmann, *Comparative Perspectives Sharî'a in Nigeria* (Ibadan: Spectrum, 2005); Johannes Harnischfeger, *Democratization and Islamic Law: The Sharî'a Conflict in Nigeria* (Frankfurt, New York: Campus, 2007).

it was used by both Christians and Muslims in the conflicts, including those in Sulawesi and Maluku.

Opponents in both countries have argued that the actual application would affect non-Muslims adversely and violate their religious freedom. Christians did not trust the promise that the rights of non-Muslims would be guaranteed under Sharî'a.[107] Nigerian Muslim supporters of Sharî'a argued that they were merely asking to be given a chance to practice their religion freely by implementing Sharî'a completely and not as hitherto in a fragmented form.

In recent years, large segments of the Muslim population in both Nigeria and Indonesia have become disillusioned due to the way in which Sharî'a has been implemented. Critics in Nigeria maintain that it is not "proper Sharî'a" that is being applied, but only "political Sharî'a." When one of the study team members asked the person in charge of implementing Sharî'a in Gusau privately why they had been in such a rush that they did not even take the time to train the judges in Sharî'a law, he was told that since the governor had promised it they had to implement Sharî'a in time for the next election.[108]

This is why many people doubted the state governor's sincerity in introducing Sharî'a laws, and why they had not implemented the economic dimensions of the law. They were too preoccupied with strengthening their own political standing and there have been no visible improvements in people's daily lives. Poor people, often women, are punished for minor moral offences[109] whereas nobody in high positions is being charged with corruption. Similar critique is heard in Aceh.[110]

This was also the critique of the radical Sheikh Ibrahim al-Zakzaky (of Zaria)[111] who held that the time was not ripe for implementing Sharî'a since Muslims do not have sufficient theological knowledge of it. He is also reported to have said that

[107] Kano was the first state in Nigeria to make it compulsory for pupils, both Christian and Muslim, in all schools (private and public), to wear Islamic dress. This new state policy came into effect 5 May 2007. *Agence France Press*, 4 May 2007.

[108] Fatih Alev in conversation in Gusau, March 2005.

[109] For instance, women using the same buses as men or riding behind men on motorcycles. Also, the poor in Aceh trying their luck by buying lottery tickets.

[110] The human rights activist, Azriana Rambe Manalu, Aceh, 2006.

[111] Ibrahim al-Zakzaky is the leader of the Islamic Movement of Nigeria which is inspired by the Islamic Republic of Iran.

> another factor detrimental to the immediate introduction of the full corpus of Sharî'a are mass poverty and institutionalized corruption, which have ensured that a small percentage of the population control the enormous wealth of the country, thus leaving the vast majority of the population impoverished. This gives rise to increasing crime rate in a society where many "genuinely steal" for the mere sake of surviving and not just for the sake of it.[112]

Al-Zakzaky believes that to be punished under Sharî'a if one has stolen out of pure need is unfair.

Some Muslims have gone as far as to say that the implementation of Sharî'a is a distortion of Islam. Rules out of context are in opposition to the spirit of Sharî'a; the rules implemented become unjust and in practice betray the intention of Sharî'a. It is like putting a façade of Islam on to the problems without going to their root, This will not solve the problems.

Because of discontent and criticism among Christians and Muslims, Sharî'a appears to have run out of steam in Northern Nigeria, and state governors have backed away from carrying out some of the harsher aspects of the system, such as death sentences and amputations.[113]

In Indonesia, including Aceh, there is a palpable sense of disappointment because the development has moved in the wrong direction. There has been too strong a focus on legislation and enforcing morality as an end in itself, and less concern with important social issues such as corruption and poverty. Bureaucratic confusion and lack of effectiveness have also been impediments.

In both countries, especially in Nigeria, heated discussions concerning the implementation and constitutionality of Sharî'a bylaws have reemerged over the years in various forms. In 2006, fifty-six members of the Indonesian parliament urged that these Sharî'a-based regulations should be overturned on the grounds of their being unconstitutional. The petition was quickly overruled by a counter-petition from 134 other members.

The two largest Indonesian Muslim organizations, NU and Muhammadiya, have clearly spoken out against the passing of Sharî'a bylaws and rejected the

---

[112] Umar H.D. Danfulani, *The Sharia Issue and Christian-Muslim Relations in Contemporary Nigeria*, (Stockholm: Almquist & Wiksell, 2005), pp. 49-50.

[113] Interviews in Gusau, Jos and Bauchi, March 2005 and "Political Sharî'a? Human Rights and Islamic Law in Northern Nigeria," in *Human Rights Watch*, vol. 16, no. 9 (September 2004).

need for Islamic law to become the basis of Indonesian law. Most Indonesians agree that the state should be based on a non-confessional ideology.[114] Most Muslims are in favor of a pluralistic state and thus against the inclusion of Sharî'a in the Constitution. Still, at a regional level there are Christians who see "Shari'azation from below" (i.e., in certain local areas) as a threat.

The Sharî'a issue has been a divisive force in Denmark, not because of its implementation or demands for such (like in Nigeria and Indonesia), but because it is constantly being problematized and stereotyped in the media, by politicians and other public figures. Like a mantra, Muslims are repeatedly asked by politicians and other opinion makers to demonstrate their democratic convictions and consequently to distance themselves from Sharî'a as such. There is no space for diversity of opinion.

After every terrorist attack connected to Islamism or other offences committed by a Muslim, Danish Muslims are urged to avow their commitment to democracy, namely the Western legal system and the Danish Constitution. This builds on the assumption that Islam is not compatible with democracy and justice, and that Sharî'a is a codex of laws, first and foremost punitive ones. This has also been a way for certain politicians to use statements made by some Muslims, especially imams, for their own political interests.

A number of Muslim politicians who were asked to renounce Sharî'a as a precondition for their candidacy for parliament or the city council decided to leave party politics. This has aggravated the feeling of not being accepted shared by many young Muslims. As a result, they have lost all interest in participating in political life. There is no doubt that the Sharî'a issue and the misunderstanding and mistrust it had created among people in Denmark was an important contributor to the controversy about the 2005 cartoons.

Effects on intra- and interreligious relationships

Religion has been both a help and a hindrance. Both Islam and Christianity have been a constructive resource for peace building and conflict transformation as well an obstacle. Religion has contributed to increasing the conflict as well as to overcoming it. This is related to what Robert Putnam calls the

[114] The leadership survey (mentioned in note 100) also reveals that 22.8 percent of the respondents want Sharî'a as the national ideology whereas the remainder prefer *Pancasila*.

contrast between the "bridging" and "bonding" forms of social capital, in this case of religious adherence.[115] Whereas in some spheres religious adherence creates social trust that will ultimately strengthen the cohesive force in society as a whole, it also has a disruptive potential by generating social ties and solidarity between members of the same religious subgroups.

Strong "bonding" social capital and strong identity may create trust in one's own group, while at the same time increasing suspicion of other groups. "Bridging" social capital forms social ties between members of different religious or ethnic groups and contributes to keeping society together. Conflict resolution usually requires investing in "bridging" capital.

We have seen that the Evangelical Lutheran Church in Denmark is very much divided on the question of its relationship to Islam and Muslims. In many ways it is only on the sidelines of the political scene and too fragmented to act and speak out. The church structure hinders the church from coming up with a clear position. The close attachment to the state makes it very difficult for the church to criticize the government. The cartoon conflict has increased this dividedness, whereas in Nigeria it strengthened the fellowship and cooperation among Christians, not only inside the Lutheran churches but also among the various denominations. They realized that they had to stand together, not in relation to Muslims, but in relation to peace for all and they have sought to include Muslims in their peace work.

In Indonesia, the conflicts have had a positive impact on intra-religious relationships and have helped to ease some of the previously existing hostilities.[116] In Denmark, the cartoon crisis did not have this uniting effect on Christians within or between churches. On the contrary, the events appear to have created stronger disagreements and harsh language among Christians, especially Lutheran pastors, who take different theological and political positions.

For Danish Muslims the conflict has highlighted the problem of lacking structures. The Muslim community is divided and their organizations

---

[115] Robert D. Putnam, *Bowling Alone: The Collapse and Revival of American Community* (New York: Simon & Schuster, 2000); Martin van Bruinessen, "Post-Soeharto Muslim Engagements with Civil Society and Democratization," in Hanneman Samuel and Henk Schulte Nordholt (eds), *Indonesia in Transition. Rethinking "Civil Society," "Religion" and "Crisis"* (Yogyakarta: Pustaka Pelajar, 2004), pp. 53-60; Theodore Friend, *Indonesian Destinies* (Cambridge, London: The Belknap Press of Harvard University Press, 2003), pp. 48f.

[116] Rev. Lukman Panjaitan meeting with church leaders, 8 June 2004, HKBP Jakarta, see note 20.

have had difficulties cooperating. This is one of the reasons why there are no purpose-built mosques (except one for the Ahmadiyya movement) and there is no overall Muslims organization or authority to represent at least a substantial number of Muslims.

Furthermore, the Muslim study team members noted a lack of intellectual discourse in contrast to the situation in Indonesia and Nigeria where there are Muslim educational institutions at all levels as well as a long-standing intellectual tradition. In Denmark, there are virtually no Muslim intellectuals, well educated in Islam, who can reflect on Islam in a Danish context. This was a blatant weakness during the crisis. The fact that spokespersons were appointed at random contributed to the deterioration of the conflict.

Later, in October 2006, a new umbrella association, the Muslim National Council (MFR), consisting of liberal Muslim organizations came into being. Its members are for the most part young people who emphasize their identity as Danish Muslims. Their aim is to unite Muslim organizations in Denmark across ethnic and national differences and around their Danish identity, to contribute to active citizenship and to work for dialogue and mutual respect in society. It is from this platform that efforts are now being made to establish a new mosque in order to gather Muslims from diverse ethnic and national backgrounds for prayer and social activities, all taking place in Danish.

A vicious circle

The cartoon crisis in Denmark must be seen against the background of a vicious circle that has developed and consolidated itself over the last decade between the media, political leaders, majority population and the Muslim minorities (fig. 1).

The circle can be entered at any point, and connections shown as crossing over. The arrows indicate impact and/or reproduction. The fact that almost on a daily basis the media portray one-sided, negative stories about immigrants in general and Muslims in particular (reproduced by politicians and in public opinion), affects the Muslim minorities who feel unwanted, insecure and unconfident. This may lead to detachment also among well-educated, second-generation immigrants and become an excuse for avoiding responsibility. It has resulted in an ingrained mistrust of the media and political processes, a lack of interest to integrate into the Danish society and taken away the energy to reflect critically and contextually on Islam. Those who do not have the necessary reserves may even become aggressive. This reaction may be aggravated by international conflicts and may lead to involvement in terrorist activities.

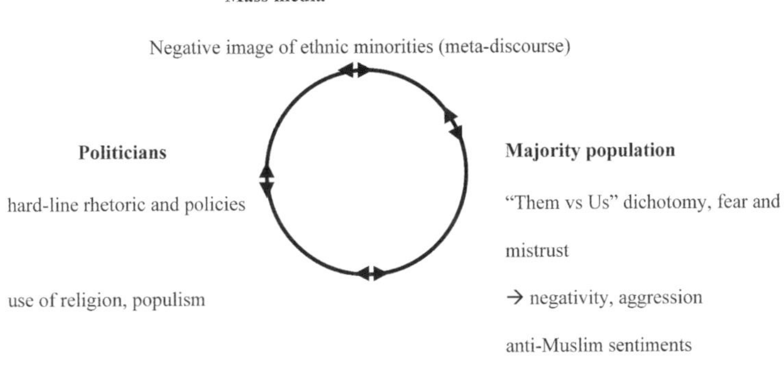

Fig. 1: The vicious circle in Denmark (nationally)

Subsequently these reactions are exploited by populist politicians and other opinion makers through harsh rhetoric and restrictive laws. The abuse of religion may be one of the tools used for this purpose, as we shall see in the following chapter.

All of the above contributes to an atmosphere of fear and mistrust, sometimes even aggressive and exclusive behavior, among the majority population who are attracted to negative stories in the media in order to have their prejudices confirmed. Also schoolchildren and youth begin to react by looking negatively at one another. The circle is complete and starts all over again.

The circle is not significant at the local level where problems are often solved before they escalate, or where there is simply no interaction between people from different cultural and religious backgrounds. In certain areas like Nørrebro, Copenhagen, there is a sense of solidarity especially among the youth.[117]

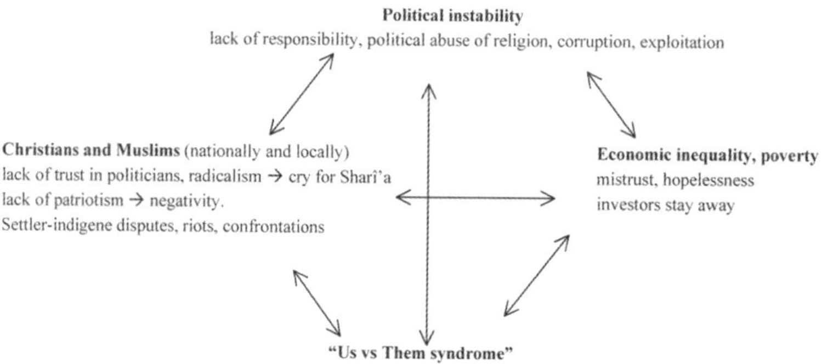

Fig. 2: Pattern of relatedness in Nigeria (locally, regionally and nationally)

The situation is rather more complex in Nigeria and Indonesia. I have tried to illustrate this not by a circle but by showing the relatedness between different levels. In Nigeria, the national and local levels are very much interconnected. Another cycle or interrelatedness, which includes other influential factors, becomes noticeable. Although media and society affect each other, the media have not had an impact on Christian-Muslim relations worth mentioning. As a result of national and regional political instability and weakness, religion is politically exploited and conflicts are not handled constructively. As a consequence, law and order break down and the dichotomy between "Us vs Them" is exacerbated, leading to the demand for Sharî'a to be introduced in order

[117] It manifested itself during violent demonstrations in March 2007 by squatters. Nearly 700 young people were arrested during three days of rioting that followed the eviction of squatters from the building that in 1982 was turned into a center for alternative youth culture. A number of young Muslims supported the demonstrations. As one of them said: "These squatters supported us during the time when a Christian fundamentalist demonstrated against Islam and Muslims in the streets and called Islam the 'devil's work.' Now it is our turn to support them."

The four-story building was demolished by the police, and demonstrators threw cobblestones and set fire to cars. The new owner of the building, Faderhuset, a Christian Pentecostal sect, announced that they want to build a Christian center on the land.

to improve the situation. Moreover, in order to garner votes, ambitious politicians have promised to introduce and implement parts of Sharî'a if they are elected.

Hopelessness spreads among those whose poverty is not alleviated, and whose conditions have not changed for the better. Mistrust and negativity vis-à-vis politicians may result leading to a lack of energy and activity. Furthermore, there where law and order have broken down, investors will stay away and poverty will increase.

In Indonesia, a cyclical pattern has manifested itself locally in situations of social inequality and economic instability. Local conflicts had economic and political roots, but the parties identified themselves and their opponents as Muslims and Christians.

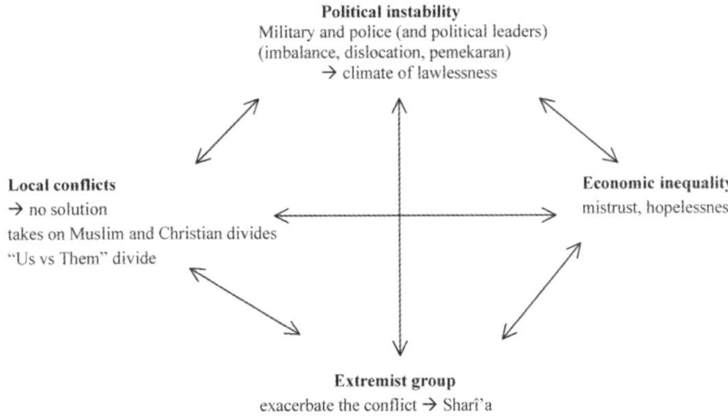

Fig. 3: Pattern of relatedness in Indonesia (in areas such as Maluku and Poso)

Political instability and economic inequality have caused and sustained conflict. In some parts of Indonesia, decentralization has added to the sociopolitical problems which has had implications on Christian-Muslim relations. Security forces have not safeguarded security but added to instability; police, politicians and the army have not interfered. The communal conflicts that erupted in Poso and Maluku are unlikely to occur again on the same scale but fears and mistrust remain and could surface if disputes over minor administrative issues are not handled expediently.[118]

The question is whether this cyclical pattern is moving toward the national level. This would mean that the main threat to peaceful coexistence and unity are not scattered violent conflicts, but political vacuum and economic crisis. The feeling of being adrift among the poor and disadvantaged increasingly fuels Islamic extremism, influenced from outside, especially from Saudi Arabia.

According to Robert W. Hefner,

> the real tension for the next indefinite time of years is not going to lie at the extremist fringe [...]. Indonesia has always had extremists and it always will have extremists. They were never numerous but they have always been there, very small, just like America. But they are not going to change the system.[119]

To this must be added the efforts of a growing number of Muslim intellectuals (i.e., The Islam Liberal Network, see p. 184, note 9) to repair the damage caused by growing religious extremism, to retain the image of Indonesian Islam as open-minded and non-violent and to develop constructive forms of communication between various religious groups in Indonesia.

In all three countries, the cycles and patterns of relatedness and impact are nonetheless major hindrances to progress. Consequently, people feel alienated and discriminated against. This has to change if coexistence is to improve. The cycle in Denmark (fig. 1) must be broken at one point in order for changes to take place whereas improvements must take place in relation to all instances and impacts in Nigeria and Indonesia (fig. 2 and 3).

---

[118] "Indonesia: Decentralisation and Local Power Struggles in Maluku," in International Crisis Group, *Asia Briefing*, no. 64 (Jakarta/Brussels, 22 May 2007), p. 10.

[119] Interview by Seth Mydans, "Indonesia Redefines Itself by 'Rolling up' Terrorists," in the *International Herald Tribune*, 17 June 2007.

Religio-political Perspectives: The Sharî'a Issue

Nelly van Doorn-Harder

The Arabic word Sharî'a means "path to the watering hole," to the good life. Sharî'a covers all aspects of what it means to be Muslim—religious practice as well as principles for the ordering of individual and social life. In this way, Sharî'a brings about unity of faith and action. Sharî'a is defined in many different ways, from the broadest to the most restrictive.

Sharî'a is not a law in the modern sense but rather a discourse embracing religion, morality and justice. For a Muslim, this discourse is eternal and unchangeable. If understood in its more concrete and restrictive sense, Sharî'a is a corpus of principles and rules extracted from Islam's fundamental sources, the Qur'ân and the Prophet's Sunnah (the way of life prescribed as normative in Islam, based on the teachings and practices of the Prophet).[1] This human process of interpretation is called *fiqh* (Islamic jurisprudence or law) and carried out by jurists and *usûliyyûn* (scholars with knowledge of the fundamental principles of Islamic law). There are many different interpretations and models rooted in specific theological and sociocultural starting points. The next step is the actual application or codification of these models in concrete legislation. Nowadays, most Muslim countries apply a mixture of laws. For example, the Nigerian system is based on English common law, Islamic law and customary law. The Indonesian system combines Roman-Dutch law, Muslim laws and customary laws. No country bases its legislation entirely on Sharî'a laws.

Some Muslims, especially in the West, who have a fixed understanding of Sharî'a as a code of law (to be introduced in an Islamic State) are conscious that it is a dream or utopia that will never be realized. Others, such as in Saudi Arabia, Iran and Yemen, claim that as a divine legal system, Sharî'a has existed since early Islam and can even today be implemented in the same form.

---

[1] Other sources used are primarily *ijmâ'* (consensus of opinion), *qiyas* (analogical reasoning) and secondarily *istihsân* (judging something good), *istislâh* (consideration linked to general interest), *istishâb* (presumption of continuity) and *'urf* (customs).

Therefore, when parts of the Muslim communities in Denmark, Nigeria and Indonesia hold on to a dream of living in a society based on or influenced by Sharî'a, they have very different understandings of what this implies. Their reasons vary as to whether it is a search for Islamic social justice, a signifier of identity, a means of political control, or to create a morally upright society. In addition, under certain Muslim regimes, local governments and activists need to gain support for their cause and/or legitimate their rule, as was the case in Nigeria.

These diverse understandings and applications of Sharî'a, in the past and present, give rise to the following questions: When did the idea of developing one sacred, unified law originate? Who were its advocates? What do they stand to gain? Why does the idea of Sharî'a evoke such fear? The idea of one unified Islamic law goes back to the nineteenth century when Muslims called for a return to the pure sources of the Qur'ân and the Sunnah. What this meant remains rather unclear, but over time some groups came to understand the reintroduction of Sharî'a as part of the quest for purity in order to revive and reinvigorate the Muslim community. By the 1970s, this ideal of returning to the pure sources was systematized by "Islamists" who opposed secularism and advocated a dominant role for Islam in the public sphere.

It is important to distinguish between Islamists who do not condone the use of violence and radical Islamists (extremists) who do. While both groups aspire to making Islam visible in public life and thus to gain political power, their methods to reach this goal differ greatly. Islamists believe that the current world order can be changed through mass mobilization and an increased presence in political life; radical Islamists are more inclined to doubt that creating political parties and organizing rallies will achieve this. Most Muslims do not consider non-violent Islamists to be radical or extremist; in many countries they find considerable support among the grass roots.

In Indonesia, the LWF study team found an example of such a group enjoying wide support among the lower classes. The team met with Agus Purnomo, head of the PK(S) ([Prosperity and] Justice Party), which had been started in 1998 and had called for the application of Sharî'a.[2]

[2] The party was established as the Justice Party (Partai Keadilan, PK) in 1998. It was reunited and renamed Partai Keadilan Sejahtera (PKS) in 2003.

However, in 2004, Purnomo told us that his party had abandoned this goal, realizing it to be "political suicide" since Indonesian society was not ready for the full application of Sharî'a. Instead, basing themselves on the methodology of Latin American liberation theologies, they had formed small base communities, consisting of ten to fifteen people, who were educated in their political rights in order to instill in them a "spirit of struggle." Purnomo furthermore explained that this party was started in order "to force the Indonesian government to adopt Islamic values." The party members decided instead to focus on providing free medical services for people and animals at the grassroots level, which led to the party's rapid growth.[3]

Today, all over the Muslim world, Muslims are increasingly discussing how Sharî'a should be understood in relation to modern society, democracy and human rights. Is Sharî'a to be understood primarily as a legal code, or is it a framework of ideas and principles, a discourse? Increasing numbers of Muslim scholars[4] perceive Sharî'a in the latter sense, which is more dynamic and all-embracing. For them, Sharî'a is a number of principles to be practiced differently today than in the early days of Islam. The most important goal of Sharî'a is to establish a moral and responsible society, with its implementation varying according to context. This perception is widely shared in Indonesia, where Muhammadiyah and Nahdlatul Ulama (NU) are engaged in reformulating Sharî'a and promoting civil society.

Sharî'a in Denmark and beyond

To many Muslims in Europe and North America, Sharî'a is a baffling concept. In Europe, those wishing to apply Sharî'a are not thinking of a political or criminal system based on principles of social justice to influence society. This discussion has begun to preoccupy many Muslims in Western countries.

---

[3] Interview, 12 June 2004.

[4] Among them are, Abdol-Karim Soroush, Tariq Ramadan, Ziauddin Sardar, Hussein Mohammad Fathy Osman, Abdullah Ahmed An-Naim and Mohamed Talbi.

In Denmark, people generally understand Sharî'a as a law codex consisting primarily of punitive laws. For instance, in October 2001, headlines featured some Muslim leaders declaring publicly that introducing Islamic law could be an option in Denmark if the Muslim population were to constitute the majority. This was based on the assumption that in forty years time every third inhabitant of Denmark will be Muslim.[5] Added to this were articles in serious newspapers quoting an alleged *fatwâ* (actually by a xenophobic Dane) calling on Muslims to drive Danes out of Copenhagen's Nørrebro district.[6]

Contributing to the stereotyping of Sharî'a have been calls for Islamic solutions from Hizb ut-Tahrîr (HT). Their spokesperson in Denmark, Fadi Abdelatif, has had regular clashes with the Danish law because of his anti-Semitic views and threats against the Danish Prime Minister.[7] Groups such as HT tend to reduce ethics, morals and Sharî'a law to *harâm* (what is forbidden) and *halâl* (what is permissible). These distinctions are often unclear and ultimately depend on factors such as individual interpretation and which school of thought one follows. Singing and playing music, for example, are activities considered forbidden by some while being avidly practiced by others.[8] Thus Dr Ismail Yusanto, HT's spokesperson in Indonesia, provided a telling example of this when the LWF team asked how his organization would handle the question of cutting hands off as a punishment for theft. According to him, whether or not someone would keep or lose their hand would depend on how much had been stolen and the reason for the theft.[9] In other words, whoever is in charge of the legal system would have the authority to make the judgment.

---

[5] Eyvind Vesselbo in Frode Holm Knudsen, "Danmarks fremtid: Hver anden er muslim" [Denmark's future: Every second inhabitant will be Muslim], in *Berlingske Tidende*, 11 October 2001. According to Eyvind Vesselbo's calculations, by around 2040 every third inhabitant of Denmark will be Muslim.

[6] See "Nu Nørrebro jeg tager" [Pop goes Nørrebro], in *Berlingske Tidende*, 12 August 2002, p. 6.

[7] In October 2002, a court in Denmark found Fadi Abdelatif guilty of distributing anti-Semitic propaganda and calling for the killing of Jews. In August 2006, a Danish court sentenced him to three months in prison for threats against the Danish Prime Minister, Anders Fogh Rasmussen.

[8] See Mona Eltahawy, "Meanwhile: Giving Muslims the Tools to take on Shariah," 14 December 2006, at **www.iht.com/articles/2006/12/14/opinion/edelta.php**

[9] Interview, 10 June 2004.

Radical views of Sharî'a generalized

While HT constitutes only a tiny group in Denmark (see p. 106), it is given much media exposure because of their sensationalist, harsh rhetoric about the West and Western democracy. This has stirred up considerable emotion among the Danish population and contributes to a generalized picture of Islam as a political ideology that Muslims believe should govern every society. Muslims are viewed as pursuing a hidden agenda of abusing democracy and manipulating the majority in order to introduce Islamic punitive laws, such as the death penalty, cutting off hands or stoning women. Radical political Islam is thus ascribed to all Muslims and Islam in general, which is seen as diametrically opposed to democracy and human rights.

As a result of this skewed perspective, a number of Danish political parties have asked their Muslim party members to renounce Sharî'a before they can stand for local or national elections.[10] Some candidates have explained that this is tantamount to asking them to renounce their religion because for them Sharî'a is a way of life and more than merely rules. One of them explained, "I can easily support Sharî'a, but distance myself from those aspects that don't fit into the year 2004. Compare it to the Constitution. Some parts are outmoded, and you might well imagine that some changes are long overdue."[11] However, many politicians, especially on the right wing, did not accept this kind of answer. According to them, there is no "but." As Prime Minister Anders Fogh Rasmussen said, "In Danish society it is not forbidden to have foolish opinions. But immigrants with such an attitude [to Sharî'a] cannot be elected for honorary office in political parties [...]. In Denmark Holy Scripture can never be superior to criticism."[12]

---

[10] Mazhar Hussain in 2000, Mona Sheikh, Babar Baig, Tanwir Ahmed in 2001, Sherin Khankan in 2002 (Social Liberal Party), Wallit Khan and Fatima Shah in 2004 (Social Democrats). All were disqualified and left their parties.

[11] "Denmark: Parliamentarians in Sharî'a-law Dilemma," at **www.jihadwatch.org/dhimmi-watch/archives/004051.php**

[12] *Berlingske Tidende*, 27 November 2004.

The stoning case

The best known debate on Sharî'a is the so-called "stoning case" in April 2002. In the *Christian Daily's* Internet forum, an imam (of Danish origin) was asked to comment on stoning in connection with the Amina Lawal case in Nigeria. The imam defended stoning as a punishment for adultery since, in his opinion, no one can change God's will. His reply, which was published in the newspaper, created an outcry among the population and gave rise to an emotional and prolonged public debate. Disagreement among Muslims over such statements has in some cases led to strong division within the community.

The stereotypical definition of Sharî'a as an exclusively punitive legislation is so solidly rooted in public opinion that other definitions are not seen as being "real Islam." Therefore many politicians and other opinion makers are eager to point out that Muslims must learn to separate religion and politics and relegate religion to the private sphere "as we Christians do." In 2004, Bertil Haarder, then Minister of Integration, said that Muslims should take a clear stance against the violent parts of Sharî'a. "Danish politicians do not have the same problem in relation to the Old Testament because religion for us is something personal, not political dogma. We have learned to separate state and church, and the Muslims have to learn that too."[13] However, the reality is that the view of an increasing number of especially young Muslims is that the Danish democratic system is more in accordance with Islamic values than any society in the so-called Muslim world.

Also, the absence of national Islamic bodies and Islamic educational institutions contributes to the inability of Danish Muslims to reflect contextually on controversial issues. There is no established authority or well-educated élite to stand up in public and explain the different understandings of Sharî'a. As a result, the Sharî'a discussion in the Danish media does not really relate to the views of Danish Muslims but is often removed from the reality of people's daily lives. It becomes the issue in a meta-debate in which Muslims do not take part because they neither identify with it, nor find it relevant.

---

[13] *Jyllands-Posten*, 26 November 2004.

Private legal councils

While Sharî'a is being debated throughout Europe, researchers are uncovering the real concerns Muslims face in their daily lives. In most Muslim countries, Islamic personal status law is applied, for example, to marriage, divorce and child custody. Consequently, in countries such as Denmark, Norway and Great Britain some Muslims want to solve these matters in private fora that apply customary rules and methods to resolve disputes. Pakistani immigrants in Denmark, for example, use these fora in family matters since going to the Danish courts would weaken their social network and identity within the community.[14]

Similar parallel legal universes have developed in civil areas in Great Britain. Somalian customary law, Jewish and Muslim law are applied through private religious boards such as the Muslim Law Sharî'a Council.[15] Those who seek advice from these boards do so, for example, because they do not want to stray from the injunctions of their religion, go against their community's customs, or are forced to have their judicial position validated. In the case of divorce, the verdict from a Western court might not suffice as a husband can appeal to Islamic law to refute this decision. In such a case, a woman might be legally divorced, but when visiting her country of origin her husband can claim her as his wife, or if she has remarried, have her jailed for bigamy. These councils can be problematic if they refuse to recognize a divorce or make decisions that infringe on basic human rights.

---

[14] See **http://tors.ku.dk/forskning/religionmigrationogglobalisering/forskere/rubyamehdi/**. This web page contains references to several articles on the issue by Rubya Mehdi, "Facing the Enigma: *talaq-e-tafweez*, A Need of Muslim Women in Nordic Perspective," in *International Journal of the Sociology of Law*, no. 33 (2005), pp. 133-147; "Danish Law and the Practice of *mahr* among Muslim Pakistanis in Denmark," in *International Journal of the Sociology of Law*, no. 31 (2004), pp. 115-129; "Ægteskab, formue og medgift: Ret og sædvane i fire pakistanske landsbyer" [Marriage, property and dowry: Law and custom in four Pakistani villages"] in Sten Schaumburg-Muller and Bodil Selmer (eds), *Retlig mangfoldighed: En fælles udfordring for retsvidenskab og antropologi* [Legal diversity: A common challenge to jurisprudence and anthropology] (Copenhagen: Jurist - og Økonomforbundets Forlag, 2003); "Separation Before Divorce under Sharî'a and the Danish Law," in *Retfærd 9*, no. 2 (2002); "Sharî'a and Customary Law and its Relationship to Danish Law," in Bente Wolff and Rie Odgaard (eds), *Alternative Dispute Resolutions: A Case of Legal Pluralism 2001. Gender and Property Law in Pakistan: Resources and Discourses* (Copenhagen: DJØF Publishing, 2001).

[15] Innes Bowen, "Law in Action," at **http://news.bbc.co.uk/1/hi/magazine/6190080.stm**.

Whereas small groups of Islamists in the West with grandiose dreams of Muslim superiority and dominance publicly demand the implementation of Sharî'a, it mostly remains a private call from Muslims who want to do what they think is right according to their religion and for their community. In the end, both groups consider their interpretation to be the right one. The Islamists' demand is more forceful as it seeks to take over the legal systems and move what belongs to the private domain into the public arena. They want to include the criminal code in their application of the law and enforce moral and ethical behavior. Punishments mostly affect women, children and the interaction between men and women. Where Sharî'a is applied, a man and a woman who are not married or blood relatives can be jailed for taking a stroll together. It seems impossible that this could ever happen in Denmark, or in any other European country, even if the Muslim community were to grow rapidly. They would be Danish and European, raised and educated in the country to which their forebears had immigrated, a pluralist society in which a secular legal system guarantees the basic freedoms necessary for such a society to function. Thus they would probably have as little patience with being governed by a publicly applied Sharî'a as do non-Muslim Danes.

Why then do liberal-minded Muslims not react and counter the Islamists' claims? Why do Muslim leaders not stand up against those with these radical interpretations of Islam with which they disagree? This is partly so because Muslims who have moved away from their country of origin are slowly taking on different identities. They do not quite know what Sharî'a stands for, and in many cases turn to religious councils in private legal matters. At the same time, many of them can study Islamic sources online and interpret texts themselves. Their values and frames of reference are different from those of their Muslim families "back home." Young Danish Muslims, born and raised in Denmark, are deciding for themselves what it means to be Muslim and Danish. Individually they seek answers from more than just the mosque and Muslim religious leaders and scholars. However, many of them would not have the courage to stand up against radical Islamists out of fear of being branded a heretic. Others are simply not very interested in the issue. This situation has motivated Islamists to work even harder to reach their goal of unification. But enormously diverse opinions prevail among scholars, reflecting the diversity within the multinational communities. Since Islam lacks one central authority there are no clear answers about who is right and who is wrong. With the exception of Islamists, few Islamic scholars and leaders would dare to claim the truth in this situation.

European Islam

As Muslims in Europe become more European they are coming to terms with their new environment, in which the majority are not Muslim. Because it is challenging for Muslims to come to terms with this situation, some are returning to when Islam spread rapidly and established Islamic rule. Islamization occurred through processes such as intermarriage, with the new converts not questioning or challenging the Islamic legal system. Today, Islamists seek to repeat this process, ignoring contemporary realities.

By studying the Holy Scriptures, some Muslims decide for themselves how and to what extent they will follow Sharî'a rules. Many want to follow at least some of the rules in order to protect the individual freedom and basic human rights of all those living in the same country. However, while protecting these rights, Danes and other Europeans (Muslims and non-Muslim) need to understand the limits of legal processes. Groups that attack or ignore the fundamental legal systems of a society have to be stopped, not only to protect the local population, but also the vast number of Muslim immigrants who are not Islamists. The protection of basic human rights and freedom is vital since the negative aspects of Sharî'a are especially borne by women and children. Their lives can become hell when there is no way out in matters of divorce, custody, child or forced marriage.

Bringing the processes and struggles out into the open is healthy and constructive. This requires study, discussion and the time to get to know and understand one another. Failing to do so can lead to distortions, such as the recent case of a German judge who refused to grant a Muslim woman a divorce by referring to Qur'ânic injunctions.[16]

[16] "German Judge Cites Koran, Stirring up Cultural Storm," in *The New York Times*, 23 March 2007.

Although there have often been dialogue initiatives, especially after traumatic events, most European countries have waited too long to engage in open and honest discussions with Muslims in their midst. After condoning or ignoring them, many Europeans now react aggressively towards them, with no real discourse or conversation.

Also, the media fuel arguments and controversies, and play crucial roles in all three countries the team visited. In Denmark, the media can freely focus on what is violent, incomprehensible and reprehensible in Muslim communities while in Nigeria and Indonesia the media are used to highlight or create controversies. Islamist journals are full of poisonous language; stories of the deep fear of the cross illustrate that in certain circles the propaganda works.

Sharî'a in Nigeria

There are many similarities in how Sharî'a law was introduced in Nigeria and Indonesia during the fourteenth and fifteenth centuries.[17] Christianity, arriving much later, was often introduced by missionaries connected to the colonizing powers. Thus, it is natural that calls for freedom from colonial influence and Muslim independence have influenced the desire to apply Sharî'a. Furthermore, the role of the media, the search for identity and the right way to live as a Muslim have fueled this call. In all Muslim countries there are continuing conflicts over who represents religious authority. Nigeria and Indonesia also struggle with issues of corruption and poverty. Furthermore, what are considered the West's moral debaucheries and movements such as feminism and Communism, are epitomized as the enemy. As in Muslim stereotypes of the Western media, these stereotypes of the West are perpetuated especially among those who have never personally interacted with someone from the West. Another growing phenomenon in both countries is the fierce competition between Muslim and Christian fundamentalists who use comparable tactics and discourses to recruit members. Often the aggressive construction of churches or mosques leads to communal violence. Incidents provide both communities with material to highlight the "danger of the

[17] Islam found some roots in Nigeria already in the eleventh century.

other." Muslims thus suspect hidden agendas of Christianization, while Christians suspect hidden agendas of "Shari'atization." These forces infest the minds of liberal-minded members of both communities, who are often slow to react to this violent onslaught.

Sharî'a controversies

In some parts of Nigeria, the presence of Sharî'a goes back to the establishment of the Sokoto caliphate in 1804. Controversies regarding its relevance to the Nigerian legal system began in 1955, when Muslims discussed among themselves the relevance of Sharî'a courts in the North.[18] Between 1977 and 1978, the issue was discussed at the national level and also involved Christians. At this point, pressure to impose Sharî'a in all of Nigeria began to be exercised. Christians feared that this was the last step toward an Islamization of the country—a process that would turn them into second-class *dhimmîs*.[19]

The debate coincided with the drafting of the new Constitution of the Second Republic. The hot issue was whether or not constitutional provisions should be made to establish a Federal Sharî'a Court of Appeal (FSCA), and Sharî'a courts at the state level. Non-Muslims and some Muslims in the Constituent Assembly found the provisions inconsistent with the secular nature of the Constitution. A compromise was found whereby the FSCA was dropped, and a section included in the existing Federal Court of Appeal that was to deal with Sharî'a cases. Eighty-eight of 230 assembly delegates withdrew for some days in protest.

---

[18] P. L. Udoma, *The Cross and the Crescent. A Christian Response to Two Decades of Islamic Affirmation in Nigeria* (London: St Austin Press, 2002), p. 101.

[19] In an Islamic state ruled by Sharî'a according to classical Islamic jurisprudence, those who are not Muslim do not enjoy equal rights and status. Christians and Jews would be considered *dhimmîs*, non-Muslim, protected minorities living under Islamic rule. According to classical interpretations, Muslims should be positioned over *dhimmîs* in key areas of society. Furthermore, *dhimmîs* should wear distinctive clothing and not proclaim or display their religion publicly. In the nineteenth century, the official status of *dhimmî* was abolished by the sultan of the Ottoman Empire. At the same time, colonial rulers forced Muslims to reform their legal systems. Remnants of its rules remain visible and palpable throughout the Muslim world. See Fatimah Husein, *Muslim-Christian Relations in the New Order Indonesia. The Exclusivist and Inclusivist Muslims' Perspectives* (Bandung: Mizan Pustaka, 2005), p. 44.

Discussions continued over whether Sharî'a should be introduced or extended, and in 1988, the Council of Ulama, among others, insisted that the whole corpus of Sharî'a be applied to all Muslims everywhere in Nigeria. The Christian Association of Nigeria (CAN) saw this as an opportunity to air their frustrations over Muslim activities, including the attempt to "victimize" Christians. The Constituent Assembly debated once again whether or not the FSCA should be established. This time the military intervened and withdrew the Constituent Assembly's jurisdiction to deal with Sharî'a.[20]

In 1994 and 1995, during the constitutional debates, Muslims attempted to have a Sharî'a court of appeal created at the federal level but again failed to achieve their objective. Since then the debate has flared up from time to time. Christians prefer a secular state while Muslims favor the term "multireligious." Muslims claim that the idea of a secular state is a Western concept, and since a multireligious society includes freedom of religion it is their right to live according to Sharî'a law.

Many Nigerians, Christians as well as Muslims, have seen these debates as a cover-up for the country's problems. During colonization, the South captured many of the jobs in the civil service and international commerce, while the North captured political power. Religion was used as a weapon in this power struggle, and harsh debates created further divisions and tensions between Christians and Muslims.[21]

One can conclude that the whole discussion has been related to the question of political power at the federal level. Northern Nigeria wanted more control over bureaucratic offices and the economy, while the South wanted more influence in the central government and the military. On the whole, Northerners generally feel that Southerners have controlled vital sectors of society for too long. Over the years, this historical competition between North and South has increasingly taken on religious dimensions, especially since the implementation in 1999 of Sharî'a in Zamfara State.

[20] *Ibid.*, p. 114.

[21] For more detailed reading on the Sharî'a debates, see also Toyin Falola, *Violence in Nigeria. The Crisis of Religious Politics and Secular Ideologies* (New York: University of Rochester, 1998); Kukah, Hassan Mathew and Toyin Falola, *Religious Militancy and Self-Assertion. Islam and Politics in Nigeria* (Aldershot: Avebury, 1996); Simeon O. Ilesanmi, *Religious Pluralism and the Nigerian State* (Ohio: Ohio University Press, 1997); Philip Ostien, Jamila M.Nasir, Franz Kogelmann, *Comparative Perspectives on Shari'ah in Nigeria* (Ibadan: Spectrum, 2005); Ghazali Basri, *Nigeria and Shari'ah. Aspirations and Apprehensions* (Leicester: The Islamic Foundation, 1994).

Reasons for implementation

In October 1999, the state governor, Ahmed Sani Yerima, implemented the Sharî'a legal system in Zamfara State. He had come to power on the promise of implementing the full Sharî'a legal system; when elected, he applied the 1999 Constitution that granted every state the right to create courts of justice and apply Sharî'a law.

While some argue that this was what Muslims had demanded but not received during previous debates on Sharî'a,[22] others claim that the move to expand the scope of Sharî'a at this point was based on the assumption that the 1999 Constitution had shifted political power from the North to the South. Therefore, many saw the introduction of Sharî'a as a form of Northern resistance to the economic, cultural, and global forces that increased the marginalization of the North. Many Northerners felt their area had long been reduced to "the periphery of the periphery," with the South seen as a being in the "vanguard of Westernization."[23] As one of the participants at the conference in Gusau said, "The North is without power nationally. Therefore, Northern politicians use Sharî'a to feel that they are 'in control'."[24]

Analyses of why Muslims choose to be ruled by Sharî'a law point to a mixture of politics, ethnicity and religious commitment. One of the main arguments is that before the British arrived, the North was governed by Islamic law. Many Muslims in the states that implemented Sharî'a laws saw it as an alternative to Western models. Dissatisfied with a failing judicial system, corruption and "moral degeneration" (for example, visible in a high rates of HIV and AIDS infection), they claimed that Sharî'a presents an alternative "internally consistent and coherent super system,"

[22] Philip Ostien, "Opportunity Missed by Nigeria's Christians: The Sharia Debate of 1976-78 Revisited," paper presented at the conference on, "The Sharia Debate and the Shaping of Muslim and Christian Identities in Nigeria," University of Bayreuth, 11-12 July, 2003, pp. 1 and 8. See Musa Gaiya, "The Complexity of the Sharî'a Debate in Nigeria," in *TCNN Research Bulletin 42* (September 2004), p. 30.

[23] Ali A. Mazrui and Albert Schweitzer, "Shariacracy and Federal Models in the Era of Globalization: Nigeria in Comparative Perspective," paper presented at the international conference on, "Restoration of Shariah in Nigeria: Challenges and Benefits," London, 14 April 2001, at **www.shariah.2001.nmonline.net/index.php?page=allpapers.htm**

[24] A Hausa-Fulani Christian from Gusau, Zamfara State, 4 March 2005.

applicable in terms of faith, morality, law, politics and culture.[25] Realizing they could not apply all its rules led to dissatisfaction. For instance, in the modern world the economic rules of Sharî'a are untenable and have to be modified, as do the rules concerning the state. Nigeria is not ruled by a caliph, but by a democratically elected president.

Fading hopes

Many Muslims at the grass roots welcomed the implementation of Sharî'a laws, believing this would create more justice and fairness. The promise that Sharî'a laws would end corruption, exploitation and poverty and restore morality gave them hope for a better life. They trusted that with the introduction of *zakât* (almsgiving), beggars would no longer be on the street, women would be able to take their husbands to Sharî'a courts and have their rights restored and men would live up to their responsibilities. Moreover, it gave them a feeling of being faithful to the Qur'ânic orders and strengthened their identity. This strong Islamic identity was coupled with a growing resistance to the West and its "decadence."

Since the introduction of Sharî'a laws their hopes have gradually faded. Sometimes those who had supported the introduction of Sharî'a laws were the first to suffer its effects. Their daily lives did not improve, social and economic divisions became wider, and poverty and corruption increased. This has led to further tensions and unrest.[26] The implementation of Sharî'a has increasingly come under fire. It is also opposed by Muslims, who criticize that Sharî'a was politically motivated as it had been introduced by politicians, not religious leaders.[27]

Another important critique is that the implementation of Sharî'a had started from the top and not from the bottom. Crime must be tackled at the roots as demanded by Sharî'a. Therefore, it is not right to introduce the punitive dimension of Sharî'a only. Before Sharî'a can be applied there

---

[25] Hameed Agberemi, "Nigeria Beyond Secularism and Islamism. Fashioning a Reconsidered Rights Paradigm for a Democratic Multicultural Society," in Mashood A. Baderin, Lynn Welchman, Mahmood Monshipouri & Shadli Mokhtari, *Islam and Human Rights: Advocacy for Social Change in Local Contexts* (New Delhi: Global Media, 2006), p. 317.

[26] Interview with Christians and Muslims in Bauchi and Gusay, Zamfara State, March 2005.

[27] Interview with a number of Christian and Muslim scholars at Jos University, March 2005.

must be appropriate social and economic frameworks. Many also question whether it makes sense at all to introduce Sharî'a in a secular state.

The case of Amina Lawal

Most Sharî'a cases that have made the headlines involve women's sexuality, as in the case of Amina Lawal, who became pregnant out of wedlock. She could not hide her pregnancy, while the child's father was exonerated: the requirement that the act of intercourse be witnessed by four adults could not be fulfilled.

Several conditions need to be fulfilled for Sharî'a to operate: it needs a reliable judicial system, police enforcement and all the conditions prescribed by law need to be met. Unlike Denmark and Indonesia, Nigeria uses Sharî'a courts to try criminal cases. It is still a process of trial and error, but some highly publicized cases have shown the weaknesses of Sharî'a criminal law and the problems it gives rise to.

While Sharî'a courts have always existed in Northern Nigeria, they previously did not sentence criminal cases. Federal Sharî'a courts of appeal do not exist. Consequently, the law of the state holds the final authority in the case of last appeal. The demand for courts of final appeal is part of the Nigerian quest for Sharî'a. Unaware of the law and its requirements, many Muslims often accept the court's verdict as a divine judgment and do not appeal. This is compounded by the fact that many judges are unqualified for the job.

The case of Amina Lawal is an example of how the system can fail.[28] The first court that sentenced her to death by stoning did not provide legal support and read the verdict in Arabic, a language she did not understand. DNA evidence not being allowed in court, the father of her child swore an oath of innocence, while Amina was asked to provide four witnesses who could prove her innocence.[29] The absence of the highest court allows the case to be tried in a non-Sharî'a court that does not criminalize consensual intercourse between two grown-ups. Since there

[28] Gaiya, *op. cit.* (note 22), p. 40.

[29] "Nigeria: Amina Lawal is Free—at Last!," in *The Wire* (November 2003), at **http://web.amnesty.org/wire/November2003/Nigeria**

is the possibility of appeal at a regular court, groups advocating for human and women's rights, as in Amina's case, are very important.

Apart from the bias against women, the case led to a battle over religious authority. When one of Amina's lawyers, a woman, stated that stoning on the grounds of adultery was not in accordance with the Qur'ân, an imam issued a *fatwâ* against her.[30] Muslims can decide whether to ignore or accept a *fatwâ*, but this rash public call for murder not only shows a radical Islamist agenda but also its corollary of male disdain for women. The punishment for adultery mentioned in the Qur'ân (24:2) is flogging, not stoning. Thus the lawyer's reasoning was as valid as the Nigerian scholar's who referred to the fact that the tradition mentions stoning.

Sharî'a in Nigeria—today and tomorrow

While the call for Sharî'a is localized, it remains part of the worldwide Islamic movement, which is fuelled by Saudi money and aims to make the Muslim world more Arab in character. "At the launching of Sharî'a in Zamfara, there was a strong delegation from the Arab and Islamic world to show solidarity."[31] A Nigerian Muslim scholar referred to Saudi Arabia's continued role as a model, observing that there were virtually no thieves there "because no Saudi Arabian indigene is a thief."[32] This analysis ignores the reality that foreigners in Saudi Arabia are mostly underpaid guest workers who have little access to the judicial system. Similarly, in Nigeria it is "cow thieves and unwed mothers" who have been punished through the Sharî'a, not the wealthy and corrupt who do not give the poor their rightful share.[33]

An Arabization is evident in the introduction of greeting one another in Arabic rather than in the local language. The focus on morality, expressed in curtailing the freedom of women, reveals a Middle Eastern Arab bias.

---

[30] Gaiya, *op. cit.* (note 22), p. 40. The punishment prescribed in the Qur'ân is flogging: "The woman and the man guilty of adultery or fornication (*zina*) flog each of them. […]," *Qur'ân* 24, verse 2.

[31] Gaiya, *op.cit.* (note 22) p. 31.

[32] Sheikh Saleh Okenwa, "Implementation of Shari'ah in Nigeria: Balancing Christian-Muslim Concerns and Aspirations." Unpublished paper presented at the conference organized by the Association of Christian-Muslim Mutual Relations in Nigeria, Gusau 1-5 March 2005, pp. 23-43.

[33] Critique reported by Sheikh Saleh Okenwa, *ibid.*, pp. 30f.

The struggle for Sharî'a in Nigeria clearly illustrates the problems confronting religious and secular authorities when trying to apply the system in the twenty-first century. If they want to highlight the system's divine justice, they need to be selective and adjust the system. Democratically elected Islamist governments have to confront the reality that it is difficult actually to apply extremist measures. From Morocco to Egypt and Indonesia, Islamist Members of Parliament have had to moderate their tone. Often they see this as a first step toward gaining full power to apply their rules and ideas. Politics involves bargaining, and unless Islamists adapt, they will lose their constituencies' support. In Nigeria, there is much bargaining at the state level. Some states apply certain rules while others do not. In the end, it is apparent that Sharî'a is not as static as some might wish it to be.

The danger is that some groups seek to create their own instant justice. Observers of the Nigerian religious climate have pointed out that extreme youth groups, displaying patterns of exclusion and intolerance, are mushrooming in southwestern Nigeria. Not being part of any social or political networks, these groups are comprised of highly educated young people in tune with global extremism. They can afford to ignore reality and produce an ideological discourse that can result in violent action.[34]

Sharî'a in Indonesia: imagination and application

Calls for Sharî'a should be taken seriously because they embody aspects of what many Muslims aspire to in their lives. However, since the concept of Sharî'a is unclear, there needs to be room to discuss the basic freedoms and human rights of non-Muslims and Muslims who do not want to live under Islamic law. Freedom of choice is one of the key elements in the Sharî'a discussion.

In Indonesia, the government tries to safeguard this choice at a national level. Sharî'a laws may be introduced at the local level, but are not backed by the national courts and cannot be enforced by the local police. Consequently, applying Sharî'a rules still remains within the realm of voluntary action or obedience.

---

[34] Agberemi, *op. cit.* (note 25), pp. 320, 321.

Books on display in prominent Indonesian bookstores deal with the ongoing struggle about what it means to be Muslim in Indonesia in the twenty-first century. Large collections offer teachings and insights on a variety of interpretations of Islam ranging from extremist, to mystical and progressive. Books promoting the Islamic law of Sharî'a and the practice of polygamy as ways of truly living out one's Muslim faith stand back to back with volumes promoting asceticism and meditation to help Muslims strengthen their spiritual life.

Extremist voices were not prominent during the thirty-two years of Suharto's suppressive regime. In spring 1998, Indonesia fell into a period of transition from an authoritarian regime to a more democratic society. Extremist Muslim groups, forced underground during the Suharto years (1966–1998), joined the struggle for political power in an attempt to realize their dreams of an Indonesian or even Southeast Asian Islamic state governed by Sharî'a. Islamist voices, previously only bare whispers, suddenly became audible nationally and internationally.

Until 1998, Indonesia had generally been a positive example of a religiously pluralist society compared to most other Muslim countries. Islam in Indonesia used to be presented as an alternative to the rigid Middle Eastern model, where religions such as Buddhism and Hinduism are forbidden. Indonesian Muslims were actively involved in developing models of democracy and religious pluralism. Although with varying degrees of success, scores of interreligious groups were and still are active all over the archipelago, setting up interfaith projects noted for their creative, novel approaches.

In 1945, Muslims, in cooperation with Christians, Buddhists and Hindus, designed a model of living together that is enshrined in the Constitution. Although the Islamic majority dictates many outcomes of legal and political processes, strictly speaking, the Indonesian state is religiously neutral and based on the philosophy of *Pancasila* that accepts the coexistence of Islam, Christianity, Buddhism and Hinduism. Liberal expressions of Islam seemed the religious mode by default, deriving inspiration from the underlying Hindu-Buddhist worldviews that had prevailed before the thirteenth-century dawn of Islam. However, *Pancasila* was accepted under great protest from certain Muslim groups who had wanted to include the Jakarta Charter in the Constitution. This charter consists of seven words mandating that Muslim Indonesians follow Sharî'a law. Discussion of the legal status of Islam has recurred regularly, even during the Suharto regime, when all expressions of extremist Islam were suppressed.

Observers of Indonesian Islam wonder whether this underlying worldview, striving for acceptance and harmonious relationships between people of different faiths, has now faded under the pressure of radical expressions of Islam.

A diverse landscape

As a result of the educational opportunities offered under the Suharto regime, the national level of education has risen and a middle class and a class of intellectuals have emerged. Nonetheless, the majority still live below the poverty line, working in agricultural and unskilled jobs; they were hit hardest by the economic crisis that crippled Indonesia at the time the Suharto regime fell. Feeling marginalized and disadvantaged, many of them saw their faith as their greatest solace.

Indonesia is a country in the process of transformation. The modern amenities of metropolitan Jakarta stand in stark contrast to the countryside, where time seems to stand still and often basic sewage systems are lacking. Even within Jakarta itself one can move between various time zones. Although the lower classes are still in the majority, a survey among 312 randomly selected villages and urban areas found that two thirds of the Muslim population believed the nation should live according to the rules of Sharî'a, which the state should enforce.[35] However, only thirty-six percent of respondents thought that the state should enforce the veil for women and even fewer were in favor of applying the criminal code of Sharî'a.[36]

---

[35] The survey was conducted by the Center for Research on Islam and Society (PPIM), a research center at the State Islamic University in Jakarta. Its results are published in Saiful Mujani and R. William Liddle, "Indonesia's Approaching Elections: Politics, Islam and Public Opinion," in *Tempo Magazine* (23-29 December 2002).

[36] Suhadi, "Discourse and Counter-discourse on the Implementation of Sharî'a Issues in the Post-Suharto Era in Indonesia," paper read at the Indonesia Study Group meeting, Australian National University, Research School of Pacific and Asian Studies, 8 October 2003, p. 3.

In the 2004 national elections, instead of voting for a government in favor of introducing Sharî'a law, only one fifth of the votes went to the parties favoring this. In addition, the majority of those in favor of Islamic law did not know what its application would mean in daily life.[37] Officially, the 1945 Constitution upholds the *Pancasila* philosophy. Under radical Muslim pressure, the Indonesian parliament discussed the matter of formalizing Sharî'a in 2002 and 2003, but the majority rejected it as a foundation of the state.[38]

Radical Muslim groups lobby for the introduction of Sharî'a as the law of the land, with some even aspiring to an Islamic state in Southeast Asia, while the majority of Indonesians long for meaning and to live an upright Muslim life. Both ways of thinking are deeply rooted in Indonesian history, but often confused with each other, sometimes even intersecting. During certain periods they emerged from the same source. Radical Islamist proponents of Sharî'a law further blur the picture. Their acts of violence have captured Western imagination and are assumed to reflect the attitudes of the entire Indonesian Muslim population. Although here and there they are intertwined, in order to understand the Indonesian Muslim landscape, we need to discuss these trends separately.

Islamist movements

Radical Islamists and Islamists came onto the scene after Suharto's fall. Their activities have received far more attention than the rest of the Indonesian Muslims, who account for eighty-eight percent of the population. Many articles, theses and books have been written describing who these radical people are, what motivates them, who finances them and what

[37] For the people of Aceh, the only province that has adopted the Sharî'a law formally, there are many other priorities. A group of NGOs found that people rank their religious needs (including morality) as number nine on a list of priorities, that has security and peace as number one and education and economic welfare as second and third. Only 1.2 percent of Acehnese expressed the view that religion should have priority, while 57 percent voted for security and peace, 14.6 percent for improved education, and 6.7 percent for economic welfare. See Lily Zakiyah Munir, "Narrative Report on the Implementation of Shariah in Aceh: Tensions, Limitations and Apathy." Report written for the Asia Foundation, Jakarta, December 2005–February 2006, p. 10.

[38] The *Jakarta Post*, 22 January 2003. See also M. N. Ichwan, "The Seven Word Controversy," in *IIAS Newsletter*, no. 30 (March 2003), pp. 23-24, at **www.iias.nl/iiasn/30/IIASNL30_23_Ichwan.pdf**.

they are up to.[39] Equally, Islamists themselves have written many volumes explaining and defending their thoughts and ideologies.[40] Whether their number is small or large, their demand to apply Islamic rules and law has influenced public discourse, opinion, mindsets, and led to proposals to change national laws. Their arguments that the models of capitalism and socialism are bankrupt appeal to those who feel crushed by the system. Yet, among liberal Muslims and among non-Muslims, their radical ideas and acts of violence sow fear and create a climate of growing polarization in which religious communities are gradually withdrawing into their own circles. From an extremist Muslim perspective, Islam is superior. This attitude can have deep repercussions for the position and role of Indonesia's Christian, Hindu and Buddhist minorities.[41]

Indonesia's radical movements did not develop in a vacuum, but some of them are deeply rooted in Indonesian Islam and can be traced back to the extremist Darul Islam movement and the modernist Masyumi Party.[42]

---

[39] The list of works in Indonesian and English is long. Some noteworthy publications in English are, Martin van Bruinessen, "Genealogies of Islamic Radicalism in post-Suharto Indonesia," in *South East Asia Research*, vol. 10, no. 2 (2002), pp. 117-154; Greg Barton, *Indonesia's Struggle. Jemaah Islamiyah and the Soul of Islam* (Sydney: University of New South Wales Press Ltd., 2004); Hasan Noorhaidi, "Faith and Politics: The Rise of the Laskar Jihad in the Era of Transition in Indonesia," in *Indonesia 73* (2002), pp. 145-169; Peter G. Riddell, "Islamization, Creeping Shari'a, and Varied Responses in Indonesia," in Paul Marshall (ed.), *Radical Islam's Rules. The Worldwide Spread of Extreme Shari'a Law* (Lanham, Boulder, New York, Toronto, Oxford: Rowman & Littlefield Publishers, 2005), pp. 161-184; Giora Eliraz, *Islam in Indonesia. Modernism, Radicalism and the Middle East Dimension* (Brighton, Portland: Sussex Academic Press, 2004); S. Yunanto, *et al.* (eds), *Militant Islamic Movements in Indonesia and Southeast Asia* (Jakarta: Friedrich-Ebert-Stiftung & the RIDEP Institute, 2003); Arskal Salim and Azyumardi Azra (eds), *Shari'a and Politics in Modern Indonesia* (Singapore: ISEAS, 2003).

[40] The number of volumes is too numerous to mention. For example, K. H. Mawardi Labay el-Sulthani, *Tidak Usah Takut Syariat Islam. Islam Agama Kedamaian-Keselamatan dan Kebahagiaan* [No need to fear the Islamic Sharī'a. Islam is a religion of peace, well-being and happiness] (Jakarta: Al Mawardi Prima, 2000).

[41] See, for example, the reflection by one of the Saudi-trained leaders of the Prosperity and Justice Party (PKS), Hidayat Nur Wahid, about Islam and other religions in which he concludes that Islam is the absolute truth, tolerant of other religions, but not pluralistic. Greg Fealy and Virginia Hooker, "Interactions: Global and Local Islam; Muslims and non-Muslims," in Greg Fealy and Virginia Hooker (compilers and eds), *Voices of Islam in Southeast Asia. A Contemporary Sourcebook* (Singapore: ISEAS, 2006), pp. 459-461.

[42] Robert W. Hefner, *Civil Islam. Muslims and Democratization in Indonesia* (Princeton: Princeton University Press, 2000), p. 44.

Others derive their support and inspiration from global transnational Islamic networks, such as the al-Qaeda network.[43]

The Darul Islam movement and the Masyumi Party emerged as political forces at the time of Indonesia's independence from Dutch colonial power. Each in its own way has envisioned Indonesia as a nation governed by Islam. Between 1948 and 1962, both groups led several rebellions against the secular state but went underground when the government broke them up.[44] Members of the Muhammadiyah movement, whose goal it is to Islamize Indonesia without using violence, heavily populated the Masyumi party.

In 1960, after being disbanded as a political party, Masyumi leaders redirected their Islamization goal by launching an organization for Islamic mission, the Dewan Dakwah Islamiyah Indonesia (DDII) (Indonesian Council for Islamic Predication). Since 1973, it has developed close ties to the Islamic World League launched by Saudi Arabia. The organization's journal is filled with stories of Islam's imagined enemies: Christians, Zionists, the West, Shiites, feminists and liberal Muslims.

In the 1970s, former Masyumi and many Muhammadiyah leaders became interested in the ideas of the Egyptian Muslim Brotherhood and its ideologues, such as Sayyid Qutb whose writings referred *inter alia* to the ideal of a modern Islamic theocracy and the justification of *jihâd* against those who obstruct Islam. Qutb also deeply opposed Western influence on the Islamic world. By the 1980s, Arab/Middle Eastern/Saudi Arabian influences became visible in Indonesia, for example, in anti-Semitic publications translated from Arabic, such as the *Protocols of the Elders of Zion*.[45] Although there are hardly any Jews in Indonesia, this type of literature has resulted in a fierce hatred of Jews and the suspicion that Jews are corrupting Islam and causing political unrest.[46] This hatred has spilled over and today also encompasses Christians. Noorhaidi Hasan, one of Indonesia's foremost specialists on radical Islamists, concludes that, "[d]ue to the insignificant presence, not

[43] The historic summary here is based on Van Bruinessen and Riddell, *op. cit.* (note 39).

[44] See Cees van Dijk, *Rebellion under the Banner of Islam: The Darul Islam in Indonesia* (The Hague: Martinus Nijhoff, 1981).

[45] Van Bruinessen, "Yahudi sebagai symbol dalam wacana Islam Indonesia masa kini" [The Jew as a Symbol in Current Indonesian Muslim Discourse], in Y. B. Mangunwijaya (ed), *Spiritualitas baru: Agama dan aspirasi rakyat. Seri Dian II Tahun I* [The new spirituality: Religion and the ambitions of the people] (Yogyakarta: Dian/Interfidei, 1994), pp. 253-268.

[46] James T. Siegel, "Kiblat and the Mediatic Jew," in *Indonesia 69* (April 2000), p. 9.

to say absence, of Jews in Indonesia, Christians have become the target of the hostility so that the anti-Zionist discourse is directly interlocked with anti-Christian discourse."[47] Anti-Christian discourse has become connected with anti-American (Western) discourse and Abu Bakar Ba'asyir (the alleged religious mastermind behind the Bali bombings) once preached that "Christians hamper Muslims from actualizing their Sharî'a."[48]

Although over time the Darul Islam movement had greatly weakened, it continued to have underground sympathizers, including Abu Bakar Ba'asyir. In 1993, he founded the terrorist network Jemaah Islamiyah (JI) which was responsible for the Bali bombings and fights a *jihâd* for the establishment of an Islamic state in Southeast Asia.[49] Ba'asyir is also the religious leader of the Majlis Mujahidin, a group focused on transforming Indonesia into an Islamic state under the rule of Sharî'a. In August 2000, about 5,000 of its members, many of whom are connected to the Darul Islam movement, met for the first national congress in Yogyakarta to discuss "the putting in place of Islamic Sharî'a".[50] Since then, they have pushed for enforcing Sharî'a at the regional level, and produced a Sharî'a draft modeled on the law in Kelantan, Malaysia.[51]

Another movement that has captured the headlines is Laskar Jihad, whose members moved into the Maluku in 2000 and Poso in 2001, evoking violent strife between Muslims and Christians. Its Yemini leader, Ja'far Umar Thalib, studied in Saudi Arabia and Yemen and promotes a strict Wahhabi interpretation of Islam. Laskar Jihad focused on defending the country according to God's orders, especially by enforcing the application of Sharî'a law throughout Indonesia. According to Thalib, "[t]here is no way to get respect from non-Muslims for Muslims except through

[47] Noorhaidi Hasan, "The Radical Muslim Discourse on Jihad and the Hatred of Christians," unpublished paper presented at the International Symposium on Christianity in Indonesia, "Perspectives of Power," University of Frankfurt, Germany, 12–14 December 2003.

[48] *Ibid.*, p. 11.

[49] Martin van Bruinessen, "The violent Fringes of Indonesia's Radical Islam," in *ISIM Newsletter*, no. 11, (December 2002), p. 7, gives an overview of the violent Islamic radical groups operating in Indonesia and their origins. At **www.let.uu.nl/~martin.vanbruinessen/personal/publications/violent_fringe.htm**. Also see his "Genealogies."

[50] Irfan Suryahadi Awwas, *Risalah Kongres Mujahidin I dan Penegakan Syariah Islam* [Proceedings of the Mujahidin Congress I and the putting in place of the Islamic Sharî'a](Yogyakarta: Wihdah Press, 2001).

[51] M. B. Hooker and Virginia Hooker, "Sharî'a," in Fealy and Hooker, *op. cit.* (note 41), pp. 178-180.

jihâd."[52] Laskar Jihad caused a storm of protests and discussions when it stoned one of its members to death for having raped an Ambonese girl. Acting with the blessings of Yemeni religious leaders to whom he turned for advice,[53] Ja'far Umar Thalib passed the sentence, which the rapist accepted "as a way of atoning for his sin."[54]

To complete the picture, fiery young male members of the Front Pemela Islam (Islamic Defenders Front), led by another Saudi alumnus, Habib (Sayyid) Rizieq Shihab, bully Christians and commit violent attacks on all forms of what they consider to be moral vices. In December 1999, they occupied the Jakarta City Hall demanding that the governor close "all discos, cinemas, pubs, restaurants, billiard halls, karaoke bars and massage parlors during the fasting month [of Ramadan]."[55] Highly publicized was their 2006 assault on the Jakarta offices of the Indonesian edition of *Playboy* magazine, which moved its headquarters to Bali from where it continues to be published.[56]

The leadership and networks of the violent fringes of Indonesian Islam are guided by an increasingly powerful Arabic/Middle Eastern influence. Leaders contact scholars from the Middle East, especially from Saudi Arabia, and in the case of Laskar Jihad, from Yemen, to ask for *fatwâs* condoning their actions. According to Rohan Gunaratna, their military inspiration derives from the Middle East; some of the leaders fought in Afghanistan where they connected with the al-Qaeda network, which is "long-standing, well-entrenched and extensive" in Southeast Asia.[57]

Furthermore, Indonesia has traditionally imported literature from the Middle East. Ideologies were brought back to Indonesia by graduates of Islamic institutions in Egypt and Saudi Arabia and by pilgrims to Mecca. By the beginning of the twentieth century, the influx of lit-

---

[52] As quoted in Riddell, *op. cit.* (note 39), p. 169.

[53] *Ibid.*, p. 171.

[54] Hooker and Hooker, *op. cit.* (note 51), p. 170.

[55] S. Yusanto *et. al* (eds), *Militant Islamic Movements in Indonesia and Southeast Asia* (Jakarta: Friedrich-Ebert-Stiftung & the RIDEP Institute, 2003), p. 52.

[56] Jane Perlez, "Playboy Indonesia: Modest Flesh Meets Muslim Faith," in *The New York Times*, 24 July 2006.

[57] Rohan Gunaratna, *Inside Al Qaeda. Global Network of Terror* (New York: Columbia University Press, 2002), p. 175.

erature from the Middle East increased and helped Indonesian Muslims gain self-confidence in their struggle against the colonial Dutch regime and its Christian influence. Over the past few decades, other journals have served as transmitters of Wahhabi ideas. The Indonesian market is flooded with cheap, heavily subsidized books espousing Saudi Wahhabi and other radical interpretations of Islam. Cyber Islam has become an important tool for transmitting these teachings. Radical groups are most adept at using modern media and translating interpretations of Islam found on global mega sites (funded by Saudi Arabia) to the Indonesian context.[58] In short, for many years the Saudis have funded radical Indonesian groups and their media productions.

Searching for religious meaning

Fearing religious strife, the Suharto regime banned political expressions of Islam and, in 1985, forced all social organizations and political parties, including the mass Muslim organizations of Muhammadiyah and NU, to accept *Pancasila*. Forgoing their political aspirations, these groups started to focus on spreading Islam via their educational and grassroots networks. Islamic boarding schools, *pesantren*, run by the NU and the Muhammadiyah schools expanded, with their mixed curricula of religious and non-religious subjects. NU and Muhammadiyah represent around sixty million Indonesian Muslims, each covering a specific interpretation of Islam. Muhammadiyah strives for a purified form of Islam, stripped of local culture and practices, while the NU allows rituals from local culture as long as these do not disagree with the normative teachings of Islam.

Public schools offered religious lessons and increasing levels of religious literacy, Qur'ân study groups, catering to a myriad of groups within society, mushroomed all over Indonesia. For example, there are study groups for women, children, mothers, teachers, students and factory workers.[59] TV programs include Qur'ân recitations and call-in shows

[58] Bruce B. Lawrence, "Allah On-line: The Practice of Global Islam in the Information Age," in Stewart M. Hoover & Lynn Schofield Clark (eds), *Practicing Religion in the Age of the Media. Explorations in Media, Religion, and Culture* (New York: Columbia University Press, 2002), pp. 242–244.

[59] Anna Gade, *Perfection Makes Practice. Learning, Emotion, and the Recited Qur'ân in Indonesia* (Honolulu: University of Hawaii Press, 2004) provides a detailed and brilliant picture

in which scholars and imams answer questions. There are also religious education programs for children. Love for God is expressed by musical groups that range from rock bands to children's choirs. Since the 1980s, the desire to be more dedicated to religion has grown and Indonesian Muslims are eager to apply their beliefs to daily life and to turn it into a tool to combat social injustices. By the 1990s, realizing that this trend could be used to strengthen his power base, President Suharto encouraged non-political expressions of Islam, embraced Islam personally and made a widely publicized pilgrimage to Mecca.

On university campuses, the ban on political Muslim activities caused students to set up religious study groups through which they channeled their discontent with the regime. These groups became part of what is now called the *tarbîyah* (education movement). Some of these groups adopted the organizational models of the Egyptian Muslim Brotherhood, a radical group that uses small, tightly knit cells or *usrah* (families) for the formation of "pious, professionally successful young Muslims" who consider Islam to be "an all-embracing and self-sufficient system."[60] "Members of these groups want to Islamize the secular universities via Qur'ân study groups that encourage strict adherence to devotional acts (*ibâdâh*), including daily prayers, fasting and the payment of alms (*zakât*) to the poor."[61] Women affiliated with these groups started to wear the veil, some even opting to cover their entire face. Through these cells, movements such as HT developed rapidly.

The struggle over interpretation

As indicated above, the majority of Indonesian Muslim believers are interested in perfecting their faith. While not everyone might pray five times daily or dress in Islamic garb, intense discussions in the media

---

of the various Qur'ân study methods and groups that sprung up during the Suharto era.

[60] Greg Fealy, Virginia Hooker and Sally White, "Indonesia," in Fealy and Hooker, *op. cit.* (note 41), p. 48.

[61] Robert W. Hefner, "Islamization and Democratization," in Robert W. Hefner & Patricia Horvatich (eds), *Islam in an Era of Nation-States* (Honolulu: University of Hawaii Press, 1997), p. 90. Also see Robert W. Hefner, *Civil Islam. Muslims and Democratization in Indonesia* (Princeton & Oxford: Princeton University Press, 2000).

and interest in religious teachings and events testify to a vibrant sense of religion. These ongoing public debates about religion challenge the actions of radical groups. The public also knows that some groups, especially Laskar Jihad, who caused the bloodbath in Maluku, are not as virtuous as they pretend to be.

In an attempt to return to what they consider to be the essential nature of Islam, the majority of Indonesian Islamists strive to hold on to the basic values of the Qur'ân. They seek political power in order to impose their agenda on the rest of society. Especially those who are willing to commit violent acts follow a narrow, highly selective interpretation of the Qur'ân and Sunnah to suit their own agendas.[62]

Unlike more progressive and liberal minded Muslims, these groups, whether violent or peaceful, have in common that they see Sharî'a as a blessing to society and thus strive to have it applied. To reach this goal, they follow a wide range of strategies. Since Suharto's fall, there have been more and less successful regional attempts to enforce Sharî'a rules.

Islamizing Indonesia via Sharî'a

In Indonesia, there has been a long and intense history of discussing the position of Sharî'a and the state's role in applying it.[63] During the Suharto regime, when Islamic political power was suppressed, at least five laws with "strong Sharî'a influences"[64]were adopted. One of these is the 1974 marriage law, the others concern charitable foundations, religious courts, Islamic banking and inheritance rules. In 1991, the so-called Compilation of Islamic Law was introduced to guide judges in the Islamic courts.

Without explicitly referring to Sharî'a, these laws have accommodated the Indonesian Muslims' wish to be governed by rules prescribed

[62] For example, the term *jihâd* come to be associated with holy war, was traditionally interpreted to refer to self-purification and the struggle against one's own sins and inner demons. Violent groups usually interpret it as a spiritual and a physical battle against those who threaten or attack Islam. See S. Yusanto, *op. cit.* (note 56), pp. 14-17.

[63] Suhadi, *op. cit.* (note 36), p. 5,

[64] Arskal Salim & Azyumardi Azra, "Introduction. The State and Sharî'a in the Perspective of Indonesian Legal Politics," in Arskal Salim & Azyumardi Azra, *Sharî'a and Politics in Modern Indonesia* (Singapore: ISEAS, 2003), p. 5.

by their religion. The marriage law, for example, allows the practice of polygamy but with strict requirements, such as the first wife agreeing to the husband taking further wives. However, this law was motivated by more than the desire to apply Islamic rules. Suharto's government wanted to curtail practices such as arbitrary divorce, polygamy and child marriage. The marriage law not only applied Islamic rules to marriage (for those wanting to follow them), but also helped to curtail poverty caused by large numbers of divorcees and population growth due to polygamous families.

Islamists who want to influence politics have no patience for this informal expression of Islamic rules. They would like to see stricter laws resembling those found in the Middle East. When local districts were given autonomy after Suharto's fall, radical groups lobbied for Sharî'a to be enforced at the local level. Groups who opposed this immediately started to analyze what Sharî'a meant in the different areas and how it was enforced. The desire to apply Sharî'a is discussed in particular in Aceh, West Sumatra, South Sulawesi and some districts in Java, where the Tasikmalaya case has received much attention.[65]

Aceh, the Indonesian province that has waged a long guerilla war to gain independence, was the first and only one of Indonesia's thirty-three provinces to formalize Sharî'a law (in 2000). This was meant to be a test and possible model for the rest of the country. It applies only to Muslims, exempting non-Muslims and military personnel. The four laws on the books so far prohibit alcohol consumption and gambling, premarital sex, oblige women to wear the veil and relate to daily ritual prayers and to fasting during Ramadan. Punishments are caning, lashing and being fined or locked up.[66] According to Muslim female activists, the majority of those punished are the poor who gamble in an attempt to add to their meager income and women who are publicly humiliated for not wearing a veil. One of the main conclusions presented during

[65] See Suhadi, *op. cit.* (note 36), pp. 8-9; Riddell, *op. cit.* (note 39), pp. 171-176. The collection of papers read at a conference about women and Sharî'a, in Rahima (ed.), *Perempuan dalam Arus Formalisasi Syariat Islam. Belajar dari Tasikmalaya, Garut, Cianjur dan Banten* [Women within the formalization of the Islamic Sharî'a. Learning from Tasikmalaya, Garut, Cianjur and Banten] (Jakarta: Rahima 2004).

[66] See Lily Zakiyah Munir, Jane Perlez, "In Religious Aceh, Islamic Law is Taking Hold," in *The New York Times*, 1 August 2006, at **www.iht.com/articles/2006/08/01/news/aceh.php**

an evaluation meeting about the application of Sharî'a was that: "When the law first came in, people were in high spirits [...] but when it came to implementing the law, everyone was confused."[67]

Tasikmalaya in West Java is a district where Sharî'a was introduced through the cooperation between the national network of Majlis Mujahidin and its local membership.[68] During the 2000 *mujâhidîn's* meeting in Yogyakarta, it was decided to shift religious influence from the private to the public sphere via local networks in districts that had been granted autonomy in 1999.[69] Tasikmalaya's population of around 1.6 million is ninety-nine percent Muslim, and with over 700 Qur'ân schools, it used to be a stronghold of the Darul Islam movement.[70] Several rules were enforced that led to a Sharî'a minded public policy. These pertained to: prostitution; alcohol consumption; segregated hours in public swimming pools and the establishment of a prayer house near the public pool; obliging students to memorize the Qur'ân and to join religious education; and obliging women to wear the veil.[71] Several other districts are subject to similar experiments. However, they do not have the means to enforce these laws, except by force or coercion, since there is neither a special police force, nor courts that can punish those who violate these laws. In fact, most of the rules applied locally are against the national law.

The following observations on the situation since the fall of the Suharto regime are striking. While only a few Indonesians actually accept these violent groups, they have nonetheless managed to influence the national mindset. Indonesian Muslims want to intensify their religious beliefs and actions, but Islamists do not go unchallenged and are confronted by formidable opponents such as women's rights activists.

Indonesian Muslims are not seduced by groups that want to impose their agenda through violent means nor by a national enforcement of Sharî'a law. At the same time, small radical groups influence the popula-

[67] Nani Afrida, "Sharia not well Understood in Aceh," in the *Jakarta Post*, 21 July 2007.

[68] Suhadi, *op. cit.* (note 36). According to Suhadi the same method of enforcing Sharî'a rules on the local population via national and local Majles Mujahidin members working together, was used in South Sulawesi.

[69] Awwas, *op. cit.* (note 50), p. 154.

[70] Suhadi, *op. cit.* (note 36), p. 8.

[71] *Ibid.*, p. 10.

tion with their anti-Western, anti-other mindset. For example, "[m]any Muslims, and not just the radicals, believe in the existence of an international conspiracy, involving the assorted enemies of Islam—Zionists, Christian missionaries, imperialist politicians and their various local allies—aiming to destroy or weaken Islam in Indonesia."[72] This "anti-minority mood" is confirmed by surveys, such as one in 1998, in which 72.5 percent of Indonesians said that those of minority faiths should not be allowed to teach in public schools, forty-seven percent objected to church services nearby and forty-two percent rejected new churches in their neighborhood.[73]

Over the past three decades, the desire to follow laws based on the Islamic Scriptures has steadily been translated into state laws. After the road to formalizing Sharî'a was blocked, Islamists are seeking alternatives within the official state system. For example, Islamist-minded former Minister of Justice, Yusril Mahendra, has presented several legal drafts to parliament that officially cannot be classified as Sharî'a, but basically are a Sharî'a model.

A recent proposal would curtail individual freedom by making adultery, oral sex, cohabitation and homosexuality illegal. Mahendra has confirmed that he intends to "introduce Sharî'a one piece at the time."[74]Another proposal would infringe on religious tolerance by prohibiting intermarriage and preventing followers of different religions from attending each other's holiday celebrations or prayers. Another bill would forbid constructing new prayer houses in neighborhoods where less than ninety grown-ups would be using it.[75]

These laws are based on the Middle Eastern model, where in most countries it is difficult to receive permission to build a church and sexual crimes are punishable by jail sentences or worse. The most visible signs

---

[72] Martin van Bruinessen, "Post-Suharto Muslim Engagements with Civil Society and Democratisation," paper presented at the Third International Conference and Workshop, "Indonesia in Transition," organized by the KNAW and Labsosio, Universitas Indonesia, 24-28 August 2003. Universitas Indonesia, Depok, at **www.let.uu.nl/~martin.vanbruinessen/personal/publications/Post_Suharto_Islam_and_civil_society.htm**

[73] Riddell, *op. cit.* (note 39), p. 175.

[74] Barton, *op. cit.* (note 39), p. 74.

[75] See Kees de Jong, "Interreligious Relations in Present Indonesia: In Between Good Cooperation and Pillarization." Forthcoming in Festschrift for Karel Steenbrink.

of the presence of Sharî'a are women who, for example, wear the veil and do not go out into the streets at night. Since their bodies serve as visible proof of the law's presence, its rules are applied to women first. The focus on sexuality brings Indonesia closer to the moral standards of the Middle East. In 2003, a worldwide survey taken on moral values confirms that "the cultural fault line that divides the West and the Muslim world is not about democracy but sex."[76] On the "barometer of tolerance" concerning gender equality, Indonesia currently ranks above Egypt, Iran, Jordan, Algeria and Morocco.[77] Clearly, Islamists want the sexual values of Indonesian Muslims to become similar to countries such as Egypt and Jordan, which more or less tolerate crimes against women, such as honor killings, and where there is a degree of gender segregation.

Many groups resist these trends toward a "Shari'azation," some from a human rights perspective, others with knowledge of Islam. The struggle against the Suharto regime helped build a strong Muslim civil society, committed to democratic values, human rights and constitutional law. As Giora Eliarz observes, "This process in Indonesia, stands in stark contrast to the Middle East. The rebuff of 'civil society' since the 1970s is closely connected with the Islamic resurgence in general and Islamic fundamentalism in particular, which rejects secular, democratic and pluralistic concepts of civil society."[78]

Muslim leaders and intellectuals such as Abdurahman Wahid belong to the founders of Indonesian civil society that has grown over the years and cannot be easily eradicated. Wahid, Indonesia's erstwhile president and former national chair of the NU, is once again in the opposition. During the Suharto years he inspired a movement within the NU that reinterpreted the Qur'ânic sources in light of the changed realities of contemporary life. Now he has opened fire on the virulent strands of Islam, which he calls "an extreme and perverse ideology in the minds of fanatics."[79]

---

[76] Ronald Inglehart and Pippa Norris, "The True Clash of Civilizations," in *Foreign Policy* (March/April 2003), p. 63.

[77] *Ibid.*, p. 67.

[78] Eliraz, *op. cit.* (note 39), p. 84.

[79] "Right Islam vs Wrong Islam," first published in the *Wall Street Journal*, 30 December 2005, also at **www.gusdur.net/english/index.php?option=com_content&task=view&id=746&Itemid=64**.

Creating space for the other

One might be tempted to brush the growth of radical Islam in Indonesia off as being unrepresentative of the general mood of Indonesian Muslims. However, historically there are many precursors for the current violent radical groups. The attraction of these radical groups is that their bold calls for Islamic supremacy convey an appealing sense of empowerment to many Muslims who feel suppressed by corrupt local and national rulers, the West and life in general. Islamists call for the resurrection of the glorious caliphate and, in March 2006, massive events were organized in several Indonesian cities. This was to show their desire for a new caliphate because, as the organizers wrote, "the world is yearning for a new system promising justice, noble civilization, peace and prosperity."

This radical discourse makes Indonesia's Christians feel like second-rate citizens. According to the Islamists' worldview there is no place for others; freedom and the basic human rights of all citizens are curtailed. The category of "others" includes not only Christians but also millions of Muslims who interpret their religion in more inclusive ways. In terms of strategies for coexistence, or even survival, Christians have powerful allies such as Abdurrahman Wahid and his followers. Wahid believes that we are facing a "crisis of misunderstanding" and the first step to overcome violence is to understand the true meaning of one's religion:

> All too many Muslims fail to grasp Islam, which teaches one to be lenient towards others and to understand their value systems, knowing that these are tolerated by Islam as a religion. The essence of Islam is encapsulated in the words of the Qur'ân , "For you, your religion; for me, my religion." That is the essence of tolerance. Religious fanatics—either purposely or out of ignorance—pervert Islam into a dogma of intolerance, hatred and bloodshed. They justify their brutality with slogans such as "Islam is above everything else." They seek to intimidate and subdue anyone who does not share their extremist views, regardless of nationality or religion. While a few are quick to shed blood themselves, countless millions of others sympathize with their violent actions, or join in the complicity of silence.
>
> This crisis of misunderstanding—of Islam by Muslims themselves—is compounded by the failure of governments, people of other faiths, and

> the majority of well-intentioned Muslims to resist, isolate and discredit this dangerous ideology. The crisis thus afflicts Muslims and non-Muslims alike, with tragic consequences. Failure to understand the true nature of Islam permits the continued radicalization of Muslims worldwide, while blinding the rest of humanity to a solution which hides in plain sight.[80]

Abdurrahman Wahid calls upon Muslims to make the courageous move of getting to know themselves before getting to know the other. Understanding allows for reconciliation and change of heart. This change of human behavior requires many steps, starting with repentance for how we ourselves have vilified the other.

In sum

Our investigations have shown that the call for Sharî'a is deeply rooted in the colonial past and the present, when in many parts of the world Muslims feel a keen sense of inequality with the West. The inner-Islamic discourse partly arose as a resistance to the West, which in the eyes of Islamists embodies Christianity. This reality does not leave Christians much room. Yet, as the team found, it is important that the communication between Muslims and Christians is not cut off. Conversations are the building blocks of peacemaking. Where Sharî'a laws harm communities, Christians together with Muslims who do not want a full application of Sharî'a, can call for justice and demand basic freedom and human rights. After all, losing one's rights always means that many others will lose theirs as well.

[80] *Ibid.*

Bridge Models
Stories of Relationships

The Story of a Christian-Muslim Association in Nigeria

David L. Windibiziri

In 1991, following the violent conflicts that had shaken Nigeria in the 1980s, a meeting of distinguished elders and religious leaders was called in Kaduna. Participants unanimously called on President General Ibrahim Babangida to establish fora for dialogue at all levels of government—federal, state and local. Here issues of common interest could be discussed, and a common understanding regarding welfare activities and their implications for the Christian and Muslim communities reached.

Since there was no reaction to this recommendation, the Lutheran Church of Christ in Nigeria (LCCN) decided to develop a vision for an interfaith dialogue association that would provide the opportunity for Christians and Muslims to meet and, respectful of one another's faith, to discuss and study together. The association was to serve as a platform for mutual interaction and the exchange of ideas.

This concept was further developed when the American Lutheran Church (ALC), now the Evangelical Lutheran Church in America (ELCA), sent Rev. Dr Ronald Miller to share with the LCCN his vision of engaging in a deeper understanding of *salâm* (peace) and building relationships between the two faith communities.

From 1992 onwards, exploratory meetings with Christian leaders were held in order to create a wider interest in the project. Although not all Christians were interested in peace, in November 1993, the vision of creating the Association for Christian-Muslim Mutual Relations became a reality. By 1999, a proposed Constitution had been decided upon.

The proposal was further debated and approved at the 2002 conference. In 2004, the association was officially approved by the federal government through the Corporate Affairs Commission.

The conferences

The first conference gathered for three days in November 1993, in Miango, Plateau State to discuss the feasibility of dialogue between Christians and Muslims in Nigeria, the theology of God's Word from biblical and Qur'ânic perspectives and the influence of politics on interreligious dialogue. The participants were Christian and Muslim religious, women and youth leaders and discussions were open and frank, albeit at times quite confrontational. Nonetheless, the fact that we could discuss together, stay together and eat together for one week was a positive experience.

The historical, political and economic causes of conflicts were identified already at this first conference. We knew that the religious aspects should not be neglected, but were aware that these were not the primary cause of conflict. They came to play a role when Christians and Muslims, because of their general ignorance of one another and one another's religious beliefs, began to use abusive and provocative language in the media and in public preaching. This led to unnecessary tensions and bitterness. As a result, one of the recommendations of this conference was to encourage mutual education regarding Christianity and Islam in order to ensure that words and actions based on sheer ignorance be minimized.

Further conferences took place in 1995, 1997, 1999, 2002 and 2005.[1] Invitations to these conferences were issued at a personal level, but there was the clear determination to see that as many states as possible were represented in order to ensure nationwide representation. Christians invited Christian participants and Muslims invited Muslim participants. A conscious effort to reach as many denominations as possible was made.[2] Some of the former participants were invited for the sake of continuity, while others were dropped so as to make room for new invitees and to ensure broader participation.[3]

[1] The first conference gathered 46 participants: 37 Christians and 9 Muslims. In 2005, the balance was 37 Christians and 42 Muslims.

[2] Representatives from the TEKAN Churches, the Fellowship of Churches in Christ in Nigeria (COCIN, ERCC, ECC, CRCN, UMCN, EYN), the Anglican Church, the Baptist Church, the Roman Catholic Church, etc. Muslims came from Jama'atu Nasril Islam, Nigerian Supreme Council for Islamic Affairs, the National Council of Muslim Youth Organisations (NACOMYO), etc.

[3] The first five conferences were sponsored by the LCCN through the ELCA, in accordance with the principle of mutuality. The sixth conference was sponsored by the Muslim community through

There was general agreement that we should be conscious of mutuality and equality. Fifty percent of the members of the planning committee, invitees and speakers should be Christian and fifty percent Muslim. The topics should be treated by a Christian and a Muslim speaker followed by discussions. Furthermore, it was agreed that women and youth should be well represented.

At the beginning we dealt with religious and ethical topics. Later we concentrated on social, economic and political issues such as poverty alleviation, the rights of women in society, national unity and a multireligious society. More recent conferences have been more practice oriented, looking at societal development, HIV and AIDS, violence and Sharî'a in relation to Christian-Muslim relations. The last conference was held in 2005, in Gusau, Zamfara State—the first state to introduce Sharî'a in Nigeria.

It is interesting to note that while discussions on social, political or moral issues were lively, there were no major disagreements. HIV and AIDS are problems that concern us all and all of us can condemn corruption. When we touched on doctrinal issues there was immediate tension, and we had to learn to accept that there are issues that cannot be discussed. In times of crisis, we had to be aware of our mutual feelings. We often found it wiser to leave what had happened to the past, because we were looking for a way to move forward.

When new participants joined many issues were raised that had been tackled at earlier conferences. These would then be dealt with in private discussions. We agreed not to expect to convince anybody of our faith convictions and to attempt to convert the other to our own faith. Rather, in light of our faith convictions, our aim was to learn to live together peacefully and respectfully. This will benefit our faith and nation.

Christian and Muslim leaders

Reasons why these conferences were so important included the growing fanatical and violent trends among Christians as well as Muslims. It was important for Christian and Muslim leaders and representatives from

---

the Nigerian Supreme Council for Islamic Affairs (NSCIA) and Zamfara State.

various religious organizations to come together and discuss common challenges so as to create awareness about the importance of Christians and Muslims working together for peace and understanding among their members, university faculties and seminaries.

Religious leaders of both communities have been known sometimes to instigate or exacerbate violence and confrontation. This has often been the case when churches or mosques have accepted politicians who subsequently used them for their own interests. These politicians were previously not recognized members of the congregation, but infiltrated and engaged in the activities of the church or mosque by financing projects and sponsoring certain groups or individuals. This made it very difficult for the clergy or elders to disagree with some of their ideas or policies. They were quickly committed to what they could not understand and found it difficult to tell the truth or reject certain ideas and policies, even when they were aware of the dangers. They were afraid that by telling the truth they might disappoint the politicians and consequently lose their financial support.

Over the years, we have been in contact with a number of Christian and Muslim leaders, and it has been up to them to share their experiences and discussions with their people. While we know that this has taken place to a certain extent, more remains to be done.

The way forward

In future, with the official recognition of the association, it may be easier for us to reach the grass roots. It is here that problems often arise because of minor issues that could easily be dealt with if the appropriate fora and people were available to handle such situations. Thus, we need committed local leaders who will take the initiative to form such local groups. In many areas, there is mutual suspicion and mistrust among people. For the sake of mutual development, it is necessary to inspire all people to recognize the importance of creating mutual understanding, tolerance and peaceful coexistence in our country.

We plan to work with interfaith projects where women and youth can meet to learn practical crafts or professions. We wish to establish sewing centers, computer centers, carpentry workshops, etc. Here, especially women and youth from both faiths could meet and learn how to take care of themselves, while at the same time creating friendships that can counteract the unnecessary violent confrontations that so easily erupt when young people are unemployed and see no fruitful future.

From the beginning, we also envisioned setting up a stationary study center with a library where people could get acquainted with one another. This would be another way of combating ignorance and promoting a better understanding of how we can achieve peaceful coexistence. It is our hope that such a center will be established in the federal capital, Abuja.

At times we may feel that the process is a very slow one and we have time and again experienced new outbreaks of violence. Nevertheless, we trust that we have made a beginning, and remember the unexpected violence in 2001, in Jos, during which a certain district in the city was spared death and destruction, because the Muslim secretary of our association organized all men—Muslims and Christians—to form a human chain around the area. This might not have happened without the mutual trust and sense of common responsibility generated by the association.

Lessons Learned after the Tsunami

Jamilin Sirait

The tsunami that struck Aceh on 26 December 2004, was the worst disaster to hit Indonesia since independence. In Aceh and Nias—the two regions most affected—114,573 people died, the majority of whom were women and children. An additional 127,774 have not been found and were declared lost. The death toll was highest in Aceh. Apart from the loss of life, thousands of houses and buildings in Banda Aceh, Lokhsemaue, Meulaboh and Sabang were destroyed. The people of Aceh experienced multiple losses: human and material. Destruction and human tragedy on such a scale present a challenge and responsibility for the victims as well as to those trying to relieve their suffering.

In the following, I shall focus on what we learned about interreligious dialogue in Aceh through the relief work of Lembaga Perduli Kasih (LpeKa) (Project for Caring Love), an NGO under the Huria Kristen Batak Church (HKBP), one of the main Lutheran churches in Indonesia.

Islam and Christianity in Aceh

Aceh is located in the very western part of Indonesia at the top of the island of Sumatra. It was among the first areas in Southeast Asia in which an Islamic state was founded in 1515, and the ruling sultan applied Islamic law. The majority of Aceh's inhabitants are Muslim and due to its connections with the heartland of Islam and its role in transmitting the Islamic faith to the rest of the archipelago, it is called the *Serambi Mekkah* (the gateway to Mecca). The Achenese are proud of their missionary role; historically, being Acehnese means being Muslim.

Some Acehnese have converted to Christianity although this is not generally accepted.[1] Thus, there is a small community of about one

[1] An Acehnese who converted to Christianity several years ago told me that his family was

hundred Acehnese Christians, all of whom live outside Aceh. However, there are many Christian immigrants—around 82,000 out of a population of 4.8 million—who have settled in Aceh to work as civil servants, teachers, military personnel, traders and in the oil industry.

For a long time, Aceh has held a special status in Indonesia. Its people have waged war against Dutch colonial dominance and were never under Dutch control. After independence, they revolted against the central government because it ignored their desire to be an Islamic area.[2] The revolt against Jakarta was inspired by the Darul Islam movement discussed in the Sharî'a chapter. In 1959, giving in to public demands, the central government granted Aceh the status of a special province and the autonomy to administer its own educational, religious and cultural affairs.

Until the fall of the Suharto regime, the Acehnese experienced recurring wars against the central government. In 1976, reacting to increasing numbers of Javanese immigrants and demanding equal distribution of Aceh's natural resources, Hasan Tiro, the last descendant of Aceh's sultan, formed Gerakan Aceh Merdeka (GAM) (Movement for a Free Aceh) and declared Aceh's independence. To crush the resistance, Aceh became an area for military operations and thousands of troops were sent to the province. GAM's demands for a separate state were not accepted and apart from the military and GAM fighters, an estimated 15,000 civilians were killed, many of them women and children. In 1999, Aceh was given special status under the name of the Province of Nanggroe Aceh Darussalam and the privilege to apply Sharî'a law. But GAM refused this status, wanting Aceh to become an independent state. After the tsunami hit, GAM declared a cease-fire. In December 2006, GAM won the elections and one of its leaders became the new governor.[3]

---

shunning him. He became a Christian after being inspired by the lifestyle of a couple he stayed with during his studies in Medan, North Sumatra.

[2] Anthony Reid, *Perjuangan Rakyat, Revolusi dan Hancurnya Kerajaan di Sumatra* [The blood of the people, revolution and the end of traditional rule in Northern Sumatra] (Jakarta: Pustaka Sinar Harapan, 1987), pp. 31ff.

[3] International Crisis Group Report, "Indonesia: How GAM Won in Aceh," 22 March 2007, at **www.crisisgroup.org/home/index.cfm?id=4715**

Sharî'a in Aceh

As in other parts of the Muslim world, applying Sharî'a law in Aceh is fraught with problems. At the national level, Indonesia has four legal systems and the status and relationship of Sharî'a in relation to these other systems have not yet been spelt out. Apart from this complication, according to Indonesia's Constitution, religious affairs continue to be managed by the central government through the Department of Religious Affairs in Jakarta. Also, Indonesia's Islamic scholars differ as to how Sharî'a should be understood and practiced.

Disagreement about its meaning and how to enforce it led to raids on women who did not use the veil. After arresting them, their hair was cut off. But the women took revenge by performing raids during Friday prayers, arresting men who were not in the mosque attending the prayer and hitting them with brooms.[4] Furthermore, there is a debate about whether or not Christian women can be forced to wear the veil, and if non-Muslims will have *dhimmî* status.[5]

Theological debates after the tsunami

After the tsunami, many discussed the social and theological factors behind the disaster. Some Islamic scholars preached that it was a warning from God to remind the people of Aceh that they had not obeyed God's teachings. Based on *sûrat al-Hâdid* (Qur'ân 57:22), other scholars claimed that it was a punishment from God because the Acehnese had left their Islamic culture.[6] According to them, virtues such as simplicity, honesty and piety were pushed aside by individualism and materialism.

Many Indonesians regarded the disasters experienced by the people of Aceh as a punishment for the bad behavior of those who had driven

---

[4] Rusjdi Ali Muhammad, *Revitalisasi Syari'at Islam di Aceh. Problem, Solusi dan Implementasi* [Revitalizing Sharî'a in Aceh. Problems, solutions and applications] (Jakarta: Logos Wacana Ilmu), p. 177.

[5] I met many Christian women in Banda Aceh who told me that it is very difficult for them to go out without wearing a *jilbâb*.

[6] Abdurrahman al-Baghdady, *Tsunami, Tanda Kekuasaan Allah* [The tsunami: A sign of God's power] (Jakarta: Cakrawala, 2005), pp. 64ff.

out non-Acehnese, confiscated their property and burnt church buildings (i.e., Meulaboh, 1986).[7] Others were neutral, considering it to have been a natural disaster. For example, scholars connected to the Liberal Islamic Network asked people to stop blaming the victims since it added to the suffering and burden of the Acehnese. They reasoned that the earthquake and tsunami could not be called God's punishment since many of the victims were innocent children and women. Moreover, the tsunami victims also included many non-Acehnese and non-Muslims from Sri Lanka, Malaysia, Thailand, etc. Besides mosques, numerous churches and other shrines were destroyed.

Seeing the disaster as a call to act generously and show commitment to and concern for the victims seemed the most appropriate way of understanding this tragedy. Overnight, the tsunami increased the number of Indonesia's poor by one million. To us in the HKBP it was a lesson in concern, not based on religious preference but on love for one's neighbor. According to the Islamic scholar Komaruddin Hidayat, the tsunami was a lesson and should encourage us to be more concerned with nature. We are responsible for protecting and maintaining the environment. In the face of nature's strength we are called to become brothers and sisters and to help one another.[8]

Christian-Muslim diapraxis

The tsunami not only destroyed lives and property, but also broke down walls separating the different religions. While the tsunami raged violently, people seeking shelter did not stop to ask about one another's religion. In Jakarta, the national Christmas celebrations of 28 December 2004 were cancelled and the money earmarked for the celebrations was sent to Aceh and Nias. Churches all over Indonesia and abroad collected money for the victims. Volunteers from various countries and organizations came to

[7] When the tsunami hit Aceh, I interviewed many Javanese people living in Medan. They said that the people of Aceh were struck by disaster because they had thrown out the people from Aceh.

[8] P. Cahanar (ed.), *Bencana Gempa dan Tsunami Nanggroe Aceh Darussalam & Sumatra Utar* [Earthquake and tsunami disasters in Aceh and North Sumatra] (Jakarta: Penerbit Buku Kompas, 2005), pp. 439ff.

Aceh to help bury the corpses and clean the place up. The word religion was never mentioned. For reasons of hygiene, many corpses were buried in mass graves. Imagine our surprise when some groups raised the matter of non-Muslim medical doctors not being able to assist Muslims.

The presence of volunteers in Aceh, including from the churches, can be understood as the follow-up to a dialogue that had been begun immediately after the tsunami. As Colin Powell, former US Secretary of State, observed: "We are not doing this because we're seeking political advantage or just because we're trying to make ourselves look better with Muslims. We're doing this because these are human beings in desperate need." Responding to the new situation, Hasyim Muzadi, national chair of Nahdlatul Ulama (NU) concluded that religion should become the rallying point towards a universal humanity.[9]

Today, real dialogue is taking place in Aceh, with people of different faiths working for the future of Aceh. Many of the Muslims I interviewed in Banda Aceh said that they were no longer suspicious of foreign relief workers but felt that many NGOs (including Christian ones) had really helped them. Two young Muslim women working for LpeKa said that they were excited and thankful to cooperate with Christians. They considered the presence of LPeKa and other NGOs to be a blessing for Aceh, and realized that this situation was unique since there was no formal cooperation between Muslims and Christians in Banda Aceh prior to the tsunami. However, many HKBP members mentioned that although there had never before been formal and theological dialogue between Muslims and Christians in Aceh, they had lived peacefully alongside their Muslim neighbors.

The future in Aceh

On the basis of interviews with a variety of people (NGO workers, the families of victims and the people who had suffered from the tsunami) and on surveys taken in Banda Aceh, I can conclude that in order truly to help Aceh we need to focus on a dialogue of *diapraxis*. However, for it to succeed, we need to pay attention to the following points:

---

[9] *Ibid*, p. 177.

- To involve the Acehnese themselves in the discussions about relief so that their culture and traditions are taken into account. Their needs and frame of reference need to be our priority. Since many have lost their jobs, income generating activities, retraining, or providing seed money to open a business should be top priorities.

- To respect feelings of loss and guilt. A Christian woman told us that she and her husband had lost three of their four children. Their house had also been destroyed. Many face similar situations and helping them to regain their spiritual strength is of great importance.

- Besides building public facilities such as schools, hospitals, mosques, churches and markets, special attention must be paid to improving human resources. Education is very important because of the high rate of illiteracy in Aceh. LPeKa runs two kindergartens with Muslim and Christian teachers. These teachers also provide sewing classes for women and men. Discussing these issues provides opportunities for Muslims and Christians to meet. Muslims even entered a HKBP church after attending discussions about the tsunami relief.

- In the near future, we might need to plan a seminar for religious leaders to discuss theologies of disaster viewed from different religious perspectives: Islam, Christianity, Buddhism, etc. Theological reflection will help us to resist the idea that the tsunami was a punishment for the sins of the Acehnese. A theological basis for *diapraxis* can be found in the sacred texts of Muslims and Christians, since one of the main purposes of religious teachings as revealed to the prophets is improving human life and relationships between human beings.

- The tsunami has produced a new generation willing to go beyond religious differences and to work together with those of other faiths. In fact, this is a return to the time when the Acehnese lived together in harmony. This situation has been disturbed for many years because of the conflicts between the central government and GAM. A byproduct of this conflict was the horizontal conflict between Acehnese and non-Acehnese. The tsunami reminded us that we are only limited and human, and that we are called upon to help each other.

Perspectives for Indonesia

We have also learned that it is important for people of various religious backgrounds living in Aceh to discuss the implementation of Sharî'a, since this law affects all. For example, the Ar-Raniry Islamic State Institute in Aceh could organize an official meeting with Muslims and non-Muslim participants in order to discuss the meaning of Sharî'a. This law is not only unclear to many, but has also become the source of many conflicts and considerable suspicion among adherents of different religions. Although the Acehnese have had long experience of living together peacefully, the new political situation has caused tensions and disagreements based on lobbying for political position.

Dialogue is just one of many tools to reach agreement between people. However, it cannot serve as a fire extinguisher; it involves a long and arduous process in which participants are truly committed to reach a level of mutual respect and agreement. Dialogue should have our common welfare in mind. Our religious leaders share in the responsibility for keeping this process going.

Much pessimism and skepticism surround dialogue. Many believe that religions are inherently different and that dialogue between believers of different faiths constitutes a mere act of politeness. Others hold that religions are to blame for many social conflicts and violence and consider religion to be a tool for political manipulation.

According to Sumartana, the Indonesian Christian theologian and founder of the institute for dialogue between religions, DIAN/Interfidei, this negative attitude towards religion is also based on the fact that those involved in it have not yet been able to create platforms that can truly intervene when social problems occur. Dialogue between different religions often takes place among specialists and thus remains an intellectual and élitist activity. When conflicts occur, this type of dialogue will not have sufficiently prepared people at the grass roots to respond adequately. Dialogue based on real-life experience is an effective tool to promote mutual understanding and agreement. When practiced at the grass roots, people learn to listen to one another while remaining both open and critical. In a natural way, people learn about on another's culture, rituals and beliefs.

Therefore, dialogue should not be seen as an easy way out when religious conflicts occur but should be practiced by every religious leader. It is the only way to overcome prejudice. Finally, in Indonesia it is important to address the issues of proselytization in both Islam and Christianity. Both Muslim and Christians believe that they are called to spread their belief to others. Unfortunately, many people understand that call to mission literally and are intent on converting the other. Christians say that the others must be baptized to become followers of Jesus, while Muslims believe that everyone has to understand the truth of Muhammad being the last prophet. These issues have to be addressed via theological dialogue, but in situations such as those in Aceh, we first need a dialogue of life.

Christian-Muslim Counseling in Copenhagen

Fatih Alev and Lissi Rasmussen

This is the story of practical cooperation between Christians and Muslims in Copenhagen, initiated in 2004 by the Islamic-Christian Study Centre (IKS) in order to establish resource networks and visiting and consultancy services for Christian and Muslim inpatients from an ethnic minority background, their relatives and health staff in the Copenhagen area.

Background

In 1996, the IKS was established jointly by Christians and Muslims. The center is working to develop, strengthen and improve the coexistence between Christians and Muslims through common study, courses, lectures, advice, information and joint projects. The counseling project is part of the attempt to create mutual understanding between Christians and Muslims.[1]

Over the past few years, a need has emerged in several hospitals in the Copenhagen area for Muslims and/or dialogue experienced persons to function as advisors and interlocutors for patients and relatives from a Muslim (and partly also Christian) minority background. Organized work in this field had not existed in Denmark previously.

In Islam there is no tradition of organized counseling, since crises are handled within the family. In Denmark and other European countries, Muslims and all other persons are viewed individualistically. There may not be a family network to assist them when needed; furthermore, many Muslim refugees do not have their relatives in Denmark. As a result, health professionals have had no one to call upon or refer to in situations where assistance is needed.

[1] For more details on the center, see **www.ikstudiecenter.dk**

Christian patients can talk to hospital chaplains, who are employed by the Evangelical Lutheran Church in Denmark and paid by church members through the tax system. Frequently, the chaplains are involved in the care of the patients. There is no imam or other Muslim to take care of the religious needs of Muslim inpatients. According to the hospital chaplains, there have been special requests such as in cases where a Muslim couple had lost their child at birth. In such situations, it is not enough for them to consult a Christian chaplain. Furthermore, Muslim resource persons have not been involved in ongoing therapeutic care in which hospital chaplains customarily play a role.

IKS has a large network in the Muslim population and a number of volunteers who have the insight and personal ability needed in cases such as the one described above. Over the years, the center has built up considerable experience in cross-cultural counseling and conflict resolution and has provided an information service on cultural and religious encounter and Islam and ethnic minorities.

In 2003, IKS was contacted by two hospital chaplains and decided to train approximately twenty Christian and Muslim volunteers from minority backgrounds in counseling. A working group was established consisting of representatives from a Muslim youth organization and IKS, Muslim medical doctors, an expert in transcultural psychiatry, the director of the hospital emergency services and two Christian hospital chaplains. The project received minimum funding to employ a coordinator for ten hours (later twenty-two hours) per week.

Education of health staff and students

The first activity was to offer a number of courses on "Islam in the health services" to staff members, nurses, doctors and students in the medical field. The goal was to give participants a wider knowledge of Islam and the various cultures that are influenced by Islam, and thus to enable them to overcome the communication barrier that might arise between staff and patient.

All the teachers are Muslims, and most of the participants are Christian, ethnic Danes. The participants have the opportunity to share their experiences and have many of their questions answered by people who are very close to the problems. Palliative care in relation to ethnic minorities, Christian and Muslim views on life, death and illness, Muslim rituals and intercultural communication are some of the subjects with which health staff need to become more familiar.

Courses on counseling for Muslims and Christians from a minority background

In a lecture room at the largest hospital in Denmark, the Rigshospitalet, seventy Muslims and Christians, mainly young people, spent five evenings together learning about conversation therapy in order to qualify as members of resource teams whose primary task is to counsel inpatients who feel the need to talk to somebody with a background similar to their own. Some of them would also assist and talk to lonely people in crisis centers, old people's homes, prisons, asylum centers and private homes.

After the first course, the coordinators selected twenty people, Christians and Muslims, for further and more intensive training in order to enter the hospital network. They completed a three-day course on crisis psychology, counseling and the problems of children and youth. The most important part of the course was the practical training in conversation therapy in smaller groups of both Christian and Muslim participants. The textbook on counseling used in the course was written by a Christian pastor specialized in conversation therapy. In both courses the teachers were Christian chaplains, Muslim doctors and imams, all of whom had theoretical and practical experience in this area.

Common training removed prejudices

During individual interviews we established that almost all participants had entered the first course because they felt a special responsibility towards patients and relatives from a background similar to their own. They were highly motivated and glad that they were needed and could do something for others, which is not something especially young Muslims usually feel. The media and many politicians often present them as a problem that needs to be tackled. In the counseling project they were given an active role: they were not passive objects or observers but necessary actors. They were not regarded negatively, but as individuals who could contribute positively. They were convinced that this project was important and that they could have a function in it. Those who are ill and alone need care. They need someone to talk to, someone who understands their situation.

Towards the end of the first course, a Lithuanian Lutheran participant told me that her prejudices and negative attitude toward Islam and Muslims, which she had developed by listening to the public debate, had vanished. She had seen the Muslims' sincere involvement and humanness and discovered that she had a lot in common with them. Later she became one of the twenty resource persons.

Practical hospital work

The project is officially recognized and supported by the management of the Rigshospitalet and Herlev hospitals. Since 2005, the resource team has been working in hospitals ready to assist nurses, patients and relatives. Team members are often called upon by nurses and other hospital staff to talk about their work and about the situation of patients from minority backgrounds, not only in Copenhagen but also in other cities.

Resource persons and the coordinator, who is now a recognized Muslim hospital chaplain,[2] are occasionally called by hospital staff to assist patients and relatives in acute situations. This is often in connection with a sudden death or severe illness. Sometimes there is a need for recurrent visits to patients who feel lonely. Patients and relatives are often surprised to realize that this assistance is available and that their spiritual needs are also taken care of. This makes them feel more at home and secure in the hospital system, and helps nurses to feel more comfortable with the situation.

[2] The coordinator, Naveed Baig, is from a Pakistani background but was born and has lived most of his life in Denmark. In connection with the project, he has taken a course on Muslim chaplaincy at the Markfield Institute of Higher Education, Leicester, England.

The resource team meet once a month for a debriefing with the coordinator (imam) and the director (pastor and author of this story), and a strong fellowship has developed among the team members.

Theological reflections

During common study and the sharing of experiences, Christian and Muslim participants have from time to time discovered new aspects of their own religious traditions. They often share how they have learned from each other, also at a theological level. For instance, Christians have realized the importance of formal prayer in order to structure the patient's day, or have come to appreciate the importance Islam attaches to gratitude to God and to patience in suffering. Muslims have recognized the need for more informal personal prayer with the patient as well as the importance of knowing how to deal with feelings of bitterness or anger in relation to God in situations of severe illness or loss, even if those feelings are not "proper" according to Islam.

Both have recognized the similarities in methodologies useful in sessions with patients in crisis and suffering from severe illness. These include narratives that give comfort and hope found in the Bible and the Qur'ân or other religious traditions. In practice, the theological basis is often very similar despite different understandings of suffering, illness and death in relation to God.

According to Islam, illness is a cleansing process that should lead to reconciliation between heart and mind, between oneself and God and between the individual and other people (*tarbiyya*). Christianity also maintains that establishing the right relationship to God, to oneself and to other people is the goal of pastoral care. In Islam, struggle and patience (*jihâd* and *sabr*) are key words in this healing process.

Perspectives

The project has created a feeling of self-confidence, togetherness and trust among the Christian and Muslim participants. By discovering their common humanity, they now have a more realistic picture of one another. At the same time, it has encouraged them to reflect theologically on the responsibility they share as believers and on the purpose and meaning of counseling. They have come to realize that in cases of serious illness and the confrontation with death, we have very similar concerns and pose the same questions: Why me? What does it mean? Has God left me alone? We may feel guilty, bitter and angry. We experience the same feelings of anxiety, unrest and grief but also the strength that we gain from our faith which enables us to be patient and reconcile ourselves to the situation.

Experiences from this counseling project have confirmed how important it is to work together towards a common goal. Discussions on religion and ethics can take place afterwards. The Muslim participants have become interested in reflecting theologically on Muslim counseling—together with the Christians. Had we begun with this reflection before we started the project, we might never have come to practice the work and additionally might have left each other with the impression that there was too much disagreement between us to cooperate meaningfully.

Engineering Bridges

Lissi Rasmussen

Bridges and interreligious dialogue

The three stories demonstrate different models of Christian-Muslim interaction. In the first section of the book, we have already identified various types of peace building activities as well as different attempts to resolve conflict and improve coexistence. Here we will reflect on these experiences and suggest further models for building bridges between Christians and Muslims. Some of these may overlap and they are by no means exhaustive. Other models could be added, relevant to other parts of the world or other situations. However, the models described here issue from our studies of the three countries and our own experiences of Christian-Muslim cooperation over many years.

Dialogue of life

What has often been referred to as "dialogue of life" exists in all three countries, and many local tensions and controversies are thereby resolved. Personal contact between Christians and Muslims takes place on a daily basis: at work, in educational institutions, on playgrounds, in hospitals, shops, the military, etc. People share the same experiences and conditions by living in the same community, or are in situations similar in other ways. Sometimes people of different faiths are linked through the intimate ties of family and friendship.

Christians and Muslims meet for celebrations such as weddings, birthdays, naming ceremonies, or even religious celebrations. They also may meet at stressful moments of their lives such as funerals, epidemics, famines, floods and terrorist attacks. All these encounters may not be religious *per se* but they are important to building human relationships.

In Nigeria and Indonesia in particular, the dialogue of life plays a crucial role whereas in Denmark there is much less contact between people from different backgrounds. Because of family ties and close neighborhood relations in these two countries, Christians and Muslims came to one another's aid during periods of conflict. For instance, they helped one another to move to other more secure places. In this section, we shall deal not so much with these informal encounters but rather concentrate on intentional, organized and more formal types of interreligious interaction.

There are examples of where both informal and more formal encounters are taking place at the same time. Yogyakarta, which has been called a model of coexistence, is such an example. Here, dialogue of life and practical interfaith solutions are a reality. Based on a long tradition of living and working together, there is a natural interaction between neighbors, families and colleagues of different religious affiliations. A common cultural foundation binds together Christians (twenty percent of the population) and the Muslim majority. At the same time, many initiatives are being taken to improve coexistence.

The most important initiative is the dialogue center, Interfidei (see pp. 185ff). The team visited Kyai Muhaimin's Islamic boarding school. Muhaimin is represented on the boards of the Indonesian Conference on Religion and Peace (ICRP) and Interfidei. At the time, he was involved in a peace initiative and busy hanging banners that called for cooperation and peaceful campaigning in the upcoming elections all over the city.

Initiatives in Yogyakarta show that in the midst of searching for new identities and reconfiguring social and religious relationships, there is great promise for future dialogue between Indonesians of various faiths. In its June 2004 issue, the national journal, *Tempo*, described a new sanctuary built by a group of religious leaders north of Yogyakarta, where worshippers of all faiths can gather to pray for the good of the nation, everyone according to their religion. This initiative dovetails with the words that the team members heard regularly when meeting with religious, political and communal leaders: "to be religious today in Indonesia means being interreligious."

Organized dialogue

Traditionally there have been at least four main categories of organized dialogue:

- **Discursive dialogue:**[1] exponents of different faith communities meet to discuss the theological, philosophical and ethical bases of their faith traditions or faith issues. The purpose is to learn about one another's religious tradition and faith by listening to one another's views on a certain topic. This may help to break down preconceived ideas and misconceptions about the other, to understand and appreciate the background and context of the other's religious tradition and to establish mutual trust.

- **Discursive-cooperative dialogue:** representatives of different groups, such as religious leaders and academics, come together to discuss subjects relevant to the communities concerned and common challenges in society. The Nigerian story is an example of this model.

- **Experience-oriented discursive dialogue:** partners expose themselves to one another's spiritual and worship life. They may participate in the other's prayer or meditation, or find a form in which both parts can participate. This is based on the belief that it is a continual endeavor to bring out the best in every person or society. This model is rather controversial in circles concerned about not compromising their own faith by entering into common spiritual activities.

- **Diapraxis (or dialogue in practice):** cooperation between people of different faiths. After working together in relation to common challenges, discursive dialogue may follow as a reflection on common practice.

In all four categories, dialogue is a process, which must be owned by both parties. One has to be prepared for opposition from other believers, from polemical writings and from networks of opposition. In this chapter we will concentrate on the second category.

[1] Discursive dialogue means the argumentative and reasoning interlocution about faith issues.

Is dialogue an antiquated term?

The term dialogue has become more and more loaded and is perceived by many, especially Muslims, as a strategy for mission. It has become a buzzword used in many contexts, often in the sense of a "civilized form" of conversation to negotiate and arrive at a compromise. Therefore, many people who oppose Christian-Muslim dialogue see it as a communicative interaction where the interlocutors try to reach an agreement and find the same answers and maybe even take over the position of the other.

In large parts of the Western world, such as Denmark, the definition of dialogue is often almost ritualized in the sense that a certain cliché-like rhetoric is attached to it (especially on the Christian side). It is often reduced to affirming its necessity without it being turned into practice. At the same time, the term is based on an approach whose starting point is that Christians and Muslims are basically different. In the face of large-scale migration and globalization, this approach is becoming increasingly difficult to sustain.

The prefix *dia-* indicates that two or more persons relate to each other across certain differences. Today there is considerable interplay between people across national and regional borders and ethnic, cultural and religious backgrounds. This means that ethnic and religious borders are broken down, not least among the young, who have played and gone to school together.

This signifies that individual identity derives not only from national, cultural and religious values, but also from values of other cultures and religions. All individuals carry layers of different cultural, ethnic and religious identities, and it becomes ever more imprecise to speak of encounters between two or more cultures and religions. The encounter takes place not only between human beings but also within each person. We are all influenced by different cultures and religions. Religion and culture are no longer confined, distinct entities as they were assumed to be before. We move, intermarry and mix. Via the Internet and the media we influence one another whether we want to or not. There is ambiguity as to where one cultural expression ends and the next begins. Culture changes through contact. This is also the reason why set categories of "Us" and "Them" are not relevant or workable.

Why interreligious dialogue and cooperation?

Why not just relate to one another as human beings, around common human problems? Why involve religion in this? On the basis of the six stories in this book, there are several reasons why religion does and should play a role.

- Religion is important in describing the other, even those who do not see themselves as being "religious" (often the case in Denmark). In this way, religion affects the division that we tend to create between people. Prejudices, myths and misunderstandings are often connected to religion. Religion is being used—by Christians and Muslims—to spread prejudice and create enemy images.

- Religion is part of cultural identity and a potential source of strength and self-assertion. Those who feel threatened by changes in the world and society, or are subject to exclusion and discrimination, often turn to religion as a source of stability and an expression of that which is immutable. As we have seen in the three countries, religion becomes a means of coping.

- Religion often becomes part of conflict. Attacks are perpetrated against religious buildings and representatives. This is often connected to the manipulation of religion and religious identity, feelings and symbols. In many countries, religion is used for political gain and to garner votes (e.g., in Nigeria and Denmark). Religion and religious leaders therefore play an important role in the process of building bridges.

- Religious appeals to human conscience and to the heart and can be a strong ethically motivating force. This can influence conflict, both negatively and positively. At the same time, it provides answers to the fundamental questions of human existence and the very meaning of life.

- Faith in God is the common motivation for Christians and Muslims to cooperate for the common good. In the Qur'ân, certain verses confirm Islam as the only true faith, but others affirm religious diversity as being willed by God. In the Bible, there are texts about Christ's uniqueness but also ones about his openness to other people irrespective of their religious background.

- Interreligious dialogue and *diapraxis* counteract fundamentalism and feelings of powerlessness. They may contribute to creating a sense of security and self-confidence so that persons are then able to open up and be themselves. It may also provoke intra-religious dialogue. We need each other to identify the weaknesses in our own traditions. We have much to learn from one another, also in terms of religion.

- Religious leaders play an important role in Nigeria and Indonesia. In Nigeria, local movements often contact these leaders in order to discuss with them problems facing the community.

From discursive to cooperative dialogue

Over the years, formal meetings and academic discussions on common challenges in society have been held in all three countries. While some were organized on an *ad hoc* basis, including with secular NGOs, others have been ongoing.

The 1980s and 1990s saw a shift in dialogue initiatives and thinking from a more formal dialogue (from "above") to a more practice oriented interaction that includes social issues of common concern (from "below"), a dialogue of commitment through practice. This refocusing was reinforced by the types of crises that necessitated an approach with more influence at the grassroots level.

Since the 1960s, Nigeria and Indonesia have had a tradition of formal, primarily intellectual, dialogue meetings in order to create better understanding and closer cooperation between Christians and Muslims. In 1962 and 1963, the first meetings between Catholics and Muslims were held on a private basis in Kano and Zaria for the purpose of improving relations between Christians and Muslims. The first "official" Christian-Muslim dialogue meeting was organized in 1974 by Fr. Chukwulozie at the Pastoral Institute in Ibadan under the theme, "How can we make our religious beliefs real and operative in this materialistic age?"[2]

[2] Victor C. Chukwulozie, "Christian-Muslim Relationships in Nigeria." Unpublished paper, Jos, 1975; Peter Clarke, "Islam, Development and African Identity: The Case of West Africa," in *Religion, Development and African Identity. Seminar Proceedings* (Uppsala: SIAS, 1987), pp. 131f. Christians and Muslims met to discuss common problems and possible solutions such as how to

In Indonesia, discussions on religious tolerance and interreligious issues first started in 1967. For instance, seminars, consultations and meetings were organized at an academic level, and the State Institute of Islamic Studies (IAIN) started religious study programs. This was promoted by the state (the state ideology of *Pancasila*). The government's program was known as interreligious concord among the people (*kerukunan antaragama*).

At first, these formal meetings involved only a few interested intellectuals from universities or other institutions of higher education, who did not have the backing of their respective religious or cultural groups. Since there was no follow-up, they had little influence on the majority of Christians and Muslims who needed to cooperate concretely at the local level. Christian-Muslim understanding and collaboration at the grass roots do not grow out of conferences and theological discussions, but out of people's social relationships. People's daily interactions and relationships influence religious beliefs and values.

As of the 1980s, recurring crises and a growing militancy among certain groups in Nigeria, coupled with common problems such as HIV and AIDS, corruption, poverty and violence, meant that peace building and cooperation at the social and political levels became more necessary. At the time, there were no organized dialogue meetings, since these were considered to be counterproductive.

In the 1990s, a new era seemed to dawn with a growing interest in interreligious cooperative activities and discussions around common challenges, such as how to overcome drug abuse and corruption. This was

---

combat materialism and to make religion more intelligible to contemporary Nigerians. A committee of five was set up to continue dialogue activities, and the journal *Nigerian Dialogue* was launched to publicize the content of the dialogue meetings and to explain the nature of dialogue from the Christian and Muslim perspectives. The committee never met but some issues of *Nigerian Dialogue* have been published.

Other meetings and efforts to promote Christian-Muslim dialogue have followed among which an important seminar for scholars and students was held in 1982 at the University of Nigeria, Nsukka, under the theme, "The Place of Religion in Education in Nigeria." In the same year, an important joint meeting was held by the Institute of Church and Society and the Islam in Africa Project in Ibadan. The theme for the meeting was the Christian churches' responses to the presence of Muslims in Nigeria. See P. L. Udoma, *The Cross and the Crescent. A Christian Response to Two Decades of Islamic Affirmation in Nigeria* (London: St Austin Press, 2002, p. 175. See also Lissi Rasmussen, *Christian-Muslim Relations in Africa. The Cases of Northern Nigeria and Tanzania Compared* (London: I.B. Tauris, British Academic Press, 1993).

when the Association of Christian-Muslim Mutual Relations in Nigeria came into existence, focusing on common challenges in society.

In both countries, the approach became more practice oriented, and religious groups together with NGOs worked for the prevention and resolution of conflict. A solid and confident cooperation developed between the leaders of the mainstream churches and the dominant Muslim networks of Nahdlatul Ulama (NU) and Muhammadiyah. Rev. Jalongos Mamillary told us that for years meetings between Christian and Muslim leaders have taken place every three months in his area in Jakarta to discuss local problems, especially in relation to youth. The local and national governments encouraged these types of meetings.[3]

During the 1990s, there were the first signs of a real, serious interest in interreligious dialogue in Denmark. Especially members of the national church took initiatives to invite Muslims for discussions, study groups, etc. Within the church, there were attempts to relate to the question of religious pluralism in a country that has been quite homogenous in religious terms. This was often done in a reactive rather than a proactive way and dealt with such questions as, What can we as Christians do? The Muslims are here, how do we relate to that problem? In the beginning, the discussions often developed in a rather polemic and apologetic way, with each party wanting to defend their own faith position.

Also, many Muslims who came to Denmark had previously not related to religions or cultures other than their own, and perhaps not even to alternative ways of being Muslim. Now they had to adapt to living in plural surroundings. Over the past decade, there has been a growing interest in dialogue, especially among second-generation Muslims. Many young Muslims are more active in society and thus need to talk to Christians who have a similar education, values and speak the same language.[4]

[3] In 2006, over 200 religious leaders of six established religions in Indonesia, Islam, Protestantism, Catholicism, Buddhism, Hinduism and Confucianism, met at a three-day national congress aimed at "revitalizing the *Pancasila* ideology as a common ethics" amid concern over decreasing tolerance among religious communities. The intention was for all religions to cooperate in finding solutions to common humanitarian problems. Ary Hermawan "Religious Leaders will Meet to seek 'Common Ethics'," in the *Jakarta Post*, 22 August 2006.

[4] In Denmark, practicing Muslims account for ten to fifteen percent of the population. See, Lene Kühle, *Moskéer i Danmark* [Mosques in Denmark] (Hojbjerg: Forlaget Univers, 2006) and a number of surveys carried out during 2006 and 2007, e.g., the survey mentioned in "Beyond the Stories," note 44, according to which only thirteen percent of Danish Muslims attend Friday prayers on a regular basis, and the report, "Values and Norms among Foreigners and Danes," compiled by

Foci of Christian-Muslim dialogue and cooperation

Christian-Muslim interaction has been formalized in all three countries. In 1993, the Association of Christian-Muslim Mutual Relations in Nigeria gathered Christian and Muslim leaders from various organizations to create awareness among their constituencies. The purpose was not merely to hold formal discussions, but also to stimulate cooperation at a practical grassroots level. The next step was to form local groups in individual states and at the local government level in order to combat ignorance and prejudice. An ongoing center for dialogue and cooperation is also being planned.[5]

The Islam in Africa Project (IAP), a para-church, NGO-style Protestant organization, also played a central role in Nigeria. It was launched in 1959, aiming "to keep before the churches in Africa their responsibility for understanding Islam and the Muslims of their region, in view of the churches' task of interpreting faithfully in the Muslim world the Gospel of Jesus Christ; and to affect the research and education necessary for this."[6] IAP first became involved in Nigeria. During the 1960s, initiatives were taken both in the more conservative, evangelical mission organizations and churches and the more ecumenically minded mission organizations and churches, such as the LWF.

In 1987, the project changed its name to the Project for Christian-Muslim Relations in Africa, PROCMURA. The project is owned by the local churches, and local programs are primarily financed locally.[7] It has played a mediating role in areas of violent conflict, enabling Christians to build relationships with Muslims by addressing matters of common

---

a think-tank under the Ministry of Integration (made public 12 March 2007). The report showed that twenty percent of Danish Muslims went to the mosque on a regular basis.

[5] Other associations have been founded to organize seminars and workshops on peaceful co-existence, e.g., the Commission for Interreligious Dialogue, initiated by the Association of the Episcopal Conference of Anglophone West Africa, AECAWA.

[6] IAP Constitution and Guidelines, 1973. IAP/PROCMURA is headquartered in Nairobi, Kenya. In Nigeria, the IAP study center in Ibadan was shut down in 1977. Subsequently, its library was moved to the Institute of Church and Society. This institute has been interested in Islam since it was founded by the Nigerian Council of Churches in 1964. Although IAP initially centered its work in West Africa it has also influenced the churches in East Africa.

[7] Some Muslims, especially Yoruba, have been actively participating in dialogue activities. Dialogue meetings have been arranged on their initiative, such as in Ilorin in 1978.

interest. Today PROCMURA is involved in twenty African countries. Local committees made up of representatives of different Protestant churches are established in each country. They arrange courses in Islam and Christian-Muslim relations for congregations and take up dialogue with local Muslim leaders.

Like the Association for Christian-Muslim Mutual Relations in Nigeria, the Islamic-Christian Study Center(IKS) in Denmark, established in May 1996 by Christians and Muslims, was from the beginning based on principles of equality and mutuality. Thus, it has an equal number of Muslims and Christians members and is backed by a number of Christian and Muslim organizations, societies and individuals. The premises are a shared home for both parties and planning, decision making and contributions are shared equally.

IKS provides training, teaching, documentation, information, consultancy, dialogue and a social network for many of its members. Over the years, the center has become increasingly study- and practice-oriented. It runs a variety of projects, the most important of which are the anti-discrimination projects and the counseling work described in the previous story.[8]

Various church organizations are beginning to think about dialogue between equal partners. For instance, Danmission, in cooperation with local partners, now focuses on *diapraxis* projects in the Middle East, and the Committee for Church and Encounter is attempting to form an interreligious national council or forum to address common challenges in society.

In Indonesia, interreligious organizations and programs were initiated in the early 1990s. A number of Muslim organizations have contributed to building bridges between religious communities. The Liberal Islam Network (JIL), the International Center for Islam and Pluralism (ICIP) and the Wahid Institute have been promoting progressive Muslim thought, democratic reform, religious pluralism and tolerance, primarily through research.[9] All have played a role in promoting interreligious dialogue and cooperation.

---

[8] Staff includes a director, a part-time staff member and a number of volunteers. Until 2003, it was funded by the Ministry of Integration. Today funds come from Christian and Muslim organizations, churches and mosques. For further information, see **www.ikstudiecenter.dk**

[9] The Liberal Islam Network was established in March 2001, see **http://islamlib.com**. The International Center for Islam and Pluralism was founded in July 2003 to create relationships among cultural and religious groups, see **www.icipglobal.org**. The Wahid Institute was established

Dian/Interfidei in Yogyakarta

Interfidei is short for Institut Dialog Antar-iman di Indonesia, or Institute for Dialogue between Religions in Indonesia. "Dian" stands for its symbol, a candle that lights itself, its environment and those who use it.[10] It is based on the ideas and vision of the Protestant scholar Sumartana who, with several like-minded scholars, religious and community leaders, founded the institute in 1991 in Yogyakarta. Since Sumartana's untimely death in 2003, the institute has been led by its cofounder, Elga Sarapung.

Its vision was to initiate studies and activities that can transform religious mindsets, create stronger networks of interreligious cooperation and, on the basis of religion, to find solutions to the many humanitarian problems facing Indonesian society. Initially, Interfidei targeted future as well as established religious leaders for whom it organized workshops and discussions. Since the beginning, its activities have covered numerous topics and groups, ranging from peace making and conflict transformation, youth forums, publications on violence, politics, democracy and religion and study groups on the religions of Abraham to fora for teachers of religion.

Especially after the fall of Suharto in 1998, Interfidei adapted its programs to the changing political and religious situation and expanded its range of activities from Yogyakarta on Java to other islands, especially those experiencing interreligious conflict.

Currently, the institute's principal objective is to make people more aware and appreciative of the Indonesian reality of religious pluralism. Three projects illustrate this: the plurality project, the forum for teachers of religion and the peacemaking project.

- **The plurality project** aims at documenting and discussing concepts of "local plurality" that will translate ethnic and religious plurality into new paradigms of understanding. The goal is to try to understand

in September 2004 by the former president Abdurrahman Wahid of Gus Dur (NU) to promote his thoughts, see **www.wahidinstitute.org** (and **www.gusdur.net**). The Muslim intellectual, Nurcholish Madjid, who died in 2005, and his Paramadina Foundation (established in 1986) have contributed to interreligious dialogue. For Nurcholish Madjid it was important that Islam become an ethical force in society to motivate tolerance, pluralism and democracy.

[10] Web site, **www.interfidei.org.id**

what it means for members of different communities to live together in the same village, town, or region. A case in point are members of Ahmadiyah in Lombok: they have lived there for decades and are highly appreciated by local communities for their services such as hospitals and schools. But when extremist Sunnis came over to enforce the *fatwâ* forbidding the Ahmadiyah movement, local villagers pushed them out to the refugee camps. If a strong, true community had been in place, extremist outsiders would not have been able to stir up this communal disturbance. The project is based on the finding that discourses on pluralism must be rooted in local concepts before they can become effective tools of interreligious dialogue. One of the methods to get to the core of local ideas on plurality is to hold writing workshops that allow authors to reflect on issues of religious and ethnic plurality in their immediate environment. The outcome of these workshops is published and used as discussion material at interreligious events.

- **The teacher forum** brings together religion teachers in middle and high schools. It seeks to develop a vision for their teaching in order to influence the young. The goal is to increase teachers' awareness of their potential to convey true understandings of diversity and pluralism to students. During a series of workshops, teachers discuss methodologies of teaching, curricula and the contexts of their classes. After several workshops, they are encouraged to set up regular meetings to continue exchanging ideas and material.

- **The peacemaking project** aims at enhancing understanding of how conflicts emerge and evolve. It consists of the study of religion, social studies and workshops based on local needs. For example, in areas where there is conflict between the two communities, Interfidei has facilitated workshops on "Deconstructing Religious Prejudices," while in areas where one religion tries to play a dominant role, it has organized workshops on "Deconstructing the Concepts of Mission."

As its activities expand, so too does Interfidei's scope; the institute has inspired the founding of similar groups all over the archipelago. Examples of such are groups called Forlog, Forum for Dialogue Among Us, and Forum Dialog Antar Kita, the Inter-congregational Dialogue Forum. These were set up in 1999 in South Sulawesi and South Kalimantan to address the growing polarization between religious groups due to the changed political climate and discussions on introducing Sharî'a rules.[11]

Solidarity born out of tragedy

> It would seem that the impact of the tsunami has if anything made for even better relations. People have reached out to one another irrespective of faith and even opened their homes to one another. Barriers had been broken, trust had been established.

With these words, Ginda P. Harahap, LWF Asia secretary, opened the LWF-sponsored seminar on "Dialogue in Life," 27–20 June 2006, in Medan.[12] The purpose of the seminar was to make use of the situation in which cooperation—healing and reconstruction during and after the tsunami—united people of the province and led to increased trust among them. A positive sense of solidarity with victims, relatives, the missing and the homeless became a learning experience, also for people from other parts of Asia.[13]

As one of the Muslim participants from Aceh, M. Syafi'i Anwar, said:

> We saw people from various faiths and different nations around the globe working hand in hand to reduce the suffering of the victims. Indeed, this

---

[11] Forlog was established as a reaction to the conflicts in the area. The forum consists of fifty members and has demonstrated its commitment to promoting pluralism and tolerance to prevent conflict by conducting activities promoted through public campaigns. It works for democratization, trauma counseling and peace journalism. The focus is on the medium and the grassroots levels. See **www.geocities.com/forlog**. In partnership with Peace Brigades International, they carried out a training of trainers workshop on conflict transformation in 2005 in Sulawesi. The workshop took place at the Center of Environmental Preservation Area. Participants included religious and community leaders who directly connected to various conflicts in South, West and Central Sulawesi as well as Ambon (Maluku). Follow-up peace building networks are currently being developed. Peace education programs, at **www.peacebrigades.org**.

[12] Two LWF study team members, Ingo Wulfhorst and Mark N. Swanson, took part in the conference.

[13] *Asia News* ran the following headline, "Brotherhood between Christians and Muslims Reborn in Post-tsunami Aceh," 29 March 2005. The words were said by the former Indonesian Minister for Human Rights, Hasballah M. Saad.

> strategy is beyond any religious, cultural, ethnic, economic or political boundaries. We saw how mosques, churches, synagogues, temples and other religious centers organized and mobilized their communities to raise funds and provide food, clothing and materials to the victims. We saw a similar phenomenon when an earthquake recently struck Yogyakarta. Again, people from various religions and nationalities were involved to reduce the fate of the victims.[14]

As a consequence of the devastating tsunami, Aceh became more open and relationships between inhabitants improved. As one inhabitant said, "Now God opened the door. Before it was closed." First, a peace agreement was brokered on 15 August 2005 in Helsinki. The rebel movement, Free Aceh (GAM), abandoned their demand for an independent Aceh and the Indonesian government agreed to extensive autonomy for Aceh's population. GAM disbanded their weapons to international monitors in Bandah Aceh and government troops withdrew from Aceh. Moreover, Aceh had to open up to hundreds of Indonesian and foreign aid organizations. Indonesian Islamists also came to Aceh to help, and the Islamic Defense Front and Indonesian Mujahedin Council participated side by side in the humanitarian work.

The post-tsunami period proved how overwhelming human solidarity can emerge in virtually no time and how the suffering of others can become one's own. The Acehnese population gained a new perspective that can be used to build a participatory social movement among people of different faiths and teach people of faith in other parts of the world to focus on humanity's real problems—environmental degradation, corruption and social violence.[15]

The common experiences during and after the disaster opened up space for Muslims and Christians to reflect together theologically. Since the tsunami, a number of dialogue meetings between Christians and Muslims have taken place during which participants explored the meaning of what occurred,

---

[14] "Pluralism and Dialogue in Life. An Indonesian Muslim Perspective," June 2006. Paper delivered at the seminar, "Dialogue in Life," 27–30 June 2006, Medan.

[15] Teuku Kemal Fasya, "Islam Sebagai Agama Hanif: Refleksi tentang Hubungan Muslim dan Non Muslim Pra dan Pasca-Tsunami di Aceh" [Islam as a Hanif religion: Reflections on the relationship between Muslims and non-Muslims before and after the tsunami in Aceh]. Paper delivered at the seminar "Dialogue in Life," 27–30 June 2006, Medan. Fasya teaches anthropology at the Faculty of Social and Political Sciences (FISIP) at the Universitas Malikkussaleh.

expressed solidarity and prayed for the victims. These meetings also helped eliminate or at least minimized misunderstandings present during the crisis.[16] Where was God? Why did God not intervene? Did all this happen as a punishment from God? The seminar in Medan provided an opportunity to reflect on such questions, and to go deeper into what had occurred.

A lesson for the world

Indonesia learned a considerable lesson from the tsunami and its aftermath. Humanitarian organizations from different parts of the world and different backgrounds came to the region to help and had to cooperate.[17] Collections were organized all over the world. In Nigeria for instance, the federal government set up a countrywide committee to collect contributions for the tsunami victims. [18] No single nation is able to solve its problems alone; it needs cooperation with other nations, including people from different cultural and religious backgrounds.

The poorest communities were hit hardest. The tsunami accentuated our common humanness and gave us the opportunity to reflect on how we act with compassion and how we set priorities.

Many people began to wonder whether the tsunami was a sign of Mother Nature striking back. Was it a warning to us that we are violating nature and one another and that we must stop being narrow-minded and short-sighted, that we must change our priorities and policies?

The tsunami forced us to reflect on the future and on our responsibility to understand and respect our interrelatedness, vulnerability and fragility. Therefore, we need to work together in solidarity for human

---

[16] Rev. Dr Jan S. Aritonang, Jakarta, "Dialogue in Life," keynote address from a Christian perspective, Medan, June 2006.

[17] On 17 January 2005, a press statement was released by Muslim and Christian religious leaders at a joint press conference concerning humanitarian work in Aceh in response to counterproductive polemics that had been reported in the *Washington Post.* Among other things, the statement clarified that all Christian communities in Indonesia reject all efforts to misuse humanitarian mission as a way of Christianizing people. The religious leaders furthermore appealed to all international Christian communities who wished to help children affected by the tsunami to work together with NU and Muhammadiyah. Press Release, "Interfaith Statement Concerning Humanitarian Work in Aceh," 19 January 2005, at **http://islamlib.com/en/page.php?page=article&id=755**

[18] Information given by LWF study team member, Nafisat Lawal Musa, Jos, Nigeria.

and environmental security instead of relying on military security. World leaders must respect life and set priorities accordingly.

Social disasters

The story of Christian-Muslim collaboration during and after the natural disasters in Aceh and Yogyakarta[19] has shown us that in situations where people of different faiths are confronted by the same frightening experience, it is easier to communicate and dialogue with one another.

Many similar stories could be told, not only from Africa and Asia, but also from Europe and the USA. Disastrous situations, where human relations or individual lives had been damaged but, at the same time, people have been brought together, have already been referred to. The violent conflicts in Jos, Poso and Maluku and the patient/medical staff counseling project in Copenhagen are such examples.

An example from my own experience is an interreligious group that met from 1989 to 2001 in the largest prison in Denmark, Vestre Fængsel, with about 550 inmates.[20] I was leading biweekly dialogue groups for Muslim and Christian prisoners, with the aim of breaking down barriers between Danes and foreigners, between Christians and Muslims. By getting to know one another and building friendships and fellowship across religious and cultural differences, they learned to appreciate each other.

Participants were able to share news, experiences and problems with on another and to discuss certain religious, existential and ethical topics related to their situations. Sometimes they prepared a meal together, especially in connection with religious celebrations. Every year, the group was in charge of Eid celebration for all Muslims in the prison, and one year they also arranged a prayer for all Christians and Muslims in the prison.

[19] 27 May 2006. Since then, a number of natural disasters have taken place: In July 2006, a tsunami struck West Java and killed at least 5,500 people; in March 2007, at least thirty-one people were killed by two earthquakes in the West Sumatran capital of Pandang. Added to this are a number of other disasters: a ferry sank in December 2006, an Adam Air passenger plane with 202 people onboard crashed, and in February 2007, fire broke out aboard a ferry and forty-two people were killed.

[20] Until the late 1990s, the prison included a number of asylum seekers who had arrived in Denmark without identity papers and therefore were confined until their identity was confirmed. Until 1989, these asylum seekers (up to one hundred) were kept in Vestre Fængsel, and subsequently gradually moved to a closed section in the camp for asylum seekers.

The group usually ended the discussions with a prayer, sometimes said by one of the prisoners. This was a very important for them, underlining the togetherness and giving them strength. At the same time, it fulfilled their need to express their feelings and experience and their religious involvement with other believers.

For many inmates, not feeling respected by others, or the loss of self-confidence, are big problems. Especially young Muslims often feel excluded, rootless and not wanted by society. They may have experienced discrimination at school, in youth clubs and on the job market and their families often misunderstand them. Even if Islam is not that important to them, because of the media's negative portrayals of Islam, they feel that they have to defend their faith. Therefore, it is important for prisoners to feel accepted, to be part of a group and to be taken seriously as human beings who can be trusted and are worth listening to.

Group counseling

We have seen that group counseling or conversation can be important for people from different backgrounds in situations where their lives have been shattered. In such a common space, persons can feel secure enough to be open, and strong fellowship and solidarity are created among participants.

During such meetings, it often was surprising how patient and tolerant the prisoners were of one another. They listened to one another's problems and histories of pain. This solidarity was also present when they were back in their wards. A Christian and a Muslim prisoner had asked to sit together in a cell in order together to study the Bible and the Qur'ân. Christians and Muslims would prepare themselves for the evening's session while exercising in the prison yard. They supported each other in different ways, and thus became counselors for one another, across religious boundaries, supporting each other in their attempts to restore their lost self-confidence.

Shared living conditions and common problems such as being locked up, loneliness, family and housing problems mean that Christians and Muslims are better able to understand and respect one another at a theological level. Sharing the same fears for the future and the struggle to survive makes it is easier to relate to and respect one another. At the same time, Christians and Muslims have a common starting point separating them from the other prisoners: faith in God, the value of prayer, human equality and forgiveness. These become more important than their differences. *Diapraxis* makes togetherness and dialogue meaningful and fruitful. People are able to assist each other, give one another strength to manage their time in prison and grow as human beings. This strengthens confidence in their own resources and values.

A shared destiny and common experiences in extreme life situations create deeper human solidarity; they open a space for dialogue. This is the lesson drawn from the tsunami and the prison situation. Does this mean that Christians and Muslims have to be locked up together or be confronted with earthquakes or other terrible disasters in order to understand one another and to work together in a meaningful way? No, of course not. It shows that the best way to create understanding and respect between human beings across different cultures and religions is to meet face-to-face, preferably in a common activity or under similar conditions, with a common goal in relation to shared challenges and needs. Genuine dialogue emerges out of experience where we learn from one another. It is not about including, excluding or generalizing. In a situation where our common humanness comes first and where we listen to the other's story of suffering and joy, changes can take place. We discover the face of the other and realize that we are equal before God.

Diapraxis for the common good

As indicated above, a paradigm shift in relation to dialogue activities has been taking place over the past few years. In 1988, I began to use the concept *diapraxis* (interreligious cooperation) as a tool not only a topic in Christian-Muslim dialogue. Already then I realized that those involved in interfaith relations were too focused on dialogue as a conversation about faith and too little on the interaction between human beings, involving larger relationships of living together, experiencing and working together.[21] The challenge of working together toward a more

[21] See my article, "From Diapraxis to Dialogue: Christian-Muslim Relations," in Lars Thunberg *et al.* (eds), *Dialogue in Action* (New Delhi: Prajna Publications 1988), pp. 277-93 and my doctoral thesis, Lissi Rasmussen, *Diapraksis og Dialog mellem Kristne og Muslimer* [Diapraxis and dialogue between Christians and Muslims] (Århus: Århus Universitetsforlag, 1997).

authentic and just international and national social order has become more difficult and more urgent. Unequal economic and political power relations and the exclusion and oppression of certain groups have resulted in reactions such as terrorist attacks. In addition, climate change, most likely due to human activity, contributes to natural disasters.

Increasingly, religion is being used politically and ideologically to incite hatred and violence. At the same time, conflicts have been globalized, especially after 9/11. A conflict in one part of the world may provoke acts of revenge elsewhere. Thus, it is increasingly important for religion to become a means of cooperation and peace, rather than part of the problem.

Cooperation between Christians and Muslims around common challenges is motivated by faith in God. As the familiar ecumenical slogan says, "doctrines divide, service unites." By serving together, Christians and Muslims can come to terms with their differences, find new approaches, develop a new openness and be challenged and inspired by others. It leads from monologue and apologetics to dialogue and contribution. Discovering the other's humanity enables us to move from concrete societal challenges to theological issues that can be tackled in more meaningful and constructive ways. Focusing on existential, concrete issues for the communities involved challenges the fundamental epistemological foundations on which we have operated in the past.

Common challenges

It is important that interreligious dialogue be proactive and not only reactive. Although dialogue often follows tensions or clashes where mistrust and hostility have been created, the long-term proactive work of creating possibilities for lasting cooperation is also needed. We should not limit cooperation to other religious people and groups but also, as in Nigeria and Indonesia, work with secular NGOs, human rights movements, trades unions, etc. Although the challenges and subsequent cooperation may not be religiously based, the motivation may be.

Christians and Muslims have a God centered vision with theologically motivated ethics. The five pillars of Islam support this understanding, and for Christians the life received from God has consequences for life with others. Thus, Christians and Muslims have a responsibility in relation to God. It matters how we treat other people and live our lives. According to Islam, faith implies submitting oneself as God's servant (Arabic: *abd*), and living one's life for God and for others. In Christianity, faith implies following in Jesus' footsteps and giving one's life for the sake of others.

The common ethical motivation is found in the belief that human beings are created by God, in the image of God, as God's *khalîfah*. From this follow respect for human life and nature and a responsibility for the common good (Arabic: *istislah maslaha*). For both Christians and Muslims, the idea of stewardship means that we do not have the right to destroy the rest of creation that witnesses to God's greatness.

Based on their respective theologies and traditions, Christians and Muslims hold widely shared concerns and obligations in certain areas.

Climate change—a common cause

One of the most important challenges humanity faces today is the threat posed by climate change. Amongst other factors, economic growth has exacerbated the overuse and degradation of natural resources and ecological systems. Global warming is thought to be most likely induced by human activity and in 2007, the UN Panel on Climate Change reported that its consequences are massive and unavoidable. Global cooperation is needed to understand and manage this situation.

The poor countries, which have only marginally contributed to the problem, will have to pay the highest price. Moreover, they do not have the capacity to mitigate the effects of global warming, having already a host of other problems to deal with. Drought and flooding will hit Africa and Southeast Asian countries such as Bangladesh, Pakistan and Vietnam the hardest. The natural disasters we have seen in Indonesia will not be the last ones.[22] The rich countries in the West will have to decide how best to adapt to the new situation and how to assist nature

[22] According to a report sponsored by the World Bank and Britain's Department for International Development (4 June 2007), Indonesia in particular is as risk. Rising sea levels would cause flooding in coastal farming areas, threatening food security and health. Thousands of farmers would have to look for other livelihoods. At the same time, the report states that activities in forestry (fire and deforestation) are the largest contributors to greenhouse gas emissions in Indonesia. *Antara News*, 5 June 2007.

to adjust. The rich countries cannot shun their responsibility. Property implies responsibility toward others. Global cooperation is needed to understand and manage this situation.

Christians and Muslims can contribute to the development of a more comprehensive worldview and sensitize people to the need to preserve the environment for future generations. Although both faiths have holistic views of what God has created, this is especially clear in Islam. The term *tawhîd* (monotheism) indicates the coherence and totality of the universe and the unity of past, present and future. God gives creation in *amâna* (trust) and human beings are responsible for the use or abuse of this trust. Creation has an inviolable integrity and order expressing God's wisdom, which must be guarded and respected.

The responsibility to care for God's creation (stewardship) is found in both religions and is an alternative to the utilitarian and materialistic view that has dominated Western culture and given rise to the ecological crisis. Created by God, nature has an ethical value in and of itself.[23]

Example 1:

Operation Noah is a community project of Christian Ecology Link in London that helps faith groups and civil society to respond to climate change. It has formed an "ethical energy partnership" with two suppliers of green electricity. Participants can sign a climate covenant promising to cut their greenhouse gas emissions and pressure governments to do the same.

www.christian-ecology.org.uk/noah

Example 2:

Cut the Carbon March, 2007. People from poor and rich countries, as well as from different religious backgrounds marched spreading the message "that climate change is not just a future problem, it is a current crisis for millions of poor people."

www.pressureworks.org/dosomething/index.html and **www.christianaid.org.uk/climatechange/index.htm**

[23] A number of conferences and seminars have already been held on these issues. For instance, the Forum for Religion and Ecology arranged a three-year series on "Religions of the World and Ecology" at Harvard Divinity School. On 24 July 2006, a seminar on "The Impacts of Climate Change on the Islamic World," was hosted at the Oxford Center for Islamic Studies (OCIS) in co-operation with the Policy Program of the James Martin Institute for Science and Civilization.

The prevention of violence and the promotion of justice and peace

Conflicts are an unavoidable part of life. We cannot remove conflicts but we can reduce violence. We can become better at handling conflict and make an effort to establish peace.

Example 1:

Conflict Resolution and Civil Society Capacity Building in Iraq is a three-year project (begun in early 2006) aiming at empowering Iraqis to deal with current and future challenges. This is done through a series of one-week workshops for Iraqi NGOs on conflict resolution and capacity building, the implementation of forty-five small-scale projects (primarily covering training in conflict resolution skills, conflict analysis, dealing with gender violence and negotiation skills), and one-week exchange workshops for youth on inter-sectarian violence in conflict and post-conflict society in Iraq and Lebanon.

The project is run by the Forum for Development, Culture and Dialogue (FDCD), a liaison between secular and religious groups based on interfaith cooperation.

www.fdcd.org

Example 2:

Through its **Peace Education Standing Commission,** the World Conference of Religions for Peace, has led the way in developing a curriculum to promote tolerance and mutual respect among young people and adults. In Israel, the project" Common Values/Different Sources" brought together Jews, Christians and Muslims to study sacred texts in search of shared values that they would practice in everyday life. The result was a book for use in schools.

www.religionsforpeace.org

Work for equal rights and recognition

It is a challenge for Christians and Muslims alike to make politicians and societies aware of their responsibility to counteract discrimination, to reduce tensions and mutual mistrust and to include rather than exclude certain groups in society. They must work together for equal rights in relation to gender, age, disability, etc.

Example 1:

Rahima, the Center for Education and Information on Islam and Women's Rights Issues, Indonesia, is an NGO that focuses on empowering grassroots Muslim women through awareness raising, dissemination of information to local Muslim groups, and *pesantrens*, seminars, workshops and discussions. Furthermore, the organization opposes an overly strict interpretation of Sharî'a and campaigns for better representation of women in politics and the media.

In recent years, **Rahima** has extended its network to women's NGOs, Islamic women's organizations, interfaith women's groups, etc. For instance, the organization has worked closely with Tim Relawan untuk Kemanusiaan (Voluntary Team for Humanity), a coalition of various Indonesian NGOs headed by the Roman Catholic priest, Sandyawan Sumardi.

www.rahima.or.id

Example 2:

Al Andalus Islamic Studies Institute in Hama, attached to the Islamic Center in Damascus, focuses on education and consultancy, and has a number of social activities for women, children, the sick and the poor. Their aim is to improve living conditions and to solve common problems of both Christians and Muslims.

www.altajdeed.org

Improvement of socioeconomic conditions

Many countries in Africa and in Asia face large-scale poverty and corruption. This leads to conflicts among people. Christians and Muslims are responsible for alleviating poverty, unemployment, combating corruption and assisting people in need. By working together for social and economic justice, we can learn from each other's experiences and ethics.

Example 1:

The **Coptic Evangelical Organization for Social Services** (CEOSS) in Cairo runs a project to improve fishermen's lives in five villages along the Nile in Ben Suef, 200 km south of Cairo. Its aim is awareness and capacity building in the villages.

Community Based Organizations (CBOs) are established to play a role in society and to administer public funds honestly and diligently. Christians and Muslims work together to assist people, regardless of their religious affiliation, to improve their living conditions.

www.ceoss.org.eg

Example 2:

Since 1998, the Christian organization, **Indonesian Dian Mandiri Foundation** (DIMAN) has specialized in allocating microcredit loans. The majority of the loans have been granted to Muslim saving clubs in the poorer areas of Jakarta and the rural surroundings. Through free loans, training, mentoring and leadership development they seek to empower the poor, in particular women, to establish their own businesses. Ninety-five percent of the clients are Muslims who have much confidence in the organization, whose main principles are transparency, integrity, accountability and solidarity. They end meetings with a common prayer.

www.dianmandiri.com

Education and training

There is a need for books and other materials with a pluralistic approach in order for schools and libraries to promote a democratic understanding that value diversity and inclusivity. Training in anti-discrimination and citizenship is crucial.

Example 1:

Through its outreach education and training program, the **Interfaith Youth Core** (IFYC) in Chicago seeks to equip and mobilize the next generation of young leaders in the interfaith movement. The organization trains, supports and networks young leaders in interfaith service and dialogue. Since 2002, IFYC staff have been working with 4,200 students in colleges, universities and schools. Three hundred students have been trained to be interfaith youth service organizers and 1,300 students have been involved in their events. IFYC can help set up training and workshops or talk on campuses or in other communities.

www.ifyc.org

Example 2:

The **Religious Diversity & Anti-Discrimination Training** project in Europe seeks to confront prejudice and discrimination and to develop individual skills and institutional strategies for creating inclusive intercultural environments. Using a highly interactive and participatory methodology, it seeks to provide adult educators with tools for situations where religious diversity and discrimination are of concern.

www.ceji.org/education/subject.php

The mass media

Editors and journalists need to be better informed about Islam and Christianity in order to avoid tendentious, one-sided reporting. Media coverage should be accurate and responsible. Enemy images must be avoided and coverage should be as impartial and objective as possible. Muslim and Christian representatives should be selected in responsible and nuanced ways and made more visible in the media. Cooperation between the media and minority groups should be encouraged. Opinion polls should be viewed critically. A culture of authentic, searching, honest and guileless debate is needed.

Example 1:

The **Center for Arab-West Understanding** (CAWU) publishes the independent weekly electronic magazine, *Arab-West Report*, dedicated to fostering understanding between the Arab world and the West. Arabic newspaper articles are translated into English, as are editorials commenting on controversial issues or issues that have been misrepresented by various media. The *Arab-West Report* has over 12,000 articles and reports dating back to 1997 in its electronic archive.

www.arabwestreport.info

Example 2:

In 2007, the **Christian Muslim Forum**, established in 2005 by representatives of Christian and Muslim communities in England, organized a one-day conference at the BBC's London offices for Christian, Muslim and Hindu pupils from different schools in Birmingham. Alongside media professionals, they explored the relationship between what they see, hear and read in the media and their own everyday experiences. Stories such as the wearing of the veil and how terrorism and Muslims are being reported on television, radio, the Internet and newspapers were analyzed. Pupils learned how the media works, wrote their own reports, interviewed journalists and examined the effect the media has on young people.

www.christianmuslimforum.org

Social space for interaction

Centers for dialogue and cooperation, where face-to-face encounters between the mainstream and minority populations can take place on equal terms and friendship, trust and respect be built, should be supported and established. It is important to create spaces where Muslims and Christians can engage in social activities and projects and jointly work on resolving common problems. Politicians and public authorities should be urged to provide financial support for initiatives to promote interaction between minorities and the majority. Moreover, minority religions must be legally recognized.

Example 1:

At the beginning of 2007, the **International Rescue Committee** (IRC) in Indonesia and the Consortium for Assistance and Recovery towards Development in Indonesia organized a sports event to help bridge the gap between the Christian and Muslim communities in Maluku Province.

Over 400 Muslim and Christian youths from different villages came together to play volleyball, football and tug-of-war. Some were also involved in the cleaning and decorating of mosques and churches. A similar program was run in Central Sulawesi in order to establish and support youth groups with the aim of strengthening ties between Christian and Muslim youth.

www.theirc.org

Example 2:

The **Interfaith Encounter Association** in Israel has formed and maintained interfaith groups or centers across the country that bring together neighboring communities. Each center is led by a coordinating team with one person from each community and becomes a “mini-community” exemplifying relations of mutual respect and friendship. For the surrounding community, the groups then act as models for how people of different faiths can live side by side in peace. Monthly sessions of faith study are held. Groups for women and youth operate in the same way.

www.interfaith-encounter.org

Common local challenges

There are numerous local challenges that Christians and Muslims can take up jointly.

Example 1:

The **Dialogue Project,** initiated in March 2007 by the Speaking Across Differences Program in Brownstone, Brooklyn (USA), is an opportunity for long-term residents and newcomers to talk face-to-face about their lives, neighborhoods and issues affecting their daily lives. The program is carried out in collaboration with a large number of community partners, religious and secular. The project seeks to create confidential space that fosters a sense of safety, allowing participants to speak honestly while also listening to the opinions of others.

www.thedialogueproject.org

Example 2:

Twin Communities of Congregations and Mosques in Nørrebro, is a project initiated by the IKS in Copenhagen. A number of communities are being established in order for Christians and Muslims to discuss problems, especially in relation to children and youth. Collaboration between public schools and Muslim private schools has been established with the support of the project in order to tackle some of the local problems, especially the harassment of children by children. Religion is used as a tool.

www.ikstudiecenter.dk

Inclusive citizenship

Since the 1980s, there has been renewed interest in "citizenship." It is a dynamic, integrative and inclusive concept whose content is defined not in terms of culture and difference but in terms of the rights and duties of every individual. The emphasis is on the horizontal, inviting collective action. Citizenship emphasizes the individual rather than culture, ethnicity and religion. Its starting point is society as a common project. Citizens are free in relation to the state and one another and free to interact and be affected by one another. Understood in this context, the term citizenship has two main aspects:

Status: the formal, negative, passive aspect (what is done to you), i.e., civil, political and social rights (to be treated justly and fairly).

Role: the normative, positive, active aspect (what you receive or achieve), i.e., social equality, political participation, social obligations to contribute to the development of society, mental representation—to do and have a value as a human being and have a sense of belonging and loyalty.[24]

In the 1990s, European countries placed more emphasis on "active citizenship," closely linked to identity and the way in which people perceive themselves. Citizenship and identity shape each other. In Asian and African countries, religion is a crucial factor in understanding citizenship.

In most countries, the harassment of one or more minorities seems to be inevitable. Many human beings feel uneasy with and are perhaps even intolerant of people who are different in terms of appearance, values, behavior, religion, etc. Victimization and scapegoating occur.

The question is how these problems are handled. Are they dealt with constructively so that people learn to regard these differences as positive, as an enrichment and dynamic development, or are they tackled destructively and used instead to generate fear? The inclination to create dichotomies is a human phenomenon. If we do not address this inclination, it may turn into a growing gap, a polarization that may lead to mistrust and even hate between "Us" and "Them," as the three conflict stories in this book indicate.

The lack of citizenship rights has been one of the root causes of the conflicts in all three countries. At the same time, it could be said that citizenship as an inclusive discourse is a key ingredient for constructing bridges. To work for inclusive and pluralist citizenship and equal recognition challenges Christian-Muslim cooperation nationally and internationally.[25] It means doing away with or limiting the categories of "indigene vs settler" and "Us vs Them," and counteracting socioeconomic conflicts and power struggles. To have a sense of belonging, dignity and value as a citizen is important for everyone. Therefore, we are challenged to educate one another to be citizens so as to make room for one

[24] On various theories of citizenship, see John Hoffman, *Citizenship Beyond* (London: Sage Publications, 2004) and K. Faulks, *Citizenship* (London/New York: Routledge, 2000).

[25] Inclusive citizenship refers to the extent to which people can claim rights and whether these rights are equal for all people regardless of their background, including rights to equal participation in society. Exclusive citizenship refers to the extent to which some citizens are denied rights and benefits, possibilities for contributing to the development of society and a sense of belonging. On exclusive citizenship, see Faulks, *ibid.*, p. 3.

another and one another's freedom and rights in our common political and social communities.[26]

Citizenship in Nigeria and Indonesia

We have seen how the indigene-settler dichotomy has led to tensions and later conflicts, especially since 1979 when the indigeneity clause was included in Nigerian public law. The categories of indigenes, settlers, etc., have undermined the very essence of Nigerian citizenship. To be born or to work one's entire life in a place does not automatically qualify a person as a citizen of the country. One's citizenship is based on one's lineage. Citizenship has become ethnicized. This raises the question of citizen rights: Who is a citizen of Nigeria? What does it entail? What does it mean to be a Nigerian?

Thus, the main issue in Nigeria today is the question of national unity, how to hold Nigeria together as one nation and how to create loyalty in a country marked by cultural, religious and geographical heterogeneity. A strong ethno-regionalism that excludes the "other" plays a prominent role in politics; there are fears that one ethnic/regional/religious group dominates the other. Therefore, constructing a pan-Nigerian identity based on equality of all citizens and common political practice is vital.

The question of national unity has become even more urgent after the April 2007 election of the Muslim President, Umaru Musa Yar'Ardua. Before the elections, many Nigerians claimed that the future president's religion and ethnicity should not matter as long as he is competent (i.e., honest) and shows the aptitude to rule. Moreover, people should vote as Nigerian citizens and for democracy for the whole people.

Today, many Christians fear that having a Muslim president could lead to the Islamization of the South, and that it will aggravate the situation of Christians in Northern Nigeria. This would erode the entire nation's liberty. It is the new government's task to create a more conducive en-

[26] A number of social scientists have dealt with the concept of citizenship and belonging. See for instance the French sociologist Dominique Schnapper, *Community of Citizens. On the Modern Idea of Nationality* (New Brunswick, N.J.: Transaction Publishers, 1998) and Stephen Castles and Alastair Davidson, *Citizenship and Migration: Globalization and the Politics of Belonging* (London: Macmillan, 2000).

vironment, to resolve internal conflicts and to restore its credentials as a trustworthy government and peacemaker.

In Indonesia, the ideology of *Pancasila* has been one of the factors contributing to cooperation, unity and dialogue and has in this way promoted a sense of shared citizenship among the population. However, the sense of shared citizenship, of belonging and being loyal to the nation, has been challenged by regional problems and struggles for political autonomy. Furthermore, a certain Islamic radicalism, connected to power relationships outside the country and socioeconomic inequalities within it, necessitates an emphasis on inclusive citizenship.[27] The debates on citizenship in Indonesia, therefore, have less frequently focused on whether citizen rights should be differentiated by ethnicity (as in Nigeria) but rather on whether they should be differentiated by religion.[28]

Citizenship and recognition in Denmark

Denmark is formally a democracy and in many ways, ethnic minorities have the same juridical rights as the rest of the population. However, there is no democratic process within society that ensures mutual respect and the inclusion of everyone as equal citizens.

For instance, political leaders still do not regard and address all citizens as equal actors in society. Exclusive citizenship and a lack of solidarity and social recognition of minorities are among the main problems. Consequently, certain symptoms (the cartoon affair) show us that minorities have no civic awareness and feel that they are not valued as human beings. In many ways, Denmark is marked by a national self-sufficiency that fails to recognize the value of diversity and multiple citizenship and the necessity of international accountability and ethical conduct. Working toward the inclusion of all citizens as equal actors in a society is therefore one of the most important challenges faced by Christian-Muslim collaboration in Denmark, as in many other European countries.

[27] On citizenship in Indonesia, see Robert W. Hefner (ed.) *The Politics of Multiculturalism: Pluralism and Citizenship in Malaysia, Singapore, and Indonesia* (Honolulu: University of Hawaii Press, 2001).

[28] Robert W. Hefner, "Introduction: Multiculturalism and Citizenship in Malaysia, Singapore, and Indonesia," in Hefner, *ibid.*, p. 34.

Recognition is the precondition for every human being to develop a socially well functioning identity. It has to be reciprocal in order to work. Everyone must be subject to equal conditions in order to become an active participant in society and to be aware of being a moral person.[29] Absence of recognition can lead to a loss of personality. Therefore, when Muslim citizens are seen as foreigners or problems and are excluded because they are Islamic, they may look for alternative cultures or means of recognition and acceptance.[30]

The development of parallel societies or subcultures among youths, even criminal gangs or extremist religious-political movements, is a symptom of this marginalization and lack of recognition. When youths from ethnic minorities feel that they are not recognized by society and are unwanted, they may develop a profound anger against society. They may segregate themselves and join other young people in the same situation. In order to regain self-confidence they must be integrated into the social community on an equal footing with the rest of society.

This requires a new inclusive rhetoric in the public debate and among political leaders. Political authorities and the media should begin to treat all individuals in terms of citizenship and not on the basis of their religious or cultural identities. As Christians and Muslims believing in solidarity and equality among human beings, our common challenge is to work together for solidarity and recognition in our societies and to view diversity as positive.

Religion and citizenship

Over the past decades, Muslims have increasingly discussed the compatibility of Islam with universal concepts such as democracy, human rights and citizenship. The discussions have not only been related to Muslims living as minorities in non-Muslim surroundings but have also

[29] This idea of equality and reciprocity in relation to citizenship and recognition forms a part of J. Rawls' notion of "overlapping consensus" or "justice of fairness" which also includes the principle of freedom of religion and equal liberty of conscience.

[30] *Cf.* Axel Honneth, *The Struggle for Recognition—the Moral Grammar of Social Conflicts* (Cambridge: Polity Press, 1996). See also Amy Gutmann (ed.), *Multiculturalism: Examining the Politics of Recognition* (Princeton NJ: Princeton University Press, 1994).

taken place in countries with a Muslim majority. For instance, in Egypt many Islamists argue that citizenship is not only compatible with Islam but that citizenship is an expression of the very essence of Islam.[31]

Furthermore, a number of modern Muslim thinkers such as Abdolkarim Soroush (Iran), Ahmad Mousalli (Lebanon), Abdullahi Ahmed An-Na'im (Sudan-USA) and Tariq Ramadan (Europe) have made attempts to articulate the concept of citizenship, most of them on the basis of Islamic principles.[32] For them, citizenship means equal political and social participation in a pluralist democracy. They emphasize the contextuality of citizenship, which they see as a process. These Muslims would agree with most Christians that exercising one's citizenship should not be dictated by religion but inspired by religious convictions. If religion were to be discredited or disqualified, pushed out of society and out of ethical debates, political life would be impoverished. Life is taken out of it and society would become poorer.

In Denmark, as in most other European countries, there is the tendency among many politicians and other opinion makers to demand the total separation of citizenship from religion. It is an important challenge for Christians and Muslims to struggle for an open political society based on pluralist principles, where religion is not relegated to the private sphere or misused for political purposes. One strategy in this case could be to promote cooperation between religious and humanitarian organizations working for human rights, equal treatment and reconciliation.

---

[31] Rachel M. Scott, "Contextual Citizenship in Modern Islamic Thought," in *Islam and Christian-Muslim Relations*, vol. 18 (1 January 2007), p. 5. See also Andrew F. March, "The Demands of Citizenship: Translating Political Liberalism into the Language of Islam," in *Journal of Muslim Minority Affairs*, vol. 25, no. 3 (December 2005).

[32] Abdolkarim Soroush, *Reason, Freedom, and Democracy in Islam: Essential Writings of Abdolkarim Soroush* (Oxford: Oxford University Press, 2000); Ahmad Mousalli, *The Islamic Quest for Democracy, Pluralism and Human Rights* (Gainesville, FL: University Press of Florida, 2003); Abdullahi Ahmed An-Na'im, *Toward an Islamic Reformation: Civil Liberties, Human Rights, and International Law* (Syracuse, NY: Syracuse University Press, 1996); Tariq Ramadan, *Western Muslims and the Future of Islam* (Oxford: Oxford University Press, 2004), pp. 165-171. Tariq Ramadan even speaks about Sharî'a as an "ethics of citizenship."

Civil society and active citizens

The term civil society has different meanings in different theoretical traditions. Here it is defined as "a sphere, sector or culture that binds together the people in a country and acts as intermediary between individuals, the state and the private sector."[33] Thus, civil society refers to public (not official) organizations and organs, cultural, educational, religious, etc. These enable individuals to discuss matters of public importance and to take part in social life outside governmental control. Civil society helps guarantee pluralism.

In Nigeria, as well as in Indonesia, there is a great need to build up a strong civil society. Especially in Nigeria, it is crucial that a more inclusive and participatory form of governance is developed so that a sense unity and belonging among heterogeneous groups in the state can be created. Our analysis of and experiences in Nigeria have shown that this development has to come from below, through the empowerment of citizens, groups and NGOs. A strong civil society can object to undemocratic political governance and pave the way for a more equally distributed development.

However, as Robert W. Hefner argues,

> To survive and thrive over the long run civil society requires a civilized state. By a civilized state I mean a state that is powerful enough to support and defend the rights of citizens and minorities in society, while sufficiently balanced and self-limiting so as not to overstep its civic-mediating role.[34]

According to Hefner, there must be synergy between state and society that deepens the democratic disposition of each. This synergy does not seem to be in sight in Nigeria. In the meantime, the aim must be to build

---

[33] Lis Dhundale and Erik André Andersen (eds), *Revisiting the Role of Civil Society in the Promotion of Human Rights* (Copenhagen: The Danish Institute for Human Rights, 2004), p. 21. Robert W. Hefner goes further and defines civil society as referring "to the network of mediating citizen organizations between the state and the family, in which civil society proponents hope citizens learn the democratic habits of participation, free expression, and tolerance." "Disintegration or Democratization? Muslim-Christian Violence and the Future of Indonesia," in *SUM Report No. 9* (University of Oslo: Centre for Development and Environment, 2000), p. 41.

[34] Hefner, *op.cit.* (note 27), p. 48.

a civil society that can challenge the new government to improve the economy so that most Nigerians benefit from the country's wealth, and for the inclusion of all major ethnic and religious groups in the future development of society. Citizens can only learn to participate, develop initiative and be responsible and loyal if their leaders live up to their responsibility to lead the country for the benefit of all.

Citizenship training

Belonging to a community, feeling secure in one's identity and having room to be oneself are important for every citizen. How can we achieve this? How can we learn to live and work together? One of the methods would be through "civic education" or "citizenship training" to strengthen the individual's universal values and enable citizens in conjunction with others to take the future into their own hands. Citizenship training should strengthen active citizenship in organizations, institutions and businesses.

It is important that schools reflect the plurality of views on life and values and emphasize the benefits of such. The religious dimension of self-identity can be seen as something that unites rather than divides. If we can create a sense of fundamental solidarity in the classroom among pupils from different backgrounds, the foundation will be laid for a society built on inclusive citizenship.

Everyone should be able to have training in citizenship, practical democracy and human rights and thus be enabled to create meaning and coherence in relation to multiple identities. The media could be involved in the process of developing a culture of social citizenship that can build bridges instead of walls.

In Denmark, a master program in citizenship was introduced at the Danish University of Education,[35] which includes historical-political and educational-philosophical dimensions as well as ethical and universal perspectives. It focuses on a number of educational and didactic problems regarding citizenship education and methodologies for analyzing politi-

[35] Web site, **www.dpu.dk/master**

cal discourse, cultural narratives, self-understanding, organizational practice and the clarification of values.

In 2002, citizenship education became part of the national curriculum in state schools in Britain.[36] In 2007, it was included in the new teacher's training program in Denmark in combination with religious knowledge and philosophy of life.[37] The goal is to prepare pupils to participate freely, equally and democratically in society. Furthermore, it seeks to develop their critical ability, enable them to take a stand, act responsibly when encountering new challenges and to live together respectful of one another's values and norms. The subject includes historical, legal, political, social and cultural aspects of citizenship. Also dealt with are ethical problems and dilemmas in relation to education of democratic citizenship.

Because of their power to help preserve or undermine cultural space or collective identity, the mass media create and sustain a common public culture. They could also play a positive role in promoting inclusiveness through educational TV and radio programs tackling such issues as socioeconomic disadvantage. Citizenship education could be channeled through the media. The effect of globalization, Westernization and the "multiculturalization" of democracy and citizenship are important themes to be dealt with.

Global citizenship and human rights

There are different forms and levels of citizenship. For instance, we are all "environmental citizens." Only few global institutions (if any) are able to ensure "environmental citizenship," because most institutions are organized in terms of nation states and linked to national interests.

Today, citizenship at the national, regional and international levels is closely interrelated. Inequalities between nations affect international relationships. As we have seen during the cartoon crisis and in the reac-

---

[36] Citizenship education is taught part of the national school curriculum and as such is compulsory in state schools.

[37] *Bekendtgørelse om uddannelse til professions bachelor som skolelærer* [Curriculum for teachers' training], *BEK*, no. 219 (12 March 2007).

tions of Muslims to the Pope's controversial speech,[38] remote problems become local problems and are used as an excuse to protest against those who have caused the problem.

Many Muslims regard the Universal Declaration of Human Rights as a Western invention which has been imposed on them. They accuse the West of interfering in the affairs of other countries and of one-sidedly accusing Muslim countries of violating human rights. In this way, the West makes Muslims feel inferior. It is seen to assume the role of global custodian of human rights and as taking away their right to be equal citizens in the international community, which is identified with the USA.

Globalization and citizenship are closely related. A global ethics of care and a consensus on human rights are needed that can be accepted across cultures and religions.[39] That means, for example, an Islamic language of human rights that is consonant with the universal discourse. Questions such as what it means to be a human being, how religion can promote human rights and strengthen the position of ethics should be addressed and discussed in Muslim circles. Thus it is not the validity of human rights as such that is at issue, but rather the question of how to base them on an international morality compatible with the norms and values also of non-Western civilizations.

Global democracy?

Who controls the public space for global citizenship? Who decides what is legitimate? Do we have a global democracy? Are we all full members in the global order, or are some marginalized? It is important that we deal with these fundamental questions of inclusion and exclusion, especially if we are to get at the roots of terrorism.

In light of the fact that we in the West claim that one of our distinguishing features is inclusive pluralism, it is important that we include Muslims and other parts of the world more positively. This cannot be done

[38] Pope Benedict XVI's Regensburg lecture, 12 September 2006, on "Faith, Reason and the University. Memories and Reflection," in which the Pope quoted a fourteenth-century Christian emperor who said that the Prophet Muhammad had brought the world only "evil and inhuman" things.

[39] On global moral, see Amartya Sen, *Identity and Violence: The Illusion of Destiny (Issues of our Time)* (New York: W. W. Norton, 2006).

by military force and threats of economic sanctions but by promoting a culture of peace. Human and environmental security must substituted for military security.

Inequality in terms of control, influence and human welfare are the root causes of many of the problems we are facing in the world today, including terrorism. Through the Internet and satellite television, these discrepancies have become much more "visible" in the world's poorer countries. It has become much more evident that the affluent Western world lacks global consciousness and empathy.

The lack of global citizenship means a lack of global responsibility. Democracy remains limited to nation states. We need a global forum or organ (not just the interstate organ of the UN) through we can enforce our common values and secure a more just distribution of power and goods.[40] Acts of terrorism show that this development cannot continue. The global agenda cannot continue to be entirely set by the Western world (especially the USA). We need what the German sociologist Ulrich Beck calls a "global cosmopolis" as an alternative to the *Pax Americana*.[41]

Interfaith cooperation aims at establishing fundamental trust between human beings. As Christians and Muslims, we must be at the forefront of the struggle to find wise ways of achieving more democratic types of citizenship and more equitable international relations.

Tolerance or hospitality?

As we have seen, trans-cultural spaces have increasingly been created by migration, communication and information technologies. Cultural, ethnic and religious borders have become porous and we have multiple identities. Therefore, religious and cultural encounters take place between people who belong to the same global community but are influenced by different cultural and religious values. This is perhaps one of the reasons why we build dividing walls. We fear losing our identity when it is no longer so clear-cut. Religion is not an easily defined and agreed upon

---

[40] Zygmunt Baumann has strongly advocated this in several of his books, for instance, *The Individualized Society* (Cambridge: Polity Press, 2001), p. 83ff.

[41] Ulrich Beck, *The Cosmopolitan Vision* (Cambridge: Polity Press, 2006), p. 132.

static entity, but changeable and variable, as is human identity. We need new, much more inclusive and equal paradigms of interaction.

In a collection of interviews,[42] the French philosopher, Jacques Derrida, stated that he preferred the concept of hospitality to the term tolerance. For Derrida, tolerance is a patronizing gesture, a condescending recognition on the side of the strong. You are allowed to be present in my home but do not forget that you are in my home. It is a conditioned hospitality in a host-guest relationship. The condition is one-sided, namely that the tolerated guest submits to the premises of the tolerant host.

Tolerance means that one part is subjected to the other and not necessarily appreciated or respected. There is neither reciprocity nor active respect of the other. You can tolerate the other without knowing him or her. Genuine hospitality, on the contrary, means that there are not guests but only hosts. It is this type of mutual hospitality that must be a helpful paradigm and the goal of our bridge building. This is what inclusive citizenship implies.

This means that to think in the categories of "Us vs Them," or "We" are tolerating "Them," no longer makes sense. It is not only stigmatizing but also outdated. It is increasingly impossible to speak about culture and ethnicity in either/or terms. We need to refer to them in relational terms. Religion is a part of this cultural and ethnic self-understanding. It not only has to do with God, but also with experience and perspectives on life and identity. At the same time, it has ever less to do with a specific territory or culture.

The paradigm we need in our postmodern societies must express the new challenge to be conscious of the interplay between different cultures and religions. This is an inclusive paradigm that relates to others not as static and confined traditional groups, closed off in fixed and dividing identities, but reflects the weaving together of life, nationally and internationally, and the complexities of overlapping identities. This must be a paradigm where multiple spaces can be created and where people meet in order to work together in search of the good life.

---

[42] Giovanna Borradori, *Philosophy in a Time of Terror. Dialogues with Jürgen Habermas and Jacques Derrida* (Chicago: University of Chicago Press, 2003).

Co-citizenship—a promise for the future

One year after the terror attacks on the USA, Desmond Tutu said in an interview:

> When God created us he made sure that none of us is self-sufficient. Sometimes one feels like crying when one sees how blind the world is to the fact that we belong together. This is what God has tried to teach us right from the beginning: we belong all of us to one humanity.[43]

The problem is that we repeatedly behave as if we were self-sufficient—often at the expense of others. Therefore, we need an approach to promote inclusive, shared and equal citizenship appropriate to a pluralistic society. The cartoon affair and its aftermath highlighted the intercultural realities of the modern globalized world. We are interdependent, and it is not enough merely to understand our own culture and values. We also have to try to understand other cultures and take seriously how they understand us.

In this way, globalization generates new forms of citizenship and global practices may transform what it means to be a human being. In a globalized world, with less emphasis on the nation-state and national independence, new approaches to citizenship are needed that take account of collective and multiple citizenship. These new challenges facing the nation-state model affect not only the nation-states of Europe and North America but also nation building in Asia, Africa and Latin America. Becoming a citizen can no longer only depend on membership in a community or in one or more cultural groups, but must be based on residence in a state's territory.

This new approach also entails that citizenship can no longer be based on antagonism between those in- and those outside. The idea of multiple citizenship, including the duties and rights that this implies, must be further developed. Our task is to act according to this new concept of citizenship that does not presuppose an enemy, an "other," but rather includes the other as a necessary part of who we are. Co-citizenship

[43] Interview, "Desmond Tutu: 'Vi har intet laert'" [We have learned nothing], in the daily *Politiken*, 11 September 2002.

as a plural and many faceted term is not a threat but a promise of our common future.

From Walls to Bridges: An Afterword[1]

Mark N. Swanson and Ingo Wulfhorst

There are long stretches of this book that make for dispiriting reading. The case studies that have been presented contain so many instances of perverse speech, betrayed hopes, rampant fears and mindless violence that one begins to wonder whether there is in fact anything constructive that can be done, or whether the more hopeful passages of the book are merely whistling in the wind. While readers committed to interfaith dialogue may note with some relief that most of the conflicts described in these pages are not in the first place religious in nature, the sense of relief is fleeting. It quickly becomes clear that religion does come to play a role in these conflicts, too often one of motivating people to engage in verbal or even physical violence. And furthermore, an analysis of the underlying causes of conflict uncovers problems that seem simply intractable. How can people of faith help to manage conflicts that are brought about by population pressures on limited land (itself suffering from the effects of environmental degradation and global warming), or poverty fueled competition for scarce resources (e.g., a zero-sum scramble to get access to "the national cake"), or demographic changes that are seen as a threat to one's very identity? What can be done when traditional leadership, governments, politicians and the media either fail to contain and adjudicate conflicts, or in fact play a role in pouring fuel on the fires that are ignited?

The following is an attempt to summarize and hold together the various stories, reflections and dialogue models in this book by focusing on some key concepts and principles.

---

[1] This chapter has been abridged from the author' original text. For a more explicitly Christian theological reflection on some of the matters treated here, see Mark Swanson's contribution to the LWF book, Simone Sinn (ed.), *Deepening Faith, Hope and Love in Relation to Neighbors of Other Faiths*, to be published in late 2007.

Genuine conversation

Throughout this study we have encountered various kinds of speech. Examples of "othering" speech have been all too common, and while this has been especially well documented in the Danish study, much of what has been discovered there can be applied to the other cases as well, and to conflicts throughout the world. We have seen how an alliance of politicians, major media outlets and opinion-makers (including religious figures) can build "a meta-discourse living a life of its own and devising its own reality" in which demeaning and even demonizing characterizations of the other are simply normalized. An echo chamber is created in which labeling others—as a "plague," "a threat," "infidels," "decadent," "medieval," "parasites"—becomes a normal part of speech. Thus, quite respectable people may join in, or at least see it as representing a "concern" that is "understandable" and has to be respected.

One obvious characteristic of this echo chamber speech is that it is always about the other; no real conversation is sought. When this speech occasionally is addressed to the other, it is often either in the form of scolding or in the form of test questions for which either a "yes" or a "no" is demanded, with no nuancing possible. The other may make an attempt to break into the monologue, but the experience is usually frustrating; "they often do not feel acknowledged and listened to."

Christians and Muslims should have no difficulty to discern what is wrong with this kind of speech. In both traditions, the God who speaks the world into being begins a conversation, not a monologue. God speaks to the human creatures, not merely about them; human words are heard. The divine-human conversation comes to a climax, for Muslims in the Qur'ân as God's revealed Word, for Christians in the incarnation of the Word.

The preceding chapters are full of signs of hope for the possibility of genuine conversation, despite the powerful forces that would control discourse and "steal" it from the grass roots. Christians and Muslims in each of the places studied have found one another and have come to be engaged in dialogue at a variety of levels, e.g., the formal dialogue meetings of the Association of Christian-Muslim Mutual Relations in Nigeria, dialogue opportunities brought about by ministries in hospitals and prisons in Denmark, and conversations—sometimes at a very deep theological level–in the wake of shared tragedy in Aceh and Nias. As

Christians and Muslims strive together to maintain or revive patterns of life together that have served well for generations, or as they confront situations "where life has been shattered," they may hope for genuine conversation. The places where such conversation takes place may seem, at times, to be islands in a sea of poisonous discourse. But as islands, they will be places of refuge for many people, of different faiths, who seek a wholesome and health giving environment.

Genuine hospitality

The concepts of "space" and "room" are important in the previous chapters. Kofi Annan's observation (concerning the cartoon crisis) that "present conflicts and misunderstandings have more to do with proximity than with distance" is borne out by several of the case studies of this book. Contesting for space (or, conflicts within a confined space) between "indigenous" populations on the one hand, and immigrants (Denmark), "settlers" (Plateau State), or transmigrants (Sulawesi, Maluku) on the other, have taken on "a religious coloration." A frequently expressed challenge and aspiration is that we "make room for each other," allow everyone to "have room to be oneself," and hold out a welcome (and a protest): "There is still room in the inn." It ought to be possible for people to feel at home.

"Making room" for others, helping them to feel "at home," are central to the practice of hospitality—a practice with deep roots in both Christian and Islamic traditions. The roots are so deep, in fact, that few people want to be accused of being inhospitable—although we have heard of proposals (in Indonesia) to introduce stricter boundaries between communities with long-standing traditions of mutual hospitality, e.g., by forbidding participation in one another's holiday celebrations. More frequently, we have heard of the way in which the concept of hospitality is manipulated in such a way so as to "blame the guest" for any difficulties in the relationship. For example, a political leader of the "indigenes" in Jos could say, "Our problem here today is that … the tenant is becoming very unruly." Guests should follow the rules! In Denmark, some have interpreted the rules to include a readiness "to put up with scorn, mockery and ridicule." According to this logic, the caricatures of the Prophet Muhammad were a sort of welcome: "We are integrating you into the Danish tradition of satire."

During its case studies, the LWF team experienced gracious hospitality from Christians and Muslims in Denmark, Indonesia and Nigeria. But more than that, we heard stories of the everyday mutual hospitality of people engaged in a "dialogue of life," of intentional efforts to provide hospitality to immigrants (particularly in Denmark), and of extraordinary hospitality in grave situations: a church in Copenhagen became a place of sanctuary, Christian and Muslim neighbors protected one another during the crises in Jos, and in one instance created a human chain around a ward of the city so as to create safe space for its inhabitants. In all three cases, we heard of instances where Christians and Muslims "made room" for meeting, conversing and sharing with one another, thereby breaking down walls and opening up new possibilities for a future together.

Fear and Hope

"Fear" and "hope" are two theologically loaded words that occur frequently in this study. Fear of the loss of (national, cultural) identity has again and again been mentioned in analyses of the Danish case; "mutual fear and mistrust between majority and minorities" featured in every case. "Hope" is often mentioned only in terms of its failure for those who have been excluded by the dominant society and/or let down by leaders, and who have concluded that "there seems to be no reason to believe in a better future." The consequences of this failure of hope are clear: for some, withdrawal and depression; for others, anger and anti-social behavior. In these situations, some "turn to their faith," but too frequently this "turn" is to a superficial, "ideologized" version of the great (Islamic or Christian) tradition, which offers simplistic answers to complex questions and divides the world into "Us" vs "Them."

Hope and fear converged in the LWF study around the issue of Sharî'a; "our hope, their fear" was a slogan used by some Muslims in Nigeria. The study helps to explain why so many Muslims regard Sharî'a as "our hope": it is not merely a code of law or a set of legal procedures, but rather a dream, an ideal for a better community guided directly by God. The implementation of Sharî'a codes in the Northern Nigerian states (since 1999) was widely welcomed: many Muslims "believed that it would create more justice and fairness" and "would end corruption, exploitation and poverty and restore morality." Unfortunately, the realities often did not measure up to the hopes, when those punished under Sharî'a law were "cow thieves and unwed mothers" rather than "the wealthy and the corrupt who do not give the poor their rightful share."

At the same time that Sharî'a represented a great hope for some, for others it was a matter of anxiety: how would non-Muslims—as well as Muslim women and secularized Muslims—be treated in states and municipalities (in Nigeria and Indonesia) where Sharî'a codes were implemented? In Denmark, support for or opposition to Sharî'a has become a test question allowing only an either-or answer. In the echo-chamber of politicians and media, the Sharî'a discussion in the Danish media "does not really relate to the views of Danish Muslims but often is far removed from the reality of people's daily life."

The Christian and Islamic traditions both have profound resources for dispelling fear and instilling hope. As Christians and Muslims have met together to share genuine conversation and hospitality, they have created fora that provide open spaces for interaction and conversation in mutual respect—beyond slogans and shibboleths—through which fears can be frankly aired and hopes explored. Some "fears-of-the-other" may be simply dispelled as people meet and talk, and perhaps forge friendships and partnerships. Some deep hopes may be fulfilled as marginalized people find themselves part of a hospitable community where they are accepted and heard.

The Sharî'a debate in Nigeria and Indonesia makes plain the very deep yearnings of Muslims in those lands for social and economic justice and the opportunity to live a decent, quiet and harmonious life. Christians share such hopes. The study team has seen many examples of Muslims and Christians working together for the sake of their communities–work that is sustained by hope and that gives hope to others.

A new conception of citizenship

The previous section of the book ended on a note of hope. Over against the "Us vs Them" syndrome that featured so prominently in all the case studies, it offered hope for "a new conception of citizenship that does not presuppose an enemy, an 'other,' but rather includes the other as a necessary part of who we are." As a political program in a world still very much defined by nations, tribes, peoples and languages, such a hope may seem naïve–even if globalization may be seen as pushing us to develop this new concept of citizenship, and even towards new conceptions of human beings. For the foreseeable future, debates about citizenship, for example, in the USA or Europe, will perhaps continue to focus on where and how to draw lines of exclusion. The vision of "a new conception of citizenship" may empower those who are grasped by it to strive to find spaces and communities in which this new kind of citizenship may be lived and experienced already now.

The places where this new kind of citizenship will be "tried on" and lived out are, necessarily, at the local grassroots level. This is where the "other" will be included, hope kindled, hospitality pursued and conversation enabled. Christians tend to claim that the first and foremost place where these practices are learned, inculcated and made a part of life will be in their congregations, and Muslims would make parallel claims for their local Muslim community. But if so, they will then, by extension, bring these practices into their neighborhoods, and to the variety of organizations and associations that neighbors concerned for the common good in a common future will create, and which often is referred to as civil society. Believers' experiences of inclusion, hope, hospitality, cooperation and conversation in the wider community may then be brought back into the gatherings of specific faith traditions, where they are interpreted in the light of their respective faiths and where they may serve to inspire others.

Throughout this study, the importance of work at the grass roots has been emphasized, and many examples cited of Christians and Muslims working together on common projects, for the common good, for a common future.[2] This, finally, is where the good news of the present study resides: that in spite of problems that seem intractable, in spite of destructive winds that blow through and destroy communities, in spite

[2] LWF general secretary, Ishmael Noko, recently reaffirmed the LWF commitment to interfaith dialogue and *diapraxis*. He noted that Muslim and Christian participants at a seminar meeting in Indonesia after the tsunami "came to realize that a dialogue in life is essential for living together in a religiously pluralistic context, because it entails overcoming economic, ethical, political, social and religious injustice through common action." "Living in Communion in the World Today: Report of the General Secretary," LWF Meeting of the Council, Lund, Sweden, 20-27 March 2007, *Agenda*, exhibit 8, p. 7.

of violence and death—Christians and Muslims in all of the case studies presented here have come together, and continue to come together, in order to create islands of vision, conversation, cooperation, hospitality and hope. They have begun to build bridges instead of walls.

Useful Information

	Nigeria	Indonesia	Denmark
Population	140 million	245 million	5.4 million
Ethnic groups	250 ethnic groups. Major groups: Hausa/ Fulani (north), Igbo (southeast), Yoruba (southwest)	300 ethnic groups. Major groups: Malay, Javanese, Sundanese, Madurese, Papuan. Also Chinese and Indian minorities	92% Danish origin, ethnic minorities from Europe, especially Turkey, Asia, Middle East, Africa
Official language	English	Bahasa Indonesian	Danish
Christians	Since the late eighteenth century	Since the sixteenth century	Since 960 CE. The Danish church was established in 1849
Percentage today	Approx. 40% (predominantly Southern Nigeria)	Approx. 8%	Approx. 87%
Lutherans	1,500,000	5,165,000	4,500,000
Muslims	Since the eleventh century	Since about 1300 CE from Persia and South Arabia through India. Islam based bylaws in many regions. Nahdlatul Ulama (NU), 30-50 million. Muhammadiya, 20 million	Since the late 1960s from Turkey, Pakistan, Yugoslavia, Iran, Palestine, Iraq, Bosina, etc.
Sharî'a	1999 Zamfara adopted Sharî'a laws. 2001 Islamic penal code in twelve of nineteen states. Many different Islamic groups. Sufi Brotherhoods widespread	2000, Sharî'a in Aceh. Islam-based bylaws in many regions	
Percentage today	Approx. 45% (predominantly in Northern Nigeria	Approx. 87%	Approx. 3.8%
Others	Traditional beliefs: 10%	Buddhists: 1%; Hindus: 2%; Others (mainly Confucians): 1%	Jews, Buddhists, Hindus, Sikhs, etc.

	Nigeria	Indonesia	Denmark
Political system	Democratically elected civil government (since 1999)	Democratically elected civil government (since 1999)	Representative democracy (since 1849)
	Secular federal republic	Secular republic	Secular state with a constitutional monarchy
	1999–2007, Olusegun Obasanjo, People's Democratic Party (PDP). May 2007, Umaru Musa Yar' Ardua (PDP)	2004, first directly elected president Susilo Bambang Yudhoyono, Partai Democrat	Coalition of Liberal Party and Conservative Party (backed by the Danish People's party since 2001)
Administrative divisions	36 states	30 provinces, 445 districts or regencies	5 regions, 98 municipalities
History	1914, amalgamation of north and south into one political unit forming the present Nigeria. 1960, independence from Great Britain. Since 1999, military rule	1949, full independence from the Netherlands. 1966–1969 Suharto regime. 1945, *Pancasila*	First organized as a unified state in the tenth century

Please note that the percentages indicated are estimates

Contributors

Fatih Alev is a board member of Islamic-Christian Study Centre (IKS), chair of the Mosque Society (Copenhagen) and a member of European Muslim Network (Brussels).

Syafa'atun Almirzanah is a Ph.D. candidate at the Islamic University, Sunan Kalijaga and Lutheran School of Theology, Chicago and chief associate professor of comparative religions, Sunan Kalijaga

Dr Nelly Van Doorn-Harder holds the Surjit Patheja Chair in World Religions and Ethics at Valparaiso University. She has taught and done research in Indonesia and Egypt focusing on gender studies, interfaith issues and contemporary daily practices.

Dr Mogens Mogensen is a part-time lecturer at the University of Copenhagen and freelance consultant on interreligious and intercultural issues. The topic of his thesis was the Fulani in Northern Nigeria.

Nafisatu Lawal Musa is a barrister at the Ministry of Justice, Jos.

Rev. Dr Lissi Rasmussen is director of IKS and part-time lecturer at the University of Copenhagen. She has thirty years of practical and academic experience with Christian-Muslim relations in Europe, Africa and the Middle East.

Dr Jamilin Sirait is the principal of the Lutheran Theological Seminary of the HKBP, Pematang Siantar, Medan.

Rev. Dr Mark N. Swanson is professor of Christian-Muslim Studies and Interfaith Relations at the Lutheran School of Theology, Chicago.

The Right Rev. David L. Windibiziri is the former archbishop of the Lutheran Church of Christ in Nigeria and chair of the board of trustees of the Association for Christian-Muslim Mutual Relations in Nigeria.

Rev. Dr Ingo Wulfhorst is a part-time lecturer at the Ecumenical Institute for Postgraduate Studies in Theology, São Leopoldo, Brazil. He is the former study secretary for Church and People of Other Faiths, LWF, Department for Theology.